Managing information

THE HENLEY MANAGEMENT SERIES

Series Adviser: Professor Bernard Taylor

Managing information

Information systems for today's general manager

A. V. Knight

D. J. Silk

McGRAW-HILL BOOK COMPANY

London · New York · St Louis · San Francisco · Auckland
Bogotá · Guatemala · Hamburg · Lisbon · Madrid · Mexico
Montreal · New Delhi · Panama · Paris · San Juan · São Paulo
Singapore · Sydney · Tokyo · Toronto

Published by
McGRAW-HILL Book Company (UK) Limited
Shoppenhangers Road
Maidenhead · Berkshire · England
Telephone Maidenhead (0628) 23432
Cables MCGRAWHILL MAIDENHEAD Telex 848484
Fax 0628 35895

British Library Cataloguing in Publication Data

Knight, A.V.
    Managing information.
    1. Business firms. Management. Information systems.
    Applications of computer systems
    I. Title   II. Silk, D. J.   III. Series
    658.4'038'0285

    ISBN 0–07–707086–0

Library of Congress Cataloging-in-Publication Data

Knight, A. V.
Managing information: Information systems for today's general manager / A. V.
Knight, D. J. Silk.
    p. cm. – (The Henley management series)
    Includes bibliographical references.
    ISBN 0–07–707086–0
    1. Business – Data processing.   2. Management information systems.
    I. Silk, D. J. (David J.)   II. Title.   III. Series.
    HF5548.2.K568   1990
    658.4'038—dc20   89–35991

1234 RB 9210

Photoset, printed and bound by
Redwood Burn Limited, Trowbridge, Wiltshire

Contents

Preface

Information is power. History is full of cases where the timely use of information has led to military, diplomatic, or business success. In the Second World War the intelligence information derived from intercepted radio messages was a vital factor in Allied military success. More recently data from surveillance satellites have been used to influence diplomatic negotiations on arms control. In the 19th century the expansion of the Rothschild banking empire across Europe was made possible by a private intelligence and communication system which gave Rothschilds market information ahead of their competitors.

It is the same for today's manager. The effective use of information is a key to business success. The difficulty is that the nature of business, and the role of information within it, are changing. At the same time modern Information Technology (IT) offers a bewildering range of choice and opportunity for handling business information. Managers cannot afford to ignore these aspects of change, but how can they get to grips with the problem while dealing with all the other pressures of management?

This book is designed to help. Its objective is to equip practising general managers to use information effectively in order to improve business performance.

Three points need to be made about this objective.

– First, the book is intended for practising managers who are not specialists in IT: its guidance is therefore practical and non-technical.
– Second, the emphasis is on using information, not just the technology: so the descriptions of IT, although necessary, are from the viewpoint of the user.
– Third, the aim is to improve business performance. The book uses real-life examples of how this can be done, and suggests a practical plan for action.

As well as giving guidance to busy managers the book is intended to be suitable for a more formal study of the subject, especially by MBA students. The book is in three parts.

– Part 1 identifies the challenge that information presents to all managers.

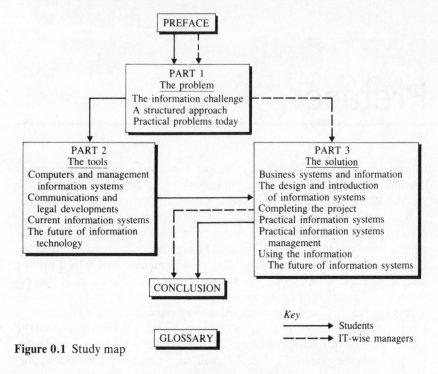

Figure 0.1 Study map

- Part 2 deals with the technology of information systems.
- Part 3 shows how such systems can be put to practical use in organizations.

Figure 0.1 shows how the parts of the book are related and provides a map for readers to follow.

All readers and students are asked to start with Part 1. Managers with a background knowledge of information technology may then, if they wish, skip to Part 3.

At the end of the main text is a Glossary of terms encountered in the field of information management and IT, a Bibliography for reference and further reading, and a conventional Index.

Throughout this book, we have tried to deal with the practical needs of today's managers and we have therefore limited the technical detail to that which has some practical relevance to managers. We have also tried to illustrate points by quoting practical applications from the world of business and management. Consequently we hope that you will find the book both enjoyable and useful.

Tony Knight and David Silk,

August 1989

Centre for Information Management,

Henley – The Management College

PART ONE
THE PROBLEM

1
The information challenge

Information is expensive; but lack of it is more so
LORD RAYLEIGH

1.1 Information as a resource

Why should managers take time out of their busy day to study Information Management? It is because information is a vital business resource.

Managers today must run efficient, profitable, and cost effective organizations. The resources that they have to achieve these results are:

- people
- money
- materials
- energy
- information.

Within the organization there may be specialist managers responsible for each of these resources but the general manager is concerned with the whole of the enterprise, not just one aspect of it. The general manager therefore needs to manage resources in a balanced way, without overlooking one or favouring another. In this book we focus on achieving the business objectives through information management, while assuming that the other resources are also being managed effectively.

Each of these resources, except information, can be counted or measured in some way and this makes the task of management easier. Information is different; it is intangible and cannot be measured. Even so, many organizations are now finding that information is one of their most important resources.

3

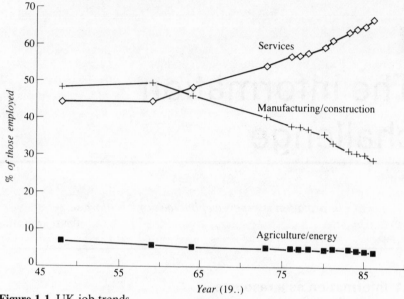

Figure 1.1 UK job trends
Source: Britain – an Official Handbook, HMSO, 1965, 1985–88

Information about economic trends, about markets, about new technology, about the skills and potential of the workforce and about what customers think, are all vital to the survival and growth of manufacturing industries. Information may be both the raw material and the finished product of the enterprise, as with a publisher. The skill and knowledge of the organization's people, delivered as an information service, may be the product, as with a professional advisory service. Recent economic trends show how our economy increasingly depends on information as a resource.

1.2 The information economy

Human societies generally evolve through three stages. The first stage is the agricultural phase, when most of the workforce is concerned with producing the food needed by the society to survive. Food is material, and can be measured.

The second phase is industrial, when most of the workforce is concerned with using machines which enhance human physical energy to produce physical goods. Energy too can be measured, and goods counted.

Next is the information or service phase, when most of the workforce is concerned with selling services, based on special knowledge or skill.

Doctors, hairdressers and consultants are examples of this, and it is difficult to measure what they are selling. At this third stage of economic development, only a minority of the workforce is concerned with providing society with food, physical energy and goods.

Many countries are now in this third phase. In the USA since the mid-19th century there has been a long-term decrease in the numbers employed in agriculture, and latterly in industry. Since about 1955, the USA has had more of its workforce engaged in information services that in anything else. The trends in the UK have been similar but slightly delayed. Figure 1.1 shows the pattern between 1948 and 1986, based on official statistics.[1]

Most of the change has occurred since the early sixties. Two-thirds of the UK workforce are now engaged in providing services. The definition of 'services' in the official statistics is rather broad. It includes: wholesale distribution and repairs; retail distribution; hotels and catering; transport; postal services and communications; banking, finance, and insurance; public administration; health; and 'other services'.

The trends within the service sector are equally important. Figure 1.2 shows the size of the six largest parts of the service sector, and the way their size has changed over the 12-year period 1976–87. The largest and fastest-growing part of the service sector is finance. The finance sector is one for

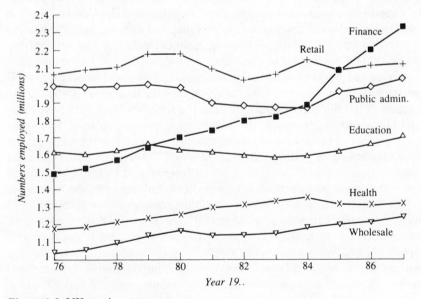

Figure 1.2 UK service sector
Source: Britain – an Official Handbook, HMSO, 1985–89

which information is its lifeblood. It has made very widespread use of modern information technology and could not work without it. A prominent financier has commented that information about money is now almost as important as money itself.

In developed countries the 'information economy' is outstripping other parts of the economy and this presents a problem. Modern Information Technology (IT) is reducing the cost of collecting, storing, processing and communicating information. In particular, the cost of replicating information is trivial, and this threatens the whole basis of an economy. If, in an agricultural economy, animals or other food-products could be replicated at low cost, the basis of that economy would very soon collapse. We must now be very careful to safeguard business information, to prevent unauthorized people from getting it and hence to preserve its economic value. Information is a valuable resource, it costs money, and it must be safeguarded and managed.

1.3 The value of information

Some attempts have been made to put a financial value on information services in the organization. A recent study[2] has suggested two approaches to estimating the value of information. One is the organization's 'willingness to pay' for information. This is measured by the budget for books, periodicals, and other sources of information, plus the individual's investment in time and effort to discover, retrieve and read the information. The second approach is to estimate the cost saving or other advantage that results from the individual having the information. A study of the US Departments of Defense and Energy showed that professionals there spent an average of 233 hours per year reading journals, technical reports, and books. Only a small fraction of this information gave the reader a specific advantage whose value could be assessed. But where the advantage could be measured it was very much greater than the cost of getting the information. It was found that the total investment in getting information was $300 million, whilst the total tangible benefit was $12 billion. This represents a 40:1 return, and brings home the value of information in a professional organization within the modern service economy. There is a risk that organizations will collect more and more data, believing it to be useful. The constant flow of data from process control systems, transaction processing, electronic point of sale terminals, and other sources can overwhelm the manager unless effective processes are established to turn the data into valuable information. Managers should at least be aware of the many sampling and analytical techniques, made easier by the use of computer software, that can help to make sense of corporate data.

1.4 Action points for managers

The following action points serve as a checklist for the general manager; they anticipate topics developed later in the book.

- As a manager, you must direct resources to achieve results. If resources don't contribute to results, in the short or the long term, then don't use them.
- Always take the point of view of a general manager, concerned with all aspects of the enterprise.
- From this viewpoint consider information as one of five resources available to you:
  - people
  - money
  - material
  - energy, and
  - information.
- When focusing on information management, ensure that all levels of the business are involved: senior managers, IT professionals, and end-users of systems. These are the three components of the 'ITernal Triangle', to be described in Chapter 2.
- Review this and other aspects of management by taking the outward, strategic view first. Consider the changing environment, the change in your market or customers, the necessary trends in your business sector, and how your enterprise will be able to win. Consider how information systems can help in this.
- Then take the internal, operational view of your organization. Identify where information is important, in the product, the process or both. Then focus on the value chain, to see where better use of IT could improve effectiveness where it matters.
- Next draw these two perspectives together, to form a coherent overview of what needs to be done in information management.
- Now resolve to work with your partners in the ITernal Triangle to make sure it happens.

1.5 Information management defined

The checklist should ensure that you treat information management in a balanced way. It is now necessary to define the term more precisely and identify what the rest of this book sets out to achieve.

Information management can be defined as

the informed response of the general manager to the opportunities of modern Information Technology.

This requires some explanation. First, what exactly is Information Technology (IT)? A simple definition is

the convergence of computing and telecommunications made possible by modern microelectronics.

The development of IT is represented on the left hand side of Fig. 1.3.

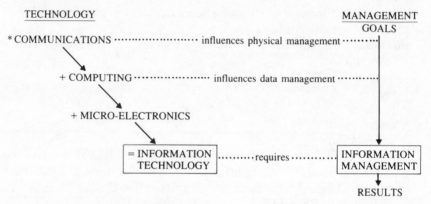

Figure 1.3 IT and management

Communications is the oldest of the three technologies, electrical communication systems having developed continuously since the 1840s. Computing was developed from the 1940s, initially for military purposes. Microchip technology was developed in the 1960s, and soon led to the rapid convergence of the older technologies into what we now term IT.

The right hand side of Fig. 1.3 relates this evolution of technology to the tasks of managers trying to achieve results in their enterprises. How have they needed to respond to the opportunities of the evolving technologies? Communications, whether physical or electrical, have always been a constraint on the physical disposition of an enterprise's resources. You cannot operate from more than one site, or in more than one country, without communications adequate to the nature of the business you wish to conduct. Managers usually had to take advantage of what the steadily-developing technology of communications could offer them.

Since computers became widely available, they have been a constraint on the way data are processed in the organization. Early mainframe computers had a major impact on structure and organization of those businesses which needed to adopt them. More recently, with the much faster growth of IT in the late-1970s and the 1980s, the available technology has been advancing more rapidly than the organization and its managers' abilities to keep pace with it. It is no longer adequate to adopt the passive attitude that emerging technology should be brought into use when it becomes available. The pace of change, and the wide range of options available, make that a disastrous course. This wealth of choice inevitably places a new responsibility on the manager – to make an informed response, rather than just an acquiescent one. The response must be by a general manager, rather than by a specialist manager on his or her own, because IT can radically affect the overall strategy of a modern business. This factor justifies the basic definition of information management.

Developing the definition indicates that there are three essential attributes needed by the general manager.

- First, the manager needs knowledge of the potential and limitations of IT itself. It is important to know just what the technology makes possible and, equally, the tasks which at present are beyond the scope of practical technology.
- Second, the manager needs an awareness of the information systems which are currently available and the legal framework within which they operate. The current market-place should be considered, to see what is available. The emphasis should be on systems, rather than on the detailed components which make up those systems; the user is interested in performance, not the technical niceties.

  The legal framework is important because recent legislation has affected the market-place, and the way we are allowed to handle information. The liberalization, or de-regulation, of the telecommunications market in several countries, and the data-protection legislation in many more countries, are major examples of this.
- Third, the manager needs the ability to assess the information needs of his or her organization, taking account of its strategy or business aims, and must play a part in formulating an information strategy for the organization. The manager must deal effectively with specialists concerned with designing and implementing new systems.

  This aspect recognizes the increasing strategic importance to the business of information management, and the fact that too often in the past there has not been an effective dialogue between general managers who understand the business and specialists who understand the technology.

Information management, then, has these three essential components:

- knowing what the technology can and can't do;
- being aware of what systems are available in the market-place; and
- being able to relate this knowledge to the needs of business.

1.6 Summary

This chapter has set information management within the context of the economy and of general management. Management is about using five resources to achieve business aims: people, money, material, energy and information. Information is becoming more important as a resource, both for the economy as a whole and for the operation of individual enterprises.

Managers must be aware of the value and cost of the information that they use and of the way in which it has been derived from the raw business data.

References

1. *Britain – an Official Handbook*, HMSO, 1965, and 1985–89.
2. King, D. W. and Griffiths, J. M. 'Measuring the value of information and information systems, services, and products', AGARD Conference Proceedings No. 385, January 1986.

2.
A structured approach

2.1 Introduction

Chapter 1 stressed the importance of information as a resource for managers to achieve business aims. Surveys show that managers are becoming more fully aware of this, and getting to grips with the issues involved. In this chapter we look at some methods which can help you relate this aspect of management to the others. There are also some definitions which focus more precisely on the problem. Thus the material provides a formal structure to the subject for those (like students of management) for whom this is important.

2.2 Information management in the business context

Management operates at three levels. Working from top to bottom in the organization, these are:

- strategic management concerned with the long-term planning of the enterprise;
- middle management concerned with mid-term decisions to ensure continuing effectiveness of the enterprise; and
- operational management concerned with the detailed day-to-day transactions of the enterprise.

The impact of IT has been in the reverse direction: from the bottom up. Computer systems first transformed the operational management of many businesses; stock-control, order-processing, invoicing, and financial accounting now rely heavily on IT support. Then IT had an impact at middle management level, with management information systems and personal computers finding an important role to support planning for the mid-term. More recently many organizations have realized the relevance of IT at the strategic level. Thus there has been a 'wave' of IT application which has come upwards through the three layers of management.

A more detailed view of management is given in Fig. 2.1.

The management map has three linked triangles labelled 'organization', 'job' and 'self'. The first is the outward-looking or strategic one. It considers the place of the enterprise in relation to its environment, and to its market or customers. The 'environment' includes all those factors over which the enterprise has little or no control; these might include the general economic situation, tax legislation, the labour market, and the political flavour of the government. Customers include potential customers, who might be attracted or stimulated, as well as current and past customers. Strategic management is concerned with the long-term relationships between these three. Knowing the aims of the enterprise at this strategic level, we know its task. This links with the second triangle, which deals with the internal structure and working of the enterprise. Here managers have to balance the sometimes competing demands of task, team, and individuals. This functional view of leadership was formulated by John Adair,[1] and is concerned with getting the task achieved by building and motivating a team of people. Each member of the team has individual needs and aspirations which we must understand and respect.

The third triangle is concerned with the individual self, comprising body, mind, and spirit. Managers contribute most directly by using their minds, but the body is important in terms of health and well-being, and the spirit is important in terms of motivation, achievement, and values and ethics. Some aspects of this triangle remain the personal concern of the individual; others, like motivation, are an important concern of management. The map helps to show how aspects of management interlink and can conflict. For example, it is unlikely that the aspirations of each individual will correspond exactly

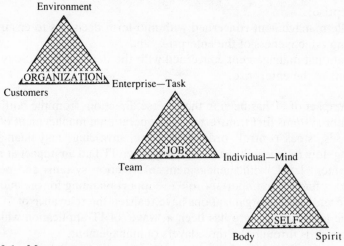

Figure 2.1 Management map

with the strategic needs of the business and the way it needs to operate in order to be effective. We can resolve such conflict by working top-down on the diagram: decide strategy first, then structure and organization, then individuals as such. During this process the manager will need to consider the possible use of the five resources identified earlier: people, money, material, energy, and information.

The map provides an agenda to consider the related aspects of management, including information management. It can be useful as a focus for brainstorming, but at some point we shall need a more detailed agenda. The approach described here has proved useful; we start with the human aspect of information management and then consider the needs of the enterprise in relation to its business goals.

2.3 Information management in the human context

Three groups of people need to be involved in information management. They are the senior managers concerned with the strategy of the enterprise, the IT professionals who know about the technology, and the middle- and junior-level staff who are (or may become) the major users of information systems. These three groups do not have the same perspective of the problem, and it is not easy to get them to agree on an effective solution.

In the past it has been possible to take the easy way out, by adopting a style of information management which does not involve all three groups. For example, some organizations have adopted a random or uncoordinated approach. This tolerates development of information systems by enthusiasts who discern its importance and have the drive to initiate new projects. Slightly more positive is to allow groups of users to formulate company policy on a wider front; this often happens bottom-up from one of the specialist areas of the organization, such as accounting. A third possibility is to allow the IT professionals to formulate the information policy for the organization. This has the danger that the IT experts often do not adequately understand business policy. Another option is top-down, where senior managers decide what should be done, in broad terms, and impose it as a series of directives. This can sometimes be valuable to get radical innovation adopted, but it is fraught with danger; senior managers are not experts (and nor should they be) about the detail of what users need or of what IT makes possible. The preferred approach, of course, is a combined one which involves all three groups in an appropriate way. It is the approach developed in this book. Meanwhile it is important to realize the human problems of trying to draw the three groups together, illustrated in Fig. 2.2.

The ITernal Triangle is a caricature of the three groups. Although exaggerated, it can help us understand the perspective which each may have. The senior manager is often ill-informed about IT and its possibilities, having worked up through the middle levels of management without needing to get involved with IT (there wasn't much around then), so why start now? Nevertheless, the manager is uneasy, having read of the startling developments in the technology and the way it is being applied to support the tasks of business, and seeing staff using it in ways he or she doesn't fully understand. The manager can give staff little guidance in this matter, and is not equipped to judge the advice given to him or her. However, the manager is reluctant to get involved, fearing that this will be time consuming, and he or she will get tripped up by experts, or will make a fool of him or herself (especially in front of junior staff) while trying to touch or use the new equipment.

In the second corner is the IT Professional possibly quite senior although unlikely to be on the Board, whose age and background make it likely that he or she started professional life in the era of mainframe computers, when these were the hub of data-processing (DP) in the organization. As the DP manager, the IT Professional enjoys heading a department which is essential to the functioning of the organization. However, the Professional often loves the technology more than he or she understands the business. Even if successful in avoiding jargon, the Professional still finds it difficult to talk with senior general managers in an easily-understood language.

In the third corner is the user of information systems, or the would-be user. Like senior management, the user is increasingly aware of what IT can offer, especially if he or she belongs to a professional institution. The user is therefore impatient to use IT for professional effectiveness. The user is not too worried about how other parts of the organization should be developing, or of the problems of coordinating IT in the whole enterprise. The user is frustrated by what is seen as the failure of the organization to provide

A caricature:

Top Manager
Ill-informed
Uneasy
Reluctant to be involved

IT Professional   *Executive End-user*
Data processing outlook   Increasing awareness
Defending the DP department   Impatient to use IT
Lacks a strategic view   Piecemeal personal computers

Figure 2.2 The ITernal triangle

the technology and systems deserved and needed. Often the user's only outlet is to buy from the petty cash, to avoid what is seen as cumbrous and obstructive approval procedures for new information systems.

The ITernal Triangle is a caricature. It is unlikely to apply in every respect. But it is very unlikely to apply in no respect at all. It helps the general manager appreciate that these three groups, even with the most constructive of attitudes, will come from different backgrounds, with different perspectives, and with different ideas of what should be done. The coordinated approach to information management must recognize this. Many organizations are now taking active steps to resolve the problems of the ITernal Triangle. For example, business managers are being put in charge of the IS function, so that the IT professionals become more aware of the business justification for the systems they develop and support. IT professionals are being decentralized, to work directly in business units alongside the users of systems; this improves understanding, and consequently improves the quality of support which the users get. Senior managers are taking positive steps to get adequate IT expertise at Board level, so that they can make an informed contribution, and where necessary take the lead. All these signs are encouraging, but there are few organizations where the ITernal Triangle does not still present some barriers to the successful use of IT.

2.4 Information management – the outward view

Assume that these human difficulties can be overcome. How then can the problem be approached within the context of managing the business as a whole? Look first on the strategic part of the management map presented in Sec. 2.2 and Fig. 2.1: the relationship between the enterprise, its environment, and its market or customers. Figure 2.3 gives a simple agenda to review the changing situation in a sector of industry or business. The diagram includes some of the deceptively simple questions which you should ask during a strategic analysis.

First consider the present size and nature of the sector. This is factual: 'Where are we now?'. The second item is to identify the pressures to which the sector is subject. There may be changes over which you have no control, but which you must take into account: 'How is the world changing?'. Such factors might include a general movement in interest rates, or rising property prices. There may be changes which directly affect the business sector: 'What are the new rules of the game?'. The Government may have changed the rules quite radically, as was done in the UK finance sector 1986–88. A new technology may be changing the old way of doing things. A new player in the market may have upset the previous balance of competitive forces. There might be a declining, or emerging, market for the sector. All these factors are pressures to which the sector needs to respond. The third item identifies that response – how the sector can survive in the changing order of things: 'What is the way to win?', 'Where do we want to be?'.

All the questions so far are to do with business strategy. As an example of strategic change in response to changes in the environment, consider the case of BAT Industries. Before 1976 it was called British American Tobacco and most of its business related to the habit of smoking. Recognizing the trend away from smoking, related to health concerns, the company changed its name to one which is not immediately associated with tobacco, and diversified its operations. By 1988 its turnover was £18 billion, in retailing, paper, and financial services. More than half of its profit was unrelated to tobacco. This shows timely strategic change.

Even in these first steps of the analysis, IT and information systems may have figured quite prominently. Any analysis of the finance sector must take account of the move towards machine-based quotations and trading. Any analysis of the travel sector must take account of the improved technology for reservations and customized holiday packages. Any analysis of the automobile sector must take account of the potential of in-car information. In any event, the last two items on the agenda of Fig. 2.3 address the information aspects.

First consider the changing needs for information systems, arising from the changing strategic situation. 'How can information systems help our people?' is the right question, not 'How can we use this new technology?'. Sometimes the pressure and trends may simply be towards greater efficiency; information systems may help. The trend may be towards a closer

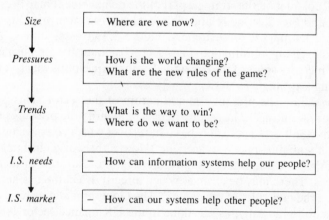

Figure 2.3 Sector analysis

contact with the customer; information systems may help. The trend may be towards greater reliance on formally-expressed knowledge and expertise made more widely available; information systems may help. By identifying where IT can contribute to strategic development, we are better placed to look internally at our organization.

The final item is to consider other markets for information technology or systems. This is obviously of interest to the IT industry itself. Less obviously, there may be a wider market for systems developed initially to meet the needs of the enterprise itself.

For example, the motor manufacturer British Leyland set up an information services division to meet its own requirements; the division became so successful that it became a subsidiary company and then a major player offering public information services (Istel). By 1988 Istel had been the subject of a management buyout, was planned for flotation on the International Stock Exchange, and more than 50 per cent of its £84 million turnover was outside the Rover Group (as British Leyland was now called). This example shows the importance of being alert to the wider market potential of the information systems and services developed initially to support core-operations.

Unilever set up a subsidiary to operate a European data communications network to meet the company's needs; this subsidiary found itself early into the field, able to offer similar services to the rest of the industry, and eventually became the subject of a takeover from a major player from the IT sector (EDS).

American Airlines were early into the market of airline reservation systems in the USA. They offered terminals to travel agents which made bookings much simpler, and presented their own flights as a first option. Not only did they increase market share but they became and remained market-leader for reservation systems. They now make more money from that than from flying aeroplanes.

It would have been difficult to foresee the eventual success of all these systems, but they made strategic sense at the time the crucial decisions were made. The question to ask is 'How can our systems help other people?'.

The sector analysis has been presented in a very simple form, but it does help focus on the changing environment within which the enterprise has to succeed in the future. This must come before any internal analysis of the enterprise.

2.5 Information management – the inward view

When looking at the organization itself, we must focus on where information systems can be used to best effect. There are two ideas from Porter[2] which can help. The first is information intensity, depicted in Fig. 2.4. The matrix focuses attention on aspects of the business which have a high information intensity; they involve information in a high proportion compared with other resources such as material or energy. The horizontal axis relates to the end-product of the business: whether it is low or high in information content. Similarly the vertical axis relates to the process by which the end-product is made within the 'factory'. These axes are independent, and so there are four types of situation which can be encountered. Cement is an example where both the product and the process are low in information content. Oil refining is an example where the product has little information content, but the process is complex and involves much use of information. In such a case IT investment would be in the process rather than the product. A newspaper is an example where both process and product are information-intense.

The second idea from Porter, shown in Fig. 2.5, offers a closer analysis of what happens within the enterprise. The value chain analyses the cost of producing the product. Hopefully, this is less than the value for which it can be sold, and the difference constitutes the margin. The diagram shows this pictorially, and also a breakdown of the elements of cost.

The primary activities relate to the sequential stages of the manufacturing, sales, and support processes, from inbound logistics to customer support. Each of these incurs cost, and some may be made more efficient with

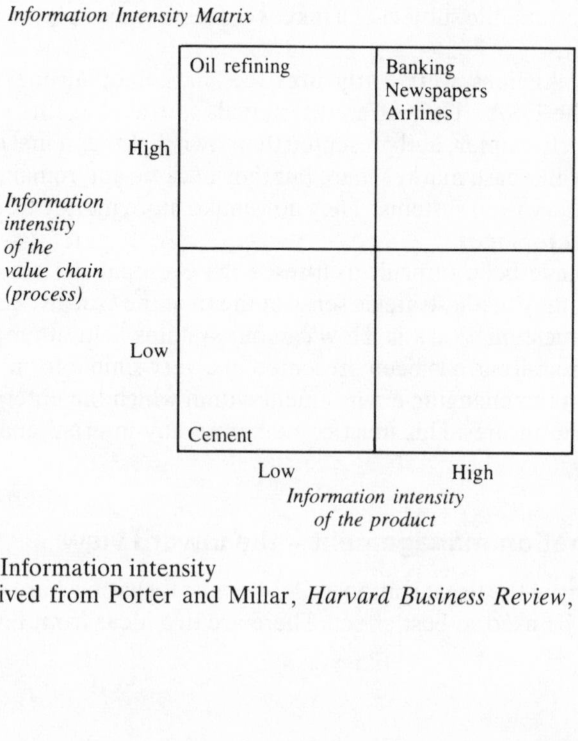

Information Intensity Matrix

		Information intensity of the product	
		Low	High
Information intensity of the value chain (process)	**High**	Oil refining	Banking Newspapers Airlines
	Low	Cement	

Figure 2.4 Information intensity
Source: Derived from Porter and Millar, *Harvard Business Review*, July–August 1985

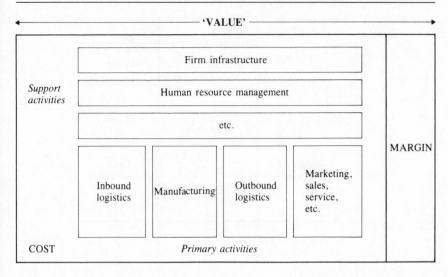

Figure 2.5   Value chain
Source: Derived from Porter and Millar, *Harvard Business Review*, July–August 1985

investment in information systems. Examples might be reduction in stock levels made possible by just in time procedures linked to the manufacturing process; use of Computer Integrated Manufacture (CIM) techniques to make production more flexible and responsive to needs; better computer-based planning of distribution, and customer support visits; help and advice services to customers over communication systems rather than with visits by the company's representatives. The support activities represent the overheads of the company rather than those costs directly attributable to stages of the production process. Infrastructure and personnel are examples. Again, information systems may improve effectiveness: for example, computer planning of the use of employee time to give greater flexibility; or management information systems which reduce the cost of reporting, monitoring, and decision making.

Information intensity and value chain analysis can therefore focus on those parts of the business which would benefit from better use of information systems, and can be a useful agenda for management review.

2.6 Information management – the overview

These two views – the strategic external view and the detailed internal view – are necessary and complementary. General managers need an overview of

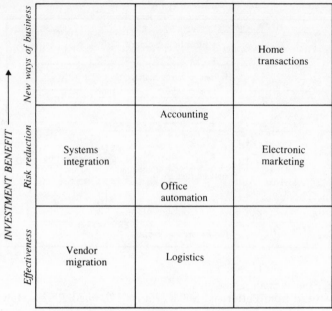

Figure 2.6   IT investment map
Source: Adapted from Peters, 'Evaluating your computer investment strategy', *Journal of Information Technology*, 1988

both, and this is not always easy. Senior managers are perhaps more used to taking a strategic external view, while middle and functional managers are more used to taking the internal view. For top management in particular it is important to have a balanced overview of the information aspect of management.

A traditional SWOT (strengths, weaknesses, opportunities, and threats) analysis of the business position is one way of doing this. Often, opportunities and threats relate to the external view from the business, while strengths and weaknesses relate to an internal analysis of the business. Bringing them together gives a more balanced perspective. Information management should be included within a SWOT analysis, but there is still a need for a method more directly related to information systems. Peters[3] has developed an IT Investment Map for this purpose, and it has been used successfully at Board level in large companies. It is shown in Fig. 2.6. The horizontal axis is the focus of the IT investment – the area of the company's activities which an existing or proposed information system supports. From left to right, there is increasing visibility to the customer. On the left therefore are the back-office systems supporting the technical operations of which the customer has no direct awareness; on the right are the market-influencing applications which do affect him. The vertical axis is the benefit of the IT investment. At the bottom are systems which improve efficiency and effectiveness; at the top are those which directly affect the market by introducing new ways of doing business; in between are systems which reduce the risk of competitors gaining spectacular advantage in either of these areas.

Marked on the map are examples of information systems, and strategic decisions about information systems. In the bottom-left corner is vendor migration. This could mean getting unlocked from a single vendor of information systems, or moving in a controlled way to another vendor whose products better suit the company's needs. In this case the effectiveness of company operations should be improved, but there will be no immediate change visible to the customer. In the top-right corner are shown home-based transactions. Here the nature of the market is changed, by using modern information systems to interact with the customer in his home instead of in a shop. The nature of the product can also change, given the new method of delivery.

As an enterprise develops its information systems, and becomes more strategic in their use, there would be a migration from bottom-left to top-right on the IT Investment Map. For industries such as retailing, manufacturing or retail banking this has broadly been the case. There is an interesting counter-example, however. In 1986 the 'Big Bang' made radical changes to the operation of the London stock market. The new regulatory environment had been pressed for by Government, and required a more rapid and competitive method of trading. Electronic dealing systems were quickly introduced, to meet the needs of this new market. The old face-to-face dealing on the floor of the Stock Exchange quickly ceased. This major investment in front-office systems, however, soon showed the deficiencies of the back-office systems which did the accounting and settlement for deals made in the front-office. In the 2–3 years following Big Bang the front-office systems had to be upgraded, but the back-office systems became the more pressing issue. On the IT Investment Map external factors had required urgent development in the top-right corner, and then internal limitations had required follow-on development in the bottom-left corner.

The IT Investment Map can be useful for senior general management to take an overview of current and proposed IT investments. It gives a simple overview of both the strategic and the operational aspects of the company's IT investment.

2.7 Some definitions

Finally in this chapter we present a few definitions which help structure the subject of information management. They are not meant to be precise in a scientific sense, but they draw important practical distinctions.

In Chapter 1 information management was defined as the informed response of the general manager to the opportunities of modern IT. An information system comprises people, procedures and technology working together in a planned way. The system will need to collect, process, store, and communicate information under the control of the plan.

There are four modes of handling information (text, data, voice, and image), and all are necessary in a business information system.

The word 'information' itself is difficult to define. Try it! In the literature there are formal definitions, such as 'patterned matter-energy that affects the probabilities available to an individual making a decision'.[4] Such definitions are scarcely helpful to the practising manager. More practical are 'Data that have been put into a meaningful and useful context and communicated to a recipient who uses it to make decisions',[5] and 'Data that has been processed into a form that is meaningful to the recipient and is of real or perceived value in current or prospective actions or decisions'.[6] These get nearer to the mark. To develop the idea, consider the set of four terms shown in Fig. 2.7.

We use these four terms rather loosely in everyday conversation; managers need to be more careful. 'Data' is used in the sense of numbers representing facts. For the manager of a supermarket, for example, the numbers of individual items on the shelves today would be data. It is a matter of style whether you think the word is singular or plural.

The other three terms build upon data (facts), but add human significance at each stage. Thus 'information' can be defined as human significance associated with some fact or facts. For the supermarket manager, the total value of the stock today (a summary of much data) is information of

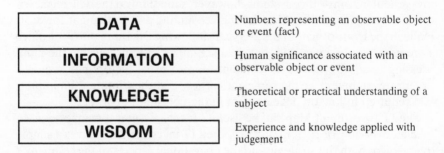

DATA	Numbers representing an observable object or event (fact)
INFORMATION	Human significance associated with an observable object or event
KNOWLEDGE	Theoretical or practical understanding of a subject
WISDOM	Experience and knowledge applied with judgement

Figure 2.7 Some definitions

significance in planning his operations. 'Knowledge' implies human under-standing, built upon relevant information. Thus the supermarket manager may be conscious that Christmas is coming and the shop needs to hold 20 per cent higher stock levels to cope with the rush of shoppers which the manager expects from a knowledge of shopping habits. Today, many forms of human knowledge can be recorded and used in electronic information systems. 'Wisdom', however, remains for the present essentially human; it is experi-ence and knowledge applied with judgement.

Data, information, knowledge, and wisdom thus form a hierarchy, each adding to the previous one in terms of human significance. The same facts may be interpreted by different people in different ways. A good infor-mation system will present data, information, or knowledge in a way which is helpful and relevant to the business user.

2.8 Summary

This chapter has given a structure for the study of information management. The management map shows the topics which general managers need to consider. You must work from a strategic view of the organization, to an analysis of the jobs within the organization, to the needs of the individuals who work there. At each stage, the information aspect must be considered alongside the others. There can be difficulty in getting the three essential players working effectively together – senior management, IT professionals, and the end-users of information systems. They make up the ITernal Trian-gle of those who must be involved in effective information management.

Developing the management map, we have presented three simple tech-niques for reviewing the role of information in support of the enterprise. The sector analysis identifies the changing environment and market within which the enterprise must succeed, to help formulate a business strategy which will include information aspects. The information intensity and value chain analyses help to look more closely at the inside working of the enterprise. The IT investment map complements a SWOT analysis in drawing this information together for the benefit of senior management who have to make investment decisions.

In Chapter 3 we shall look at specific examples, to make these ideas more concrete and to form the basis for illustration thoughout the rest of the book.

References

1. Adair, John, *Training for Leadership*, Macdonald, 1968.
2. Porter, M. E. and Millar, V. E., 'How information gives you competitive ad-vantage', *Harvard Business Review*, July–August 1985, pp. 149–60.
3. Peters, Glen, 'Evaluating your computer investment strategy', *Journal of Infor-mation Technology*, Vol. 3, No. 3, September 1988, pp. 178–88.

4. Rogers, E. M., *Communication Technology*, The Free Press/Collier Macmillan, 1986.
5. Burch, J. G. and Grudnitski, G., *Information Systems: Theory and Practice*, Wiley, 1986.
6. Davis, G. B. and Olson, M. H., *Management Information Systems*, McGraw-Hill, 1985.

3.
Practical problems today

3.1 Introduction

We have now set information management into the context of general management and given a formal structure to the subject. In this chapter we look at some practical examples of information systems and management.

General managers need to take first an external strategic view and then an internal analytical view of the enterprise they work for. To illustrate this, we shall take an external view of three business sectors, and then an internal view of five functions which are often represented within a business. The examples all relate to the UK situation in the late 1980s, but have been chosen so that managers from different sectors or countries can relate them to their own situation. They are not intended as detailed surveys for those working in the sectors or functions concerned; they are examples for people in other areas to consider and relate to their own work. The business sectors are:

- manufacturing,
- retailing, and
- finance.

The functional areas are:

- finance,
- human resources,
- marketing,
- planning, and
- operations.

Each has its own section in this chapter, and then there is a brief conclusion.

3.2 Business sector 1: Manufacturing

Size

In 1986 some 24 per cent of UK employees (5.2 million people) worked in the manufacturing sector, and produced about 24 per cent (£79 billion) of the Gross Domestic Product (GDP). The hundred largest companies accounted for one-third of this. The biggest four companies by turnover were: BAT £12.5 billion, ICI £10.5 billion, Unilever £6.5 billion and GEC £5.2 billion. Between 1955 and 1984 the UK's share of the world market for manufactured goods dropped from 20 per cent to 8 per cent. In 1986 we exported £73 billion and imported £86 billion worth of goods. The largest part of the manufacturing sector is electrical, electronic and instrument engineering, accounting for one seventh of the total.[1]

Pressures

There is immense pressure from overseas competition, where labour is cheaper and technical skills are becoming more widespread. In the UK the pressure is therefore to cut costs and to increase efficiency using new technology such as robots. Between 1984 and 1986 the number of industrial robots in the UK doubled but was still below the level of our European competitors. A survey in 1985 showed that a quarter of managers in the manufacturing sector said there had been no significant change in production process in the previous five years; one-third said that new technology had had no impact; two-fifths of companies had no strategy for adopting new technology. So many of the smaller companies are not responding vigorously to the challenge. The industry carries high levels of stock; at the end of 1984 they were estimated to be worth £41 billion and costing £10 billion each year to maintain. Thus there is pressure for techniques such as Just In Time (JIT) to reduce stock levels.

Trends

In manufacturing, lower stock levels and greater use of automation are important. There is also a need to be more sensitive and responsive to the needs of the market. For example, the clothing industry can survive overseas competition if it can reduce production costs and then exploit an important advantage: speed of response to the changes of the domestic fashion market. In general we need a faster reaction time from design to production, using integrated systems, and the ability to customize products without losing the advantages of mass production. Computer Integrated Manufacturing (CIM) or Flexible Manufacturing System (FMS) are umbrella terms used to describe the bringing together of parts of the total process: Computer Numerically Controlled (CNC) machines, Computer Aided Design (CAD) and Management Information Systems (MIS).

Information systems

IT has a vital role in all these manufacturing systems. It is important (but difficult) to link together systems which were originally designed in isolation for different purposes. The industry is now pressing for information systems and local area networks which will link the various equipments in a modern factory, and allow them to work effectively together. Protocols (standards) are being developed for this, notably the Manufacturing Automation Protocol (MAP) initiated by General Motors in the US, and the broader Technical Office Protocol (TOP) initiated by Boeing. This is a good example of user-pressure to achieve more efficient, effective, and rapid-response manufacturing systems. We shall look more closely at networks and standards in Chapter 5.

Some examples will illustrate these issues.

1. A small specialist manufacturer of sheet-metal components invested in CNC machine-tools with a linked CAD system. This enabled it to speed up the response it could offer its customers for specialist, small-batch items. They saw a strategic opportunity to extend the CAD system into customers' premises, and possibly link into customers' own CAD systems, as a way of working even more closely with them. This 'locking-in' of customers, to mutual advantage, can give a lasting competitive edge to a company.
2. A UK clothing manufacturer was under heavy price competition from overseas. It responded by moving further into the ladies fashion market, where style changes quickly. By using Point of Sale (POS) data about sales in retail stores, the company was able to watch the market more closely and plan its production more accurately to track demand. This speed of response gave it an advantage over the overseas competition.
3. An overseas clothing manufacturer responded to this situation by setting up a small design team in London. They watched the fashion market closely and then used CAD equipment to design the clothes. The data from the CAD system was sent by satellite link to the overseas manufacturing facility, which could then enter production much more quickly. By moving up-market the margins allowed use of air-freight to get the product into the market quickly enough to compete with UK-based producers.

4. European car manufacturers cooperated to set up a common network for data exchange between suppliers and manufacturers (Electronic Data Interchange, or EDI). This would give them all a benefit of speed and economy, by replacing paper-based ordering procedures with faster electronic ordering. However, one major manufacturer withdrew from the project, believing that it was in its best interest to run a separate system with which it could continue to 'lock-in' its suppliers.

3.3 Business sector 2: Retailing

Size

In 1986 retail distribution was the second largest part of the service sector, with 2.1 million employees.[1] In 1984 there were about 231 000 businesses in the UK whose annual turnover exceeded £18 700. Their total turnover was £82 billion. Since then, there has been a reduction in the number of retail businesses, with a shift towards large multiple retailers; they now account for 58 per cent of retail turnover. The largest multiple is Sainsbury, with 279 stores and a turnover of more than £5 billion in 1987–88. The largest mixed-multiple is Marks and Spencer, with sales of £4.6 billion in 1987–88.

Pressures

Demographic trends, including increased personal mobility, have altered the pattern of shopping. There is a greater demand for out-of-town shopping, in complexes which offer a wide range of goods associated with free car parking. Customers expect convenience, as well as value for money. For many families, shopping has become a joint activity done in the evenings or at the weekends. Customers want easy and convenient methods of payment.

Trends

The Government is encouraging the trend towards larger stores. By the end of 1986 there were 375 superstores and hypermarkets, and planning permission had been granted for 87 more. The purpose-built shopping centres in Manchester, Tyneside and Milton Keynes cover more than one million square feet, and are among the largest in Europe. For the motorist, the number of petrol stations is declining, but there is a trend to self-service (42 per cent of the 20 641 stations at the end of 1986). Competition has become more intense, leading to some focusing of business. For example, in 1986

Woolworth and British Home Stores decided to withdraw from food retailing. Mail-order shopping reached a peak in about 1980, but some 20 million people now shop by post, accounting for 7 per cent of non-food retail sales. Electronic systems such as viewdata make home shopping more attractive and popular.

Information systems

Technology has contributed to greater efficiency in stock-control, particularly with Electronic Point of Sale (EPOS) systems. In supermarkets, laser-scanning electronic check-outs have increased rapidly since their first introduction in 1979. In 1987 a major UK supplier, ICL, estimated that the number of EPOS systems would grow from 58 000 to 410 000 by 1993, covering 80 per cent of larger retail outlets. The extension of EPOS to Electronic Fund Transfer at Point of Sale (EFTPOS) allows the customer to pay by authorizing an immediate debit from his bank account. EFTPOS has been slower coming, because it is unclear who benefits and should therefore bear the cost: retailer, bank, or customer. However, trials are in progress, and a national EFTPOS network supported by the Clearing Banks is planned. Another trend is for electronic ordering by retailers from wholesalers. Electronic Data Interchange (EDI) is the generic name for this. EDI networks, such as Edinet from Istel and Tradanet from ICL, transfer orders between users' computer systems even if they are made by different manufacturers. Tradanet has endorsement until 1990 by the Article Numbering Association which coordinates the bar coding of retail products.[2]

Large retailers are therefore heavily committed to the use of information systems. An increasing challenge will be the integration of the different types of system mentioned: stock control; POS at the check-outs; EDI to interface suppliers; EFTPOS to allow electronic payment; and home-based systems to permit home shopping. Detailed data from POS systems can be a valuable source of marketing information. The retailer can monitor, very closely, the volume of sales of any particular item, and identify any regional or time variations. This information can be used to plan advertising and other marketing activities. The same data is of interest to the wholesale suppliers; retailers may find they can sell data to them as a by-product of introducing EPOS systems. In 1989 Boots became the first major retailer to announce that it was investing in a large POS system not primarily to improve stock-control but rather to improve marketing. It enabled them to identify much more accurately the profit being made on individual items. As a result of having such detailed information, they dropped certain pet-food lines.

3.4 Business sector 3: Finance

Size

Finance is the largest and fastest-growing part of the service sector of the UK economy. In 1986 it employed 10 per cent of the workforce (2.2 million people) and generated 16 per cent (£52 billion) of Gross Domestic Product (GDP). Overseas earnings were £9.4 billion, making an important contribution to the balance of payments.[1] London is a major international financial centre. The International Stock Exchange in London quotes some 6650 different securities with a market value of £1693 billion, while the London foreign exchange market is the largest in the world with daily transactions exceeding £70 billion. In the UK there are 19 retail banks, with total liabilities and assets of £218 billion. They have 11 800 branches, of which 81 per cent are owned by the 'Big Four' (NatWest, Barclays, Midland, and Lloyds). There are 151 building societies, with assets of £141 billion. The three largest (Halifax, Abbey National, and Nationwide Anglia) account for about half of this.

Pressures

The Government has exerted pressure to increase competition in the financial sector, with three major pieces of legislation. The 1986 Financial Services Act set up a supervisory framework for City institutions, operated by the Securities and Investments Board (SIB). It oversees a number of Self-Regulating Organizations (SROs) which draw up and then monitor the operation of rules for individual sectors of the industry. The 1987 Banking Act improved supervision of the banking sector, while the 1986 Building Societies Act allowed societies to diversify their activities and compete with banks, estate agents, insurance brokers, and stockbrokers.

Trends

Increasing competition and the growth in the volume of transactions has led to greater use of technology. The change in the regulation of the City in October 1986 was termed 'Big Bang'; the new style of operation required electronic systems for quoting and dealing in the market. The trend was to form large financial conglomerates, which became the market makers. Several smaller companies withdrew from trading, and the traditional face-to-face trading on the floor of the Exchange all but disappeared. The more competitive and faster-moving market, based on electronic dealing systems, has sometimes caused or aggravated instability in market prices; this happened in September 1986 and in October 1987 for example.

In the retail finance sector, a similar growth in transactions has encouraged further automation. Nevertheless the number of paper-based transactions is still increasing. For transactions between banks there are electronic networks like SWIFT for international payments, and Clearing House Automated Payment System (CHAPS) and Bankers Automated Clearing Services (BACS) for payments within the UK.

To reach individual customers, there are now 10 000 Automated Teller Machines (ATMs, or cash-dispensers) in the UK. Many of them use networks which are shared between more than one bank or building society. Home banking, using viewdata terminals in the home, is still on a modest scale; a service by the Bank of Scotland and the Nottingham Building Society was introduced in 1982, but the larger banks have not yet marketed extensive systems. In contrast, the use of credit and debit cards has increased very fast. There are some 23 million credit and charge cards in use in the UK, the average debt per household exceeds £1400. Telephone payment by quoting a credit card number is the fastest growing method of payment.

The growth in electronic money systems has led to an increase in fraud. It is difficult to estimate the size of this problem, because institutions which have suffered are often reluctant to admit the fact. However, a study in 1986 showed that the annual loss to UK business due to computer fraud was between £25 million and £30 million per year. The average size of fraud increased from £31 000 in 1983 to £250 000 in 1986. In about half of the detected cases the culprit is found, but only 5 per cent are successfully convicted. The Department of Public Prosecutions only has time to deal with cases of fraud involving more than £1 million.

Information systems

The major markets in the City need electronic quoting and transaction systems which are reliable, able to handle peak transaction rates, and are resilient in the event of failure. When major new systems are introduced, as with Big Bang in October 1986, it is not easy to meet all these criteria at once. A second need is for decision support systems which can help traders be effective in rapidly changing situations. Today's dealers have only a few seconds to react to a change in the market, make an offer, and close a deal. A third need is for electronic systems to help organizations comply with the new regulatory framework. This is particularly important for financial conglomerates which may act in different capacities for different clients. There must be 'Chinese Walls' which confine financial information to those entitled to receive it within the organization. In the past, Chinese Walls have been physical safeguards, but now we must enclose electronic information as well. All financial networks, of course, need security features to prevent fraud by outsiders, or by insiders with privileged access to the computer networks involved.

For the retail finance sector, large networks are needed to serve increasing numbers of ATMs, branch offices, and home-based customers. More significant will be the growth of EFTPOS systems (see Sec. 3.3), where the customer authorizes an electronic transfer of funds at the time a purchase is made. In France, a trial of 'smart cards', with embedded microchips, is aimed at supporting 10 000 ATMs, and 400 000 EPOS terminals by the early 1990s. In 1987, 40 European Banks announced their intention of making their cash and credit card systems compatible by 1990. Here are two further examples of strategic use of IT in the finance sector:

1. The Friends Provident insurance company developed an electronic system which linked their branch offices to the Head Office; this improved the efficiency of conducting business internally. In 1982 they extended the system to insurance brokers and agents, using the Prestel viewdata system. Over the period 1975 to 1986 the productivity, in terms of new policies per member of staff, had increased four-fold and the market share doubled in about six years. Much of this success was attributed to being at the leading edge of the use of new IT.
2. The Bank of Scotland built on its home-banking link with the Nottingham Building Society by offering a service for small businesses which lacked accounting and financial expertise. This is an example of providing a specialist function over an electronic information system to the customer. Once such an electronic link has been established, there is opportunity to offer a wider range of services with only a small increase in overheads.

All these examples from the three business sectors show the importance of monitoring the external or strategic situation: the relationship between the enterprise and its customers in a changing environment. Today, this is vital for the public as well as the private sector, and also for the non-profit sector as well as the profit-making sector of the economy. Sector analysis provides a simple approach to linking business strategy with the use of information systems.

3.5 Management functions: Introduction

The modern manager in any discipline is expected to be able to react quickly to a wide range of problems. At one moment there may be difficulties over a budget or some item of office expenditure, at the next there may be some crisis in the factory, or trouble with a member of staff. At the same time as dealing with these immediate matters the manager must also be concerned with the overall well-being of the organization, now and in the future.

The manager may be thought of as a juggler, keeping several balls in the air at once. Each one demands a little of the juggler's attention, but to concentrate on one or the other would inevitably lead to the others getting out of control. These different activities, or functions, may be grouped under five headings:

- finance
- human resources
- marketing
- planning
- operations.

The practical manager will look for help in coping with these functions: that help may come from colleagues, inside or outside the organization, and now from Information Systems. The intelligent use of information systems by managers can have the same effect as a good set of tools in gardening or do-it-yourself activities: just as mechanical tools extend the reach and power of the human hand and arm, so information systems can extend the reach and power of the human brain to achieve results that previously would have been unthinkable.

3.6 Management function 1: Finance

We are all concerned with money. Either we have too little of it, or perhaps too much. If we are managers then we are concerned with our organization's income and expenditure and with our costs. Our position in a competitive market-place will depend on effective cost controls and realistic pricing; our survival may depend on our profit margins and annual investment of capital. Even the most efficient and sophisticated businesses can run into money problems if they are not able to process information quickly enough for it to be of any use. Cash flow will suffer if bills are not sent out quickly or if debts are not collected.

A small engineering company specialized in the repair of machine tools. Their competitive advantage was their speed of response and their 24-hour service. A customer would report a fault or would request attention for a machine overhaul; a mobile technician would be sent to the site. A preliminary estimate for the work would normally be given to the customer after brief consultation with the repair company's office, although in urgent cases the work would be started immediately. The preliminary estimate was based on a schedule of standard manhours for typical jobs together with an estimate of parts required. If the machine was a large one it might be repaired *in situ*, smaller machines would be transported to the repair company's works.

No detailed costing of the work could be done until the job had been completed and the worksheets had been returned to the accounts department. Extra work or special parts were often required; urgent jobs might be done overnight when the accounts personnel were absent. Worksheets sent to accounts often lacked important information, especially if the work had been urgent, consequently there were long delays in preparing accounts and in sending out bills to customers who often queried the details. To compensate for this inconvenience to customers long periods of credit, as much as two months after the date of the bill, were granted to most customers and special discount terms were available to favoured customers.

The work-load on the company increased and the company appeared to be successful, but cash flow problems also increased and became serious. The company was unable to forecast income or expenditure and was not able to meet demands from its suppliers or from its workforce.

How could this company improve its financial control procedures? Some method of collecting information, perhaps directly from the mobile technicians, and feeding it into a computerized worksheet could be investigated. The computer could allocate standard costs for manhours and parts, thus allowing a preliminary estimate to be given. A worksheet could be issued for the job and could act as a data input document for additional work or parts. Alternatively the data could be entered directly into the computer from keyboards in the works. By this means it should be possible to prepare properly costed bills for each job as it leaves the works. Linking the costing information system to the accounts system would allow expenditure and income to be controlled. Other benefits of linking stores, ordering, personnel and other systems together could also be obtained. The key ingredient for success in this case is information: the right sort of information, collected, stored, processed and communicated efficiently to improve financial performance. Apart from helping with cash-flow problems, information systems may be used to assist managers with a wide variety of money-related matters. Tax and VAT returns, budgets, investment analysis and accounts are all grist to the computer's mill. These applications may be beneficial on their own, but the advantages of integrating management information systems, as in the case of the repair company, will be considerable.

At the highest organizational level the manager may be concerned with investment policy, with new business ventures requiring new capital, with dividend policies and so on. As will be described later, information systems are able to provide decision-support at the strategic level of financial management as well as at the operational levels.

3.7 Management function 2: Human resources

It is recognized that an organization's most valuable resources are the people that work for it. People are not like things, they have aims and aspirations, they need consulting, coaxing, encouraging and paying. However, like goods or machines, people can be moved around, assigned to specific tasks, or trained for new ones. For that reason every organization needs to keep careful records of the people that it employs, their conditions of work, hours of attendance, pay, pensions, and so on. There may be training schemes or management development schemes for the staff which need to be triggered by information in the personnel files. The organization may wish to recruit people for jobs, in which case job profiles may be prepared together with descriptions of the ideal qualifications for candidates. Managers may wish to consult the personnel records to select a candidate for some special job or for promotion.

Personnel records usually contain confidential material, but the organization will gain from some integration of the personnel files with other business information systems, such as those for accounting and for production. Problems of security of information will need careful treatment, with different levels of access to the information being granted to persons with appropriate authority.

3.8 Management function 3: Marketing

All managers must be concerned in some sense with marketing. They may actually be responsible for producing and selling goods or services in a competitive market-place, or they may have to 'sell' their knowledge and expertise within the organization in competition with their colleagues. Marketing is clearly an area where information is power. The effective manager must have information about the products, services and skills that the organization or the individual can offer. There must be detailed knowledge of demand for the organization's products or services, both now and in the future. Forecasts will have to be based on the best available information, much of it from outside the organization. Much current management literature refers to the 'competitive advantage' that effective management of information can bring: as with military intelligence, the role of information is to give the manager early warning of trends, an indication of opportunities, and a means of planning for action.

Since successful marketing depends on satisfying the present and future needs of customers it will be necessary to collect and to process information about them. Most businesses have simple mailing lists of current and potential customers, but more information is needed. Indications of customer preferences, of their likes and dislikes, details of products and services that they already use, information about their businesses and other facts and figures will enable the manager to plan a campaign or to design and sell a new product. Such information may be collected by the organization itself, or it may come from market research by outside organizations. This information will need to be processed and presented in a form useful for management decision making. Mathematical analysis may have to be performed on figures, econometric forecasting models may be constructed, graphs and charts will be required. All this is facilitated by modern information systems.[2]

The computer has an enormous capacity for 'number-crunching' and there are easy-to-use statistical and graphical packages that can reduce apparently meaningless numbers to concise and meaningful reports in minutes. The use of information systems in the marketing function enables the marketing manager to be quicker and better than a competitor: in today's competitive world the advantage may make the difference between fortune and failure.

An example of the power of information systems in marketing is seen in the case of the American airline that established a seat reservations system for its own use. The system was so successful that it was decided to market the facility to other airlines. However, the designers ensured that when a user interrogated the system for flight information, the first flights to be offered were always those of the original owners of the system.

3.9 Management function 4: Planning

Planning is the process of directing the resources of the organization, now and in the future, towards its longer-term goals. All managers have to plan. For some, planning is simply a matter of arranging the diary for a week, or a month ahead. For others it may involve complex strategic plans for new product development, or for major capital investment over several years. In each case accurate information is required about the organization's activities and about factors outside the organization likely to affect the plans. As planning looks further and further ahead it may be difficult or even impossible to get good information. Managers will have to use their experience and judgement to forecast what may occur in any set of circumstances.

Information systems may be seen as providing tools for managers in organizations, helping them to work faster, more accurately or more effectively. The potential for information systems is much greater. If they are applied to planning and decision making at the higher, strategic, levels of organizations they can have a revolutionary effect. Because the computer can simulate and explore business opportunities without constraints of resources or time planners have access to a wide range of alternative strategies.

In Chapter 13 we will look at ways in which computers and information systems can be used in business modelling and decision-support.

3.10 Management function 5: Operations

Apart from managing money, people, markets and plans managers will be concerned with managing the work that flows through their organization and the processes that are applied. That work may be in the form of goods bought, sold or produced or may be in the form of services. The efficient management of goods and services is another potential application of information systems. Imagine the situation in a large public service industry, such as gas, electricity or telecommunications. Large stocks of materials, cables, pipes, domestic appliances, components, tools and so on, must be kept in the stores. These stocks are used every day, often in an unpredictable manner. To reduce costs the stockholding must be kept to a minimum, but the level of stocks must be sufficient to avoid shortages of key items. Some method of recording inventories and the movement of stocks is required and needs to be linked to an ordering procedure for replenishment of stocks. A service organization, such as a garage, a post office, or a hospital, is concerned with the rapid movement of cars, customers or patients through the system. People should not be kept waiting and should be satisfied that they have received quick and careful attention.

The problem is particularly acute where the organization handles perishable goods, such as food. Products must be manufactured, stored for a minimum period, transported to distributors and retail outlets and then sold to customers, often in a matter of days or even hours.

> One company in the North of England, manufacturers and distributors of seafood, meat and other foods, has computerised its operations by means of a truly distributed information system. Trucks are equipped with microcomputers, powered from the vehicle batteries. Drivers are able to process invoices and sales details on the spot, VAT calculations are done automatically. Customers receive invoices that have been printed by the computer in the truck. Not only is the individual truck's stock list kept up-to-date but at the end of each week the floppy disk from each computer is used to update the company's central records.[3]

A further development of this system would be to link the mobile computers to the central computer by means of a cellular telephone network. In this way stock control, invoicing, customer orders, route scheduling and other functions could be controlled in real time.

The effective management of any of these processes requires information; in one case information about stock levels, consumption and likely demand for stores; in another case information is needed about the level of demand, nature of the task and resources needed to provide the service. Modern information systems are easily able to handle such information and to assist in its effective management.

In a manufacturing environment the manager will be concerned with the design and development of new products and with their economical manufacture. The increasing use of computer-controlled machines and automated processes implies an enormous increase in the information required to be processed. Information systems can now handle computer aided design (CAD), computer aided manufacture (CAM) and computer integrated manufacture (CIM). The kinds of information to be found in such systems include design, production control, machine loading, machine control, quality control, work-scheduling, costing, maintenance control, etc. Manufacturing information systems can collect, store, process and communicate such information quickly and efficiently. The information can be used for process control, or for design and production planning, or to reduce waste and to improve quality. Information may also be used in a simulation of the production process, allowing experimental changes to be made to the processes or products to achieve maximum efficiency and cost-effectiveness.

3.11 Management functions: Integration

Information systems are capable of dealing with many specialized management problems, but they are wasted if operated in isolation. The real power of information management comes from the integration of the various management functional systems into one overall information system. An organization may then have a central database of management information, operational data, records, etc. which can be accessed by a number of different systems. Information for any particular application can be extracted and formatted as required for use. Information in the database may come from within the organization, or from outside it. Some information systems include the facility of automatic monitoring of external databases for significant information, for example, the movement of stock or commodity prices. Whenever there is a significant change the system will signal the users most concerned who can then plan for the most appropriate action.

3.12 Conclusion

In this chapter we have looked at three sectors of UK business, and five functions of management within business. In each case we have identified, in broad terms, the place where information systems can and should play a part. You should relate these examples to your own experience and organization, to help you focus on the needs and opportunities there.

This completes Part 1 of the book; see the map at Fig. 0.1. If you are familiar with the details of Information Technology and current systems you can move straight to Part 3 (Chapter 8). Otherwise you should continue with Part 2 (Chapters 4–7), which deals with the tools for building information systems.

References

1. *Britain – An Official Handbook*, HMSO, 1988.
2. Parkinson, L. K., and Parkinson, S. T., *Using the Microcomputer in Marketing*, McGraw-Hill, 1987.
3. 'Delivering the goods in style', reported in *IMPAQ*, 2Q87, p. 16.

PART TWO
THE TOOLS

4
Computers and management information systems

4.1 Introduction

Business information systems comprise people, procedures, and technology. In that sense there is nothing new about information systems; they have used the technology of paper and ink for thousands of years, and the technology of the telephone for more than a hundred years. Some business systems can still operate effectively using only those technologies and the principles of information management still apply. However, modern IT does offer new and more effective ways of handling information. In this part of the book we shall be considering information systems in the narrow sense: electronic systems which use modern IT for the collection, processing, storage, and communication of data, information and knowledge.

Some people use the term 'information system' only in this narrow sense. However, the manager must always remember the wider meaning, and we shall return to it in Part 3. Meanwhile, here we focus on IT and the electronic information systems it has made possible. These are the tools with which to build business systems.

4.2 Electronic information systems

The functions which are needed in IT systems are:

- *signals* to represent the data or information;
- *transmission* to convey it;
- *switching* to select where it is sent;
- *processing* to manipulate and present it.

These four functions can be illustrated by the familiar telephone system.

When we speak, the sound is converted by the microphone of the telephone handset into an electrical representation, or signal. That signal is passed over a transmission facility (usually buried copper wires) to the local telephone exchange. There, the exchange performs the switching operation in response to the telephone number which we have dialled; it selects a path through the huge network of transmission facilities to reach the person we wish to speak to.

Occasionally there may also be some processing, in the form of storage and retrieval of the signals representing our voice if the person we wish to speak to is not immediately available but has an answering machine or a voice messaging system connected to a telephone.

With modern IT microelectronics is the technology for handling the signals; communications is the technology for transmission and switching; and computing is the technology for processing. Modern information systems bring the functions and the technologies closely together. This chapter deals with microelectronics and computing, Chapter 5 deals with communications, and Chapter 6 shows how they come together. Finally, Chapter 7 describes some future trends in information technology.

4.3 The development of microelectronics

Electronics depend on devices where a small amount of electrical power can be used to control a larger amount of power. Such 'active devices' enable signals to be stored and manipulated; they are the basis of all modern IT. A brief account of the development of active devices will show how the underlying power of IT has expanded, and how it is likely to expand in the future.

The first important active device was the thermionic valve, invented in 1906. It uses a lot of electrical power and has a limited life. It dominated electronics from 1906 until the invention of the transistor in 1948. The transistor is much more reliable and operates at lower electrical power levels. It is a solid-state device made from materials called semiconductors which have special electrical properties. The material most commonly used is silicon.

The transistor made a major impact on electronics from the 1950s. Electronic circuits could be made using Printed Circuit Boards (PCBs) in which the electrical conductors were made by etching patterns of copper onto a rigid sheet of insulating material. This made electronics more reliable, and suitable for mass-production. Eventually devices were made in which a number of transistors and their interconnecting wires were fabricated on a single small piece of silicon called a 'chip'. This technique dates from the

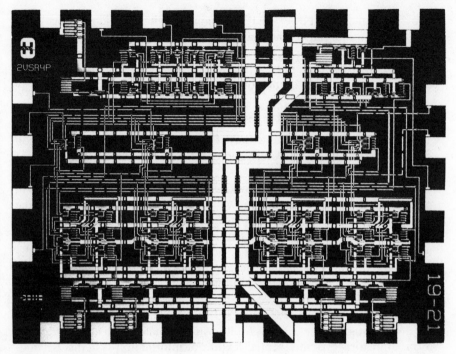

Figure 4.1 Integrated circuit

early 1960s. Figure 4.1 shows a magnified view of such an Integrated Circuit (IC); the chip of silicon is only a few millimetres in each direction.

Besides having all the advantages of transistors, ICs had much greater functional power, because so many transistors could be fabricated onto a single chip. The rapid growth in the power of ICs is shown in Fig. 4.2. The number of components which can be fabricated on a chip is increasing ten-fold every five years. By 1975 there were ICs with more than 10 000 components; this was termed Very Large Scale Integration', or VLSI. This

YEAR	COMPONENTS PER CHIP	NAME
1960	10	Small Scale Integration (SSI)
1965	100	Medium Scale Integration (MSI)
1970	1000	Large Scale Integration (LSI)
1975	10 000	Very Large Scale Integration (VLSI)
1980	100 000	
1985	1 000 000	
1990	10 000 000? (for FGCS)	Ultra Large Scale Integration (ULSI)

? GROWTH: initially 'Double every Year' (Moore's Law) latterly 'Times 10 in 5 Years'

Figure 4.2 VLSI development

immense functional power of ICs, compared with individual transistors, explains the major impact they have had on electronics. The rapid expansion in the power of silicon ICs is continuing, and has not yet reached the fundamental physical limits. The increasing power of chips will give a corresponding increase in the power of IT devices.

4.4 Analogue and digital technology

This development of electronics has affected the way in which information systems work. The signals which represent data within a system can be of two kinds: analogue and digital. With analogue signals, the size of some physical quantity is represented by an electrical voltage whose size varies in proportion to that quantity. This is well suited for quantities which can take on any value within a defined range. Examples are the temperature in a room, the pressure of the oil in a car, or the air-pressure of the soundwave which we utter when speaking. A device called a transducer represents the size of the quantity by an electrical voltage. In the examples quoted, the transducer would be an electrical thermometer, a pressure transducer, or a microphone.

Valves and transistors were good at handling analogue signals. But there are disadvantages. First, it is difficult to store signals which are in analogue form, and storage is an essential feature of information systems. Second, there are some types of data or information which are not suited to an analogue representation anyway. Text, for example, consists of a series of letters and other written characters. The letters of the alphabet cannot take any value within a range; they can only be one of the 26 letters defined in the alphabet. In such cases, we have to devise a convention which labels each of the permitted values with an identity number. This is called digital technology. One convention uses the decimal numbers 065 to 090 to represent the capital letters A to Z inclusive; thus the word 'BOOK' would be represented by the series of numbers 066 079 079 075.

Integrated circuits are good at handling signals which can be in only one of two states. These states are usually called '0' and '1'; physically they might be represented by a positive or a negative standard voltage, with no intermediate voltage being allowed. In this form, called binary (or two-value), the signals can be stored as well as processed. It is simple to convert from decimal numbers to binary numbers, and the word 'BOOK' would be represented by the series of binary numbers 01000010 01001111 01001111 01001011. If you type the word BOOK on a word processor or computer, that is the pattern of 0s and 1s physically stored to represent the four letters of the word.

This representation of data by binary-number signals is called digital technology. It is useful to be aware of some of the terminology used. A 'bit' is a single element, a 0 or a 1; it is short for 'binary digit'. Usually, bits are handled in groups of eight called 'bytes'. Note that each letter in the binary example above was represented by one byte, consisting of eight bits. In computer code an 8-bit byte is used to represent each character; this gives 256 possibilities, of which the capital letters A–Z account for 26.

The capacity of a computer memory is usually measured in bytes (characters). A 'Kilobyte' or 'K' is about a thousand bytes. The exact number is 1024 (the number 2 raised to the 10th power), but the figures are usually rounded for convenience. A 'Megabyte' or 'M' is about a million bytes. A 'Gigabyte' or 'G' is about a thousand million (or billion) bytes. To set these numbers into perspective, it is worth remembering that one A4 page of text holds about 3000 characters or 3K bytes. Modern IC memory chips can store 256K bytes, equivalent to nearly 100 pages of text. The hard disk store in some modern personal computers can store 100M bytes, equivalent to 40 000 pages of text. For comparison, the text of the Bible contains 3.6M bytes.

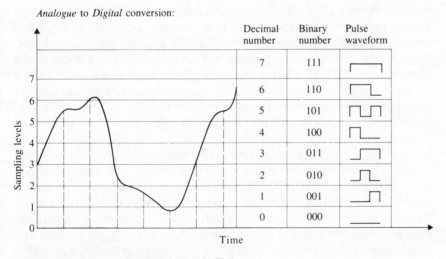

Figure 4.3   Pulse Code Modulation (PCM)

Computing technology is now almost entirely digital, and communications technology is rapidly becoming digital. Where necessary it is possible to convert an analogue signal into a digital form so that it can be handled more effectively. This is illustrated in Fig. 4.3 for the case of a telephone system. The smoothly-varying curve on the left of the diagram represents the analogue signal coming from the microphone; it corresponds to the changes in air-pressure. In an analogue system, this smoothly-varying voltage is transmitted right through the telephone system. However, it is possible to convert the signal into a numerical form instead. The analogue signal is examined, or sampled, at regular intervals (8000 times per second in practice) and for each sample the size of the signal is measured and recorded as a number. The diagram shows a 3-bit number, which can represent eight different levels; in practice 8 bits are used to get greater precision. The binary numbers can then be sent, one after the other, as a digital signal. The telephone signal thus becomes 8000 8-bit numbers per second, or 64 000 bits per second. This conversion from analogue to digital, and the reverse operation, can be done quite simply with a special chip. Once in digital form, the signals can be stored, processed, and communicated using all the features of modern IT.

4.5 Computers: Fundamentals

What exactly is a computer? It is a general-purpose machine which is made to perform a particular job by a set of instructions called a program. There are two important points about this definition. First, the computer is a general-purpose machine; it differs in that respect from almost any other tool that humans have made. Most tools do one job, or a set of related jobs. A screwdriver will drive in screws but will not undo nuts; for that you need a different tool. To type a letter you use a typewriter; if you want to add up numbers you have to use a calculator. A computer can be told to prepare text or process numbers exactly when and how the user wishes. This unique flexibility of computers explains their remarkable success.

The second point is that the machine and the program (the set of instructions) are of similar importance. The physical machine and the items connected to it are termed the hardware. Hardware is what you can see and touch. Software is more subtle. Strictly it is quite abstract or intellectual: it consists of the program (the instructions to the hardware) and the data which the hardware will need when it carries out those instructions. In practice the software must be recorded in some physical form which can be read and acted upon by the hardware. So software is often recorded on a magnetic diskette which the machine can read. For the human user, it is also documented and explained in a manual. Nevertheless, the value of the physical storage medium is trivial compared with the intellectual investment in devising the program, or the cost of assembling data about a business. A diskette which itself might cost £1 could hold a program whose commercial value is £400; a diskette might hold data which has cost a business thousands of pounds to assemble and process.

With advances in IT, hardware is becoming cheaper, more powerful, and more reliable. Software is becoming more complex, but still requires a huge investment of human effort to prepare and prove it. Software is therefore becoming the major cost of modern computer systems.

4.6 Computer architecture

A simple block diagram of a computer is shown in Fig. 4.4. The diagram is a specific version of the general one for an information system; it has the features of collection, processing, storage, communication and control. The lower four blocks represent the hardware: data is entered via an input facility (such as a keyboard), it is manipulated in the processor and the final version is delivered through an output facility such as a Visual Display Unit (VDU) or printer. Data needed for the processing, or generated during processing, is held in a store or memory. The top block represents the software which controls the whole operation. The application program is the set of instructions needed to make the machine do the particular task desired; the software control function orchestrates the operation of the machine to achieve what the program requires. In practice much of this software is also held in the memory of the machine.

The first generation of computers using this structure or 'architecture' was built from about 1946. Valve technology was used, and this limited the complexity possible. From 1959 the second generation used transistors, and from 1964 the third generation used ICs. Up to this time computers were large and required specialist operators, only the largest organizations could afford them. These 'mainframe' machines had to be operated in a centralized location. Data were taken or transmitted to them for processing in a

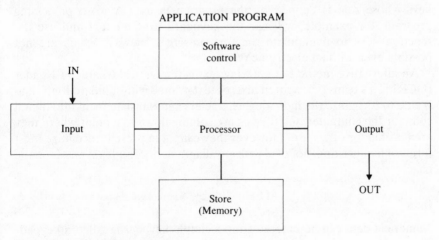

Figure 4.4 Computer architecture

batch, usually on some regular cycle of operations. In business, mainframe computers became the hub of data processing for such applications as payroll, stock-control and financial recording within banks.

With the rapid development of ICs, computers became more reliable, compact, and powerful. Minicomputers were developed which could operate in a normal office environment and therefore be taken much closer to the user. Eventually, from 1980, the microcomputer or personal computer (PC) became feasible, as a desk-top device for individual use. During the 1980s PCs became more compact and powerful, and a range of portable machines gave PC facilities to individuals on the move. These developments in computer technology have had important effects in business.

4.7 Computer input

In this section we consider computer input devices which operate in the four modes:

- text
- data
- voice
- image.

Text

For text the commonest input device is the keyboard. For letters and numbers this uses the same layout as the typewriter. In addition there are some control keys to give instructions to the machine, and a set of function keys whose role is defined by the program in use. A word processing program, for example, will use the keyboard to enter text and use the function keys to manipulate the text on-screen in ways which are not possible even with an electronic typewriter.

An alternative method of entering text is the Optical Character Reader (OCR). This scans typewritten text, or text printed with standard fonts, and is able to recognize the individual characters and translate them into digital code for the computer. OCR costs are coming down to a point where they are feasible for office use. However they cannot at present recognize most forms of handwriting, nor deal with any diagrams or complex symbols on the page.

Data

Numerical data can be entered from a simple keyboard, called a keypad. This is satisfactory for small amounts of data, but becomes tedious for large amounts. Faster methods are now available, such as the bar code reader. Items held in stores, goods sold in supermarkets, and books issued by libraries can be marked with an optical bar code. This is a pattern of broad and narrow black lines printed onto a white label fixed to the item. An optical reader, which has a light and a detector mounted inside a device like a pen, is stroked across the pattern of bars and reads it as a digital code. Laser scanners which scan an item automatically and search for and read the appropriate type of pattern are now widely used at supermarket check-out points; they enable the stock-number of each item sold to be read into a computer system which identifies the current price of the item, and alerts the stock-control system to the fact that one such item has been sold. Besides optical bar codes, there are magnetic ones similar to the brown magnetic stripe on the back of most credit cards. Such stripes can hold a few hundred characters (more than the optical version) but they require a special reader and hands-off scanning is not possible.

Much greater volumes of data can be held optically on items such as credit cards. These patterns are read by a laser, but this time the card must be placed in a special reader. It is possible to store gigabytes of data in this way, so that personal details, medical history, and even data to form a colour picture of the individual can be held on a credit card.

Voice

Entering voice into a computer system is more difficult, for two fundamental reasons. First, the way that individuals pronounce the same words differs widely. Besides the different voice characteristics of the two sexes, there are regional and national variations. Even one person will utter the same word in a different way depending on the context, if he or she has a cold, or is under stress. When speaking we do not separate the words clearly; they merge into each other. The problem of recognizing continuous speech uttered by a wide range of people has not yet been solved. At present, it is possible to recognize a few words (such as the numbers one to ten) when spoken slowly and distinctly by large numbers of people. Alternatively, it is possible to train a voice-recognition system to recognize several thousand words spoken distinctly by one individual. There is a second, and more fundamental problem. The structure of spoken language is imprecise and not always used consistently. When we talk to other people we make many assumptions about the way they will understand us; computers are not yet very good at being understanding listeners, even if they can make out the words. The practical application of voice input is therefore limited at present.

Image

Image is even more demanding than voice. Firstly, a computer image consists of a very large number of picture elements (called pixels) each of which may have a different colour or shade of grey. The screen of a VDU is often made up of 640 × 400 pixels: a total of 256 000. To define one of eight colours or shades for each pixel requires one 8-bit byte. For the whole screen this makes 256K of data. Putting even a coarse image like that into a computer system takes a very large amount of data. However, scanners based on TV technology make it possible to record images in this way. It is more usual to represent the essential elements of the image (usually the lines) by a geometrical description. This is much more economical in terms of data; a simple description of the image is stored, rather than the image itself. This helps with the second major problem associated with using images: getting the computer to recognize the structure of the image, so that processing is possible. The essential elements of the image can be entered using a 'digitizing pad'. This is a flat calibrated surface over which a cursor, or 'mouse' is moved; the computer monitors the position of the cursor, so that it can record the shape of a line along which the cursor is moved, or the precise position of the significant points indicated by the operator pressing a button on the cursor or mouse.

4.8 Computer output

Every personal computer has a VDU or flat screen which displays what is currently going on. Text will appear when it is typed, and it can then be examined with a view to changing it. Data entered in tables can be examined, and then plotted on the screen as graphs to decide their significance. The screen is invaluable while the computer is at work, but a more permanent form of printed output is needed for the final product. This is called 'hard-copy'.

For text and data, the commonest type of hard-copy output device is the printer. The cheapest form is called dot-matrix; the characters are printed by a set of small rods or pins which hit the paper via an ink ribbon. Dot-matrix printing is flexible; it can print coarse images as well as text. The quality depends mainly on the speed of printing and the number of pins. Dot-matrix printers are now available with 24-pins which give quality which is acceptable for most business correspondence.

The daisywheel printer is another kind of impact printer, but uses preformed letters arranged on stalks around a central disk. The appearance of this set of letters, like flower petals, on a disk gives the name daisywheel.

Such a printer gives high-quality print, similar to that of an electric type writer. It will not, however, print anything other than the characters (usually about one hundred) available on the daisywheel.

Of increasing importance is the laser printer. This uses a technology similar to photocopying. The image to be printed (which may be a shaded picture, a diagram, or print in a variety of fonts) is scanned with a small laser beam onto the sensitive drum of the printer. This electrostatic action attracts the black toner powder, which is then printed and sealed into the paper. The quality of laser printers is extremely high because the definition is good: typically achieving a resolution of 12 dots per millimetre, compared with 2 or 3 dots per millimetre for most dot-matrix printers. Laser printers are falling in cost, and because of their flexibility and quality are beginning to dominate the office printer market.

If large volumes of output are involved then a more compact form of hard-copy than paper may be needed. An example is Computer Output Microform (COM). The output from the computer is recorded photo-graphically onto one of the standard microform formats: usually microfiche (A6-sized transparencies, each with images of about 40 A4 pages) or micro-film (35mm transparencies in a roll of film). This is very useful for archiving large amounts of text, data, or images.

Voice output from computer systems is limited at present. Technically, it is not very difficult to synthesize a representation of the human voice. Words can be translated into the corresponding sounds, but they are un-natural to the human listener. For some limited purposes it is useful, like alarm systems trying to gain human attention or public telephone-enquiry systems.

Image output is very important and becoming more widely used. This is because the human brain is very good at taking in information presented visually. Without conscious effort, the brain will look for pattern and signifi-cance in an image; this is sometimes more effective than statistical manipu-lation of data. With an image the eye takes in the data at a glance and identifies its significance. There are dangers: the brain will look for pattern at all costs, and this is the basis for many optical illusions.

Generally, then, computer displays are necessary to monitor what is going on but usually some permanent hard-copy output is also needed. Paper and microform can be used for text, data, and image records. Image, although demanding in computer capacity, is becoming increasingly important and is a very effective way of presenting information to people for them to assess its significance. Voice output, like voice input, is limited in its practical value at present. There are many ways of getting data into and out of a computer system. The combinations used will depend on the application.

4.9 Computer storage

The store or memory element of a computer (see Fig. 4.4) has two main tasks. First, it must be able to store relatively small amounts of data for short periods, such as interim results during complex calculations. For this purpose the speed of storage and retrieval is more important than the volume of data stored. The second task is to store much larger amounts of data which it does not need to access so quickly. Archiving of data for lengthy periods, or the recording of data which needs to be used much later by the same computer or another system, are examples of this. The volume of storage is then more important than the speed of access.

Computers use different technologies for these two types of storage. Section 4.4 showed how digital data is measured in bits and bytes. An A4 page of text contains about 3K bytes; digitally-coded speech from a telephone generates 8K bytes per second; a simple image might contain 256K of data; a high-quality image would contain 3M or more. This illustrates the vast increase of storage needed to move from text to voice, and then from voice to image modes.

In a computer, the short-term requirement is met with semiconductor storage using ICs. A single VLSI chip can now store about 256K of data. Semiconductor storage can be of two types.

1. Random Access Memory (RAM) is for general storage use; in this case data can be read quickly into the ICs and will be stored for as long as power is maintained to the IC (that is, the computer remains turned on). As soon as the power is turned off, the data is lost, so RAM is only suitable for short-term storage where the final results of the processing will be stored in a more permanent form in another way. For long-term storage of data, a different kind of semiconductor storage can be used.
2. Read Only Memory (ROM). This holds only predetermined data, which is not lost when the machine is turned off. ROM can be useful for storing the initial instructions for a computer start-up procedure, or to define the conversion between digital computer code and the letters and numbers which will be displayed on the VDU. ROM chips for such standard applications can be mass-produced very cheaply, and do not clutter up other storage media with standard data. There is a variant called Programmable Read Only Memory (PROM) which is for storing data which the user wants to define once and then not change. Another descriptive name is WORM (Write Once, Read Many times). If the data needs to be changed, but only occasionally, then EEPROM (Electrically Erasable Programmable ROM) is used. The data can be changed when necessary;

this is an elaborate procedure, using special equipment, and cannot be done during the normal operations of the computer system.

For more general long-term storage, it is necessary to have a storage medium of high capacity to which data can be written, and from which the data can later be read. The commonest media for this purpose are magnetic. They store the data as magnetic patterns on a medium such as tape or disk which moves in relation to the sensing head in the drive-unit. The oldest example is magnetic tape, which is stored on reels and can hold huge amounts of data. Tape is still used for mainframe computers and for large archiving applications. More widely used now are so-called hard disks (or Winchester disks) which use a rigid disk, or set of disks coated with the magnetic storage material. The read and write head rides on a cushion of air, while the disk rotates very rapidly beneath it. The time needed to retrieve a particular piece of data is much faster than with tape (milliseconds rather than seconds), and the capacity is measured in gigabytes. Small hard disk units are used in personal computers (when the capacity is typically between 10 and 100M), and will operate all the time the machine is turned on. The data are safely stored in the magnetic imprint when the machine is turned off, but a major loss can occur if the head accidentally crashes into the surface of the disk. It is therefore very important to keep back-up copies of data held on a hard disk.

Cheaper and more convenient are the flexible diskettes, or floppy disks, used in PCs. They consist of a thin, flexible disk of plastic, coated with magnetic material and kept inside a cover which allows the drive mechanism and the read/write head to access the disk. When activated, the drive mechanism rotates the plastic disk at about 300 rpm inside its protective cover and the head touches the disk on the appropriate circular track of data. There are two popular sizes of floppy disk. The first is 5.25 inches in diameter, and will typically store about 360K of data, corresponding to about 100 pages of A4 text. The second and more recent size is 3.5 inches in diameter and is held inside a rigid plastic cover with access points which are uncovered only when the disk is inserted into the drive. This makes the diskette more convenient and safe to carry about. The capacity is usually 1M or more, and recent versions can store 3M of data. All floppy disks, but especially those with exposed surfaces, need careful handling. As with hard disks, a back-up procedure will safeguard against inadvertent loss of data.

Although magnetic storage is the commonest form of long-term storage, the high-capacity storage medium of the future is probably the optical disk. Here the data is stored as very small pits burned by a laser on the metal coating of a rigid plastic disk. CD-ROM uses the same technology as compact disks in home hi-fi installations. The disk is rotated by the drive

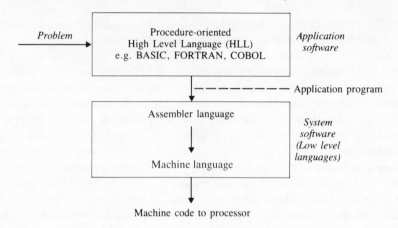

Figure 4.5 Software architecture

unit, and is read by a laser detector. They can store gigabytes of data, but at present it is not easy to change (re-write) the data on an optical disk. It is best used for cheap duplication of large amounts of data which does not need to be changed. Updates can be achieved by issuing a new version of the disk. An optical disk has adequate capacity for image storage; several hundred thousand images can be stored on a single disk about 30cm in diameter. There is considerable development work under way to make an optical disk where the data can be changed many times. Another recent development is digital paper; this is a paper/plastic laminate which can be manufactured in great widths and lengths. Data are stored in the same way as CD-ROM, with a laser burning marks on the surface.

4.10 Computer software

Referring to the block diagram of a computer (Fig. 4.4), we have now briefly reviewed the hardware technology for input, output, and storage. The processor, which is the heart of the machine, is usually a powerful integrated circuit or set of ICs working together. In a PC it is a single IC, called a microprocessor, located on one of the printed circuit boards within the system unit. The function of the processor is vital. It requires a set of very detailed instructions, called machine code, corresponding to the set of software instructions contained in the application program. The final box of the block diagram, labelled software control, is concerned with achieving this. Here, it will be described in terms of what the user and the computer do, in turn, to solve the user's particular problem; see Fig. 4.5.

Only the user understands the problem, the computer is merely a machine to help solve it. Today's third generation computers will only work step by step, following a well-defined procedure. The user must therefore first analyse the problem, and decide how it can be solved in a sequence of steps, using specialist help from a systems analyst or programmer if necessary. For example, the user may have to define the steps necessary to evaluate a formula, or calculate the statistics from marketing data. When the user is clear about the procedure, a procedure-oriented programming language is used to write the program; this is the set of instructions telling the computer exactly what to do.

The languages are called High Level Languages (HLLs), because their instructions are in words which bear some similarity to spoken English and are therefore convenient for the user to learn and remember. They are procedure-oriented because they are structured to make the machine follow a well-defined sequence of steps, as required by this type of computer. Examples of popular HLLS are: FORTRAN (which stands for FORmula TRANslation, and was developed for scientific calculations); COBOL (COmmon Business-Oriented Language); and BASIC (Beginner's All-purpose, Symbolic Instruction Code). BASIC is available on all personal computers, and includes such instructions to the computer as READ, PRINT, LOAD, STOP. A program consists of a numbered list of such instructions, which the computer must perform in strict order. An example of a very simple set of BASIC programs is given in Fig. 4.6.

Even without a knowledge of BASIC you may be able to see the structure and purpose of such simple programs. Program 1 prints the integers 1 to 15. Although very simple, this program illustrates an important point; it is very easy to make computers do a similar operation by going many times around a loop in the program. The FOR ... NEXT instructions make the machine

Program 1	Program 2	Program 3
10 FOR A = 1 TO 15	10 FOR A = 1 TO 15	10 FOR A = 1 TO 15
	15 FOR B = 1 TO A	15 FOR B = 1 TO A
20 PRINT A;	20 PRINT A;	20 PRINT A*B
	25 NEXT B	25 NEXT B
27 PRINT	27 PRINT	27 PRINT
30 NEXT A	30 NEXT A	30 NEXT A
40 END	40 END	40 END

Comments:
A 5-line program which prints the integers 1–15. Line 27 moves the print position to a new line on the screen.	A second loop has been added inside the first. For each value of A, the integers from 1 to A are printed.	Changing line 20 makes the program print the product of A and B each time

Figure 4.6   BASIC programs

do a similar task (print a number) 15 times. Program 2 adds a second such loop, inside the first; it prints the integers 1 to A for each of the 15 values of A. Program 3 prints the product of A and B each time. BASIC programming is suited to such well-defined procedural operations.

A program written in a HLL like BASIC to solve a particular problem is called an application program. In principle it can then be used to run on any computer which supports that particular HLL. In practice, things are not that simple; there are many dialects of the standard languages such as BASIC. Assuming the right dialect of the HLL has been used, and the program fed into the computer, what does the machine have to do? This is shown in the lower part of Fig. 4.5. It has to bridge the gap between the application program, written in high-level language, and the processor, which requires detailed machine-code instructions. This translation from HLL to machine code is usually done in two stages. There is an intermediate level of language, called Assembler Language, for which there is usually one easily remembered instruction corresponding to every Machine Language instruction. The conversion from HLL to Assembler is followed by the conversion from Assembler to machine code. Most application programs have already undergone the conversion process and are in machine-code form, suitable for a particular type of microprocessor.

It should now be clear that there are two main divisions of computer software. The user is responsible for the 'application software' written in a HLL to solve his problem. The computer manufacturer must provide the 'system software' with each machine. This will include the interpreter/compiler to convert from HLL, and also the operating system which will manage the operation of the computer and its peripheral devices such as tape-readers and printers.

All this sounds rather complex, especially for the user who is not an expert in computing. There are several ways non-experts can get help. First, by seeking the help of an expert. Second, by using one of the modern fourth generation systems which make it easier for the non-expert user to express exactly what they want done. The system will then construct the detailed program to achieve it. Thirdly, if the problem is a fairly standard task, a software package can be bought which is marketed commercially to meet such a need. For most users, this is the commonest way of acquiring complex computer programs.

4.11 Application packages

What are these applications which are widespread enough to justify the marketing of packages? Figure 4.7 shows some of them. The figure shows the four modes of handling information and the input and output devices suitable for each, as described earlier. At the bottom are shown the typical applications for which packages are available.

The commonest is word processing (WP). Text is entered from the keyboard, displayed on the VDU, and can be manipulated on-screen before the final version is stored or printed. This gives much greater flexibility in revising and changing text, and has led to significant increases in productivity in typing pools. For the manager, the PC-based word processor may be a valuable aid if he is reasonably proficient on a keyboard, or prepared to invest the time to become so. WP can mean that the time and effort to process a written document is much less than the time needed to compose and structure the message it contains. WP can lead to thinking at the keyboard, where ideas can be rearranged and the logic of arguments improved without the delay of drafting, typing, redrafting, and retyping. Each manager needs to form their own view on the value of WP at the personal level and at the corporate level of their organization.

Perhaps the second most widely-used application is the spreadsheet. This is for handling numerical data such as sales figures, financial plans, and other quantified data. A spreadsheet (sometimes called a worksheet) is an array of 'cells' into which data or labels or formulae can be entered. The most popular spreadsheet package is Lotus 1–2–3; it can be considered as a very large sheet of paper, only part of which is visible on the screen at any one time, as shown in Fig. 4.8. Numerical data can be entered into the cells of the spreadsheet, and then formulae entered to calculate totals or other statistics. An example of a spreadsheet is given in Fig. 4.9. This spreadsheet analyses UK employment trends. The data from the official publications has been entered into rows 9, 12–14, and 27–36. The text has been entered into other

Mode	Text	Data	Voice	Image	Mech.
Input	Keyboard OCR	Keypad Bar codes Mouse	Recognition	Digitiser Facsimile TV	Sensor
Output	VDU Printer COM	VDU Printer	Synthesis	Plotter COM	Actuator
Use	Word-processing	Database Spreadsheet	Telephone-interface	Graphics	Robots

Personal computer (PC) – WP, Database, Spreadsheet, Graphics
WIMPS: Window, Icon, Mouse, Pull-down-menu Systems

Figure 4.7 Computer applications

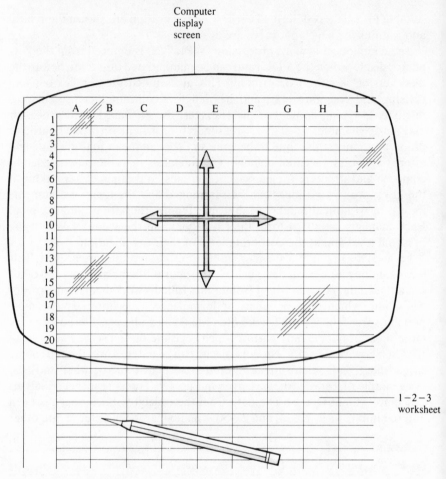

Figure 4.8 Lotus 1–2–3 Worksheet
Source: Lotus 1–2–3 Manual, p. 22

cells to make the layout clear. In row 37 formulae have been entered to calculate totals for rows 27 to 36 inclusive. If any of the data is changed, then the formula will automatically recalculate the total. In column P formulae have been entered to calculate the percentage increase between 1976 and 1986; this enabled the three fastest-growing parts of the service sector to be identified: finance, other services, and hotels and catering. The package also allows graphs to be plotted immediately from the data; Fig. 4.10 is an example, showing the data from rows 12–14.

Another popular application for personal computers is graphics. The value of graphical presentation has already been emphasized, and packages

(Print A1..P40)

A	B	C	D	E	F	G	H	I	J	K	L	M	N	O	P
5	YEAR:														
6	19..	48	59	64	73	76	77	78	80	81	83	84	85	86	
7															
8	TOTAL NUMBERS IN CIVIL EMPLOYMENT (excluding self-employed)														
9	(M)	21.5	23.2	24.2	22.7	22.6	22.6	22.8	22.9	21.9	21	21.2	21.5	21.6	
10															
11	% WORKING IN EACH SECTOR:														
12	1	6.9	5.9	5.3	5.2	4.9	4.9	4.9	4.7	4.9	4.8	4.6	4.4	4.0	
13	2	48.5	49.6	46.2	40.4	37.9	37.8	37.2	35.7	33.6	31.4	30.7	30.3	28.9	
14	3	44.5	44.5	48.4	54.4	57.2	57.3	57.9	59.6	61.5	63.8	64.7	65.3	67.1	
15															
16	Sector 1: agriculture, forestry, fishing, energy, water supply														
17	Sector 2: manufacturing and construction														
18	Sector 3: Services – see next page														
19															
20	NOTE: Page 2, below, gives a breakdown for Sector 3														
21	BREAKDOWN OF SECTOR 3 (SERVICES)														
22															
23	Thousands (as at June)														
24															
25	YEAR (19..)					76	77	78	80	81	83	84	85	86	% Increase, 1976-86
26															
27	Wholesale dist & repairs					1039	1058	1096	1163	1137	1147	1179	1194	1208	16.3
28	Retail dist					2061	2087	2102	2175	2092	2060	2143	2086	2110	2.4
29	Hotels & catering					864	877	892	978	943	964	1015	1061	1085	25.6
30	Transport					1025	1030	1051	1046	987	894	882	911	904	−11.8
31	Post & Communications					431	419	415	437	438	430	429	434	437	1.4
32	Banking, finance & insurance					1494	1519	1569	1697	1738	1822	1887	2083	2203	47.5
33	Public administration					1990	1989	1995	1985	1899	1875	1869	1962	1984	−0.3
34	Education					1618	1602	1622	1628	1615	1583	1590	1619	1656	2.3
35	Health					1174	1184	1212	1254	1293	1331	1349	1312	1316	12.1
36	Other Services					1193	1204	1242	1327	1322	1323	1393	1530	1592	33.4
37	TOTAL					12889	12969	13196	13690	13464	13429	13736	14192	14495	12.5
38															
39															
40															

Figure 4.9 Spreadsheet example
Source: Britain – an Official Handbook, HMSO, 1965, 1985, 1986, 1987, 1988

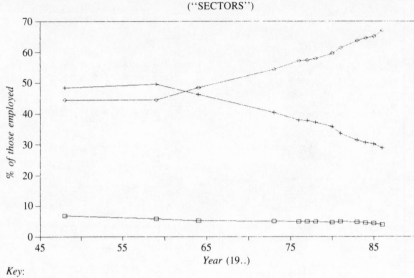

Key:
□ Agriculture/Energy
+ Manufacturing/Construction
◇ Services

Figure 4.10 Employment trends in three sectors

are available to take data, or rudimentary graphs like Fig. 4.10, and process them into a more professional format. The Freelance package was used to process the Fig. 4.10 graph to produce the version used in Chapter 1. Note that the labelling of the graph can be done more flexibly, and titles added to improve appearance. The graph was printed on a laser printer.

The fourth common application is database. This is the electronic equivalent of a paper filing system. The database contains a complete record of the facts, but those facts may be accessed in a way which suits the particular needs of the user. For example, a database which contains the holdings of a library could be accessed to find all the works of a given author, all the works published since 1985 on a particular subject, or all the works which are both by a given author, and on a particular subject, and published since 1985.

As the power of PCs has increased, so there has been a trend towards 'integrated packages' which include all the popular functions and enable the user to move from one to another quite flexibly. Another trend is towards use of better graphics to assist the user to interact easily with networks and computer packages. Here the acronym WIMPS is used for Window, Icon, Mouse, Pointer, Screen-based systems. Figure 4.11 shows the icons of a popular office-automation product. The icons resemble items in a paper-based office: in-tray, out-tray, filing cabinet, etc. This enables the user to think in a way which is familiar. The right-hand side of the diagram shows the fresh set of icons displayed when the In Tray icon is selected from the first screen; the user can now read, store, and reply to incoming electronic mail over a network of PCs. Icons can be more helpful to inexpert users than complicated computer codes, in the same way that graphs can be more helpful than large amounts of computer print-out.

So much for information-based processing. Figure 4.7 also shows, on the right hand side, the increasing use of computers as part of mechanical systems. In this case the input to the computer is a sensor which produces a digital signal to monitor a physical quantity. This might be the temperature of a part of a chemical process, or the position of the arm of an automatic welding machine, for example. The output is taken to an actuator which controls some physical device. In the examples it might be a valve which controls the flow of chemical fluid, or a motor which moves the arm of the welding machine. This broad area, where computers interact with the physical environment, is called robotics. It is the basis for automated production techniques called Computer Aided Engineering (CAE). These in turn are often linked with Computer Aided Design (CAD) systems, because they need to share the same data about the articles to be manufactured. The composite system is usually termed Computer Integrated Manufacturing (CIM).

Once a computer program has been written it is not essential that it should continue to be held on disk or tape as software. For certain well-defined and unchanging tasks it is feasible to hold all the program in a ROM semiconductor store. This in effect creates a microprocessor dedicated to the performance of one particular task, and enables the machine to be directly associated with other hardware. Examples are in mass-produced processors controlling domestic appliances such as washing machines and television sets. In most cases, however, it is better to retain the basic principle of a general-purpose hardware machine, whose performance can be controlled by the modification of software. It is easier to modify and update software than it is to change and modify hardware.

4.12 Management Information Systems (MIS)

Let us now see how computers can help managers in their work. Individual software packages can help managers process text, data, and image for particular tasks. A Management Information System (MIS), is more complex. It is a computer-based system designed to give managers information relevant to their work, not just provide tools for their personal use. Remember that information is different from data; it must be easily understood by

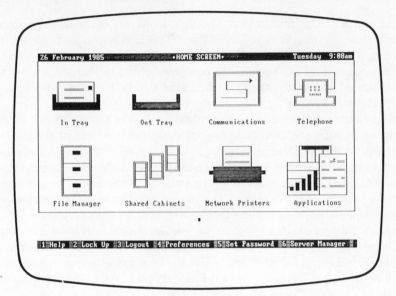

(a) Home screen

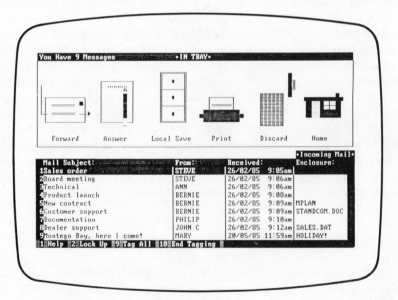

(b) In Tray screen

Figure 4.11 Computer icons
Source: 'Tapestry' workstation pack (Torus)

the user and relevant to that user's problem. Managers must be critical about information, to make sure it contributes to decision and action.

Figure 4.12 shows the types of MIS which are appropriate to each level of management. We shall examine each in turn.

- Transaction Processing Systems (TPS), are the simplest. They deal with the routine aspects of operations like payroll, stock-control transactions, and invoicing. They do not in themselves provide information for longer-term decision making.
- Information Provision Systems (IPS), provide summaries and reports based on the detailed data held by TPS or entered manually. The summary may be an aggregation of the data, or a sample of it. Reports may be produced either routinely, or when called for by a manager with a particular problem.
- Decision Support Systems (DSS), are quite different. They contain a model of some aspect of the real world, and enable the manager to investigate the available options. The model might be a financial one, or a model of a physical system such as a chemical plant. The manager asks 'what if' questions, and gets the model to predict the outcome of possible decisions. It is important for the manager to understand the nature of the model contained in the DSS (which may have been prepared by someone else) and the assumptions which it makes, or the predictions may actually be misleading. Used carefully, DSS can be a valuable aid to decision making at middle and senior level.

These three types of MIS can be considered as the first wave of information systems in organizations. TPS came first, often based on large mainframe computers. Often they made substantial savings of clerical and other people. Next came IPS, which began to make some of the routine activities of middle managers unnecessary. DSS is now making a significant impact on decision making at more senior levels.

The second wave of information systems is now under way, and means that computer-based systems are increasingly trusted to initiate actions

Management Information Systems (MIS):	Level of Management:
• Transaction Processing System (TPS)	Operational control
• Information Provision System (IPS)	Management control
• Decision Support System (DSS)	Strategic planning
• Programmed Decision System (PDS)	
• Expert System	
• Intelligent Knowledge-Based System (IKBS)	

Figure 4.12   Management Information Systems (MIS)

which were previously initiated by people. For example, the next type of MIS listed in Fig. 4.12 is a Programmed Decision System (PDS). This is programmed to take decisions automatically in accordance with criteria specified by management. For example, the middle-manager responsible for stock control might traditionally have taken monthly outputs from an IPS, analysed the stock and consumption rates and then decided how much should be ordered from suppliers in the forthcoming period. Normally the rules for such decisions are well-defined, and the computer can be told exactly what to do. It is often possible to give the supplier his order in a machine-readable form, so that apart from defining the ordering policy the manager is not involved. Likewise, the automated control of chemical plant or production facilities can be considered as a form of PDS.

The four types of MIS mentioned (TPS, IPS, DSS, and PDS) are in common use today. The next type of MIS is beginning to make itself felt. Expert Systems operate in a different way from traditional computers; they apply rules rather than follow a well-defined procedure of individual steps, and they are based upon human knowledge rather than mere data. These systems can fulfil part of the role of a human consultant, acting as an adviser to the manager who has to take decisions. They are examples of a more general development towards Intelligent Knowledge-Based Systems (IKBS), and will be considered further in Chapter 7.

We therefore have several types of MIS needed to support the various levels and functions of management. There was an early and enthusiastic view that all these functions could be integrated onto a single large MIS. In practice the disadvantage was that different types of data and information were being used by each system, and that the various types of MIS were at differing stages of development. The preferred view is shown in Fig. 4.13.

The one thing which is common to all the MIS is the data representing the facts about the enterprise. This database should be viewed as a corporate resource, and maintained and safeguarded accordingly. Individual MISs can interact with the corporate database, abstracting data from it and giving updated or processed data to it. Each individual MIS can be the responsibility of the part of the organization which it is supporting directly, and can evolve with more independence and flexibility than with a single large MIS. Database Management Systems (DBMS) enable the enterprise to manage corporate data as a central resource and allow individual MIS to interact with it.

4.13 Conclusion

In this chapter we have defined the functions of electronic information systems and seen how microelectronics has developed. Digital technology

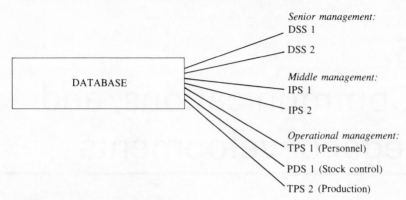

Figure 4.13 MIS/Database

has become pre-eminent. We have seen what computers do, and the technology and devices which make up the hardware of a computer system. We have examined the role of software, and the application packages which are now widely available. These are valuable to managers, but Management Information Systems (MIS) have a more important role in business. The first wave of these systems penetrated organizations from the bottom up, and the second wave is now taking effect. Today, five types of MIS are of practical importance, and database technology enables them to co-exist in the enterprise and share the corporate database of facts.

5.
Communications, and legal developments

5.1 Introduction

In Chapter 4 we looked at electronics technology, and the development and management applications of computing. In this chapter we examine the other main constituent of IT, telecommunications, together with legal developments in the UK which affect the use of information systems.

The functions of electronic information systems were listed in Sec. 4.2: the use of signals to represent, transmission to convey, switching to select, and processing to manipulate information. It is useful to consider the historical perspective given in Fig. 5.1.

Communication is as old as humankind, but for our purpose the technology of telecommunications started in the 1840s with the introduction of the electric telegraph. There has been a steady growth in communications capability ever since. The middle column of the diagram shows the

Year	Transmission	User services
1840s	Metal cable	Telegraph
1880s	Multiplex cable	Telephone
1900s	Submarine voice cable	Telex
1910s	Valve repeaters	Facsimile
1920s	Automatic switching	Radio systems
1930s	Co-axial cable	Television
1940s	Submarine repeaters	Mobile radio
1950s	Atlantic voice cable	Data communications
1960s	Satellite communication	International services
1970s	Fibre-optic cable	High-capacity services
1980s	Submarine FOC	Mobile services
1990s	Signal processing?	Image-based services?

Figure 5.1 Telecommunications

development of transmission media, starting with simple metal cables and working through to the glass (fibre-optic) cables which are so important today. The right hand column shows the kind of services which became possible for users at about the same time and which depended on the developments in transmission capacity. Note that very few services have disappeared; each has grown and been steadily improved. The telephone system is the most widespread, but we also have facsimile, telex, data, mobile radio, viewdata, and many other services available today. In Chapter 6 we shall look more closely at current systems; the point to note here is the very rapid growth in user-services in step with the increases in transmission capacity.

5.2 The communication process

A communication system will need to handle all four information modes (text, data, voice, and image) if it is to support people and computers effectively. What is involved? Figure 5.2 shows the process of communication between two points. The sender of the information has to encode it, or put it in a form suitable for the communication channel over which the message is to be passed. Electrical signals do this in modern systems. Transmission over the channel is not always perfect, and may be spoilt by noise. Noise includes any unwanted signal which interferes with effective transmission. On a telephone line, noise might come from other calls, electrical machinery, lightning, or anything else which disturbs the line. After reception, the receiver decodes the signal into the form required. For the telephone line, the earpiece of the handset converts the electrical signal back into audible sounds. This model is quite general. The written word, for example, can be considered as a channel of communication. In that case the words are encoded into letters of the alphabet which are written onto paper.

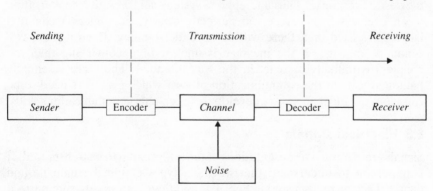

Figure 5.2   Communication process

Line	Text	% sent
1	O, who can hold a fire in his hand	100
2	By th_ nkin_ on the _ rosty Cauca_ us?	89
3	Or ___oy the hu_ gry __dge of _ppet _te	80
4	By ba_ e ima___ na__ion of _ fe_ s _?	71
5	O_ wa___ow nak___ in Dece____ _ n _w	59
6	_y t___nki _ g o_ _ an _ a _ tic_____m___'s _ea _?	51
7	___ n___ t _ e __p _ re___ n___ o of t___ _o _ d	41
8	_____b___ _h _ gr___ter_____i____ _o _____ _o _ s___	30
9	____ ____r____ _ o ____ne____r___l _ ____re	19
10	____ ____n___ _i__ s____ _ a____ ____ ____ ____e	11

Figure 5.3 Noise on a text channel

Source: Richard II, Act 1, Scene 3, lines 294–303

Noise may result from poor printing, or blots of ink which prevent us reading the text properly. Figure 5.3 illustrates a text channel degraded by noise, so that in successive lines of the text more and more characters are lost.

The example makes an important point. The human brain is able to re-construct the message even when some of it has been lost because language has evolved to be tolerant to moderate losses of this kind, and reflects an important principle in designing information systems. People cannot absorb undiluted data; it must be presented in a form which contains some redundant information and so can tolerate some loss during the communication process. In that respect people are different from machines. It is the reason for the traditional advice to a lecturer: 'Tell them what you are going to say, say it, and then tell them what you've said'. Repeating the message in a slightly different form makes the communication more effective.

Our message needs to be received, convey the right meaning, and evoke the desired response. Thus a telephone system can transmit a conversation to an overseas business person perfectly clearly, but unless a common language is used then there will be no understanding. Even if there is a common language, if the message is unclear or unconvincing then the recipient is unlikely to react in the way intended. These are essentially human aspects of the communication process which managers need to be conscious of, and if necessary develop their personal communications skills.

5.3 Electrical signals

Signals are electrical representations of the information to be transmitted. It is important to understand the two main types of signal: analogue and digital. They were discussed in Sec. 4.4, and their features are summarized in Fig. 5.4.

Analogue signals vary continuously, in sympathy with the physical quantity being represented. They have some advantage of simplicity (especially for the telephone), but they also have serious disadvantages. They need analogue transmission, which cannot then easily be used to carry other types of signal, such as computer data. Once an analogue signal is corrupted with noise (unwanted electrical interference, present to some extent in all equipment) it cannot be restored. Thus long-distance calls on an analogue telephone system may degrade seriously in quality. Analogue equipment is more difficult to maintain, and is more liable to give rise to 'cross-talk' between different channels.

Digital signals are quite different. They represent the information numerically, so that it can be transmitted as a series of two-state (0 or 1) binary digits, or bits, in the same way as a computer stores and processes data. Some types of information are naturally suited to digital representation: computer data is already in that form; the signals from a keyboard can easily be denoted by numbers; and black/white images likewise. For some signals, like voice, it is necessary to convert from the analogue representation to a digital representation. Figure 4.3 shows how it is done. After transmission through the communication system, the signal can be turned back into analogue form if necessary.

A digital signal has several advantages over an analogue representation. It requires digital transmission which can be used for other digital signals as well. The signal is not progressively degraded, as an analogue one is, but can be regenerated and its quality maintained irrespective of distance transmitted. This is an important advantage for today's worldwide communication systems. Microelectronics are very effective at handling signals in a digital form, and the storage media discussed in Chapter 4 can also handle them easily. The trend, therefore, is towards wider use of digital technology within communication systems.

A particular advantage is that digital signals can easily be interleaved together for transmission over high-capacity facilities, and then separated out at the far end. This process is called multiplexing and is shown in Fig. 5.5 It shows four individual channels multiplexed together to pass over a single channel working at four times the speed of the individual channels. On the left is depicted one byte from each of the four channels, A to D. They are

| ANALOGUE | Continuously-varying 'analogue' of physical quantity; progressively degraded during transmission. |
| DIGITAL | Numerical representation, with binary digits ('bits'); signal can be regenerated, and quality maintained during transmission. |

Figure 5.4   Electrical signals

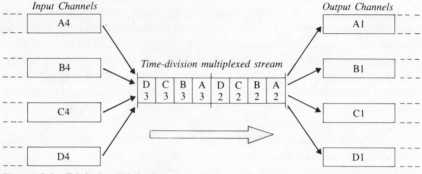

Input Channels

A4

B4

C4

D4

Output Channels

A1

B1

C1

D1

Time-division multiplexed stream

| D 3 | C 3 | B 3 | A 3 | D 2 | C 2 | B 2 | A 2 |

Figure 5.5 Digital multiplexing

labelled A4 to D4 and will be transmitted rapidly in turn over the transmission channel. The diagram shows the earlier bytes A3–D3 and A2–D2 interleaved in this way and actually being transmitted. At the receiving end the bytes are separated out into individual channels. Thus bytes A1–D1 have already been sorted and delivered to the respective output channels. The diagram is a snapshot, showing multiplexing on the left, transmission in the centre, and demultiplexing on the right. The users of the individual channels are unaware that they have shared transmission with other channels, but the provider of the communications has made more effective use of the resource. It is a very important feature of modern communications, and digital signals make it much easier.

Analogue signals and digital signals are fundamentally different. There has been a huge investment in analogue equipment in the past, because it was the easier of the two to use for telephone systems and because micro-electronic technology was not available. However, digital technology has many advantages, and is essential for providing communication for computers and other devices. So the pressure is to move towards wholly-digital communication systems which can carry all types of traffic.

5.4 Transmission systems

Having represented the information by a signal, how is that signal transmitted from one point to another? There are many techniques available, and it is useful to classify them by considering the frequency of vibrations which they use. Frequency is measured as the number of complete vibrations every second, and is expressed in Hertz (Hz), after a famous German physicist. The spectrum is an arrangement in order of frequency, and is illustrated in Fig. 5.6. The scale at the top shows an immense range of frequency. The index (the small number written top-right of the 10) means the number ten raised to that power (or the number one followed by that number of noughts). For example 10 with the index 6 means 1 000 000. The three parts of the spectrum of most interest for communication purposes are marked: sound, radio, and light. Some everyday examples are shown. Thus the Alternating Current (AC) mains supply in the UK has a frequency of 50Hz, which corresponds to a low-pitched hum within the audible range of sound. The musical note 'A' to which musicians tune is 440Hz, and near the middle of the sound range. A good domestic hi-fi installation will handle frequencies from about 30Hz to 20 000Hz (or 20kHz). Adequate telephone transmission requires much less: about 300Hz to 3.4kHz. Radio waves in principle cover the whole band, but the range of practical importance is shown. The UK national transmission, BBC Radio 4 on Long Wave, is about 200kHz. The Very High Frequency (VHF) radio band used for Frequency Modulation (FM) broadcasts, is shown at about 100 million Hz (or 100MHz). Finally, the band of visible light is shown. Light is a vibration similar to radio waves but of a very much higher frequency. Thus red visible light is about 400 million million Hz. Light is usually measured by its wavelength (the physical distance between successive peaks of the wave); for red light this is about 0.25 micrometres (or one ten-thousandth of an inch).

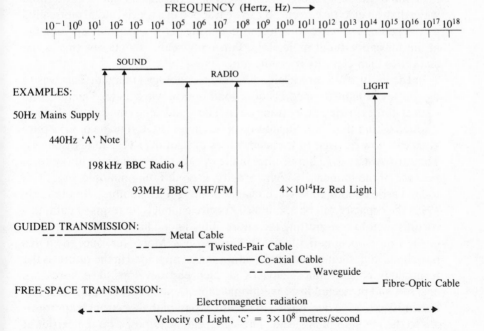

Figure 5.6   The spectrum

Why all this emphasis on frequency? The important point is that the higher the frequency used the faster the communication channel can work. With multiplexing, more and more signals can be combined together to use this greater capacity. Thus communications transmission has evolved to use higher and higher frequencies of transmission.

The lower part of Fig. 5.6 shows the various methods of transmission appropriate to different parts of the spectrum. Guided transmission uses cables of various types. This has the advantage that you know the signal will go exactly where you lay the cable, and nowhere else. Cables have usually been made of metal (copper). For the mains supply, there are usually three conductors (two for power and one protective earth), each insulated from the others by a plastic sheath. This is fine for high power, at low frequency like 50Hz. If such a cable is used for communication at higher frequencies it becomes inefficient; it will lose energy by radio emission and also pick up unwanted interference (noise). The performance can be improved by twisting the pair of wires carrying the signal together, but this is only effective up to a few MHz. The next step is to have a central conductor shielded by a woven cylindrical sheath of copper. This is called co-axial cable and is widely used for connecting TV aerials to TV sets. It operates effectively up to the high end of the radio spectrum. Beyond that, the signal is more like a radio wave than an electric current. It can be trapped in a special metal pipe called a waveguide. The waves bounce off the inside of the waveguide and emerge at the far end without major loss. For many years, people saw this as the answer to high-capacity transmission.

In the early 1960s a radically different technology emerged. This was to use pulses of light trapped inside a solid optical waveguide. The hair-thin optical fibre is made of very transparent glass, and bends the light so that it is trapped within the fibre. Such fibre-optic cables (FOCs) made of very pure glass can now be used to transmit pulses of light over very long distances. They are of increasing importance in the world's telecommunication systems because of the immensely high capacity offered. Using multiplexing, FOC today carries about 2000 voice channels along a single fibre. By the early 1990s the capacity will be about 40 000 voice channels; in terms of data, this is equivalent to transmitting the entire Bible in one hundredth of a second, or the Encyclopaedia Brittanica in four seconds. Moreover, once the fibres have been laid, their speed of operation can be upgraded in the future as the technology of the optical devices at each end develops. The fibres are encased and protected in conventional cable sheaths before being laid. For transmission, a 'carrier' is used in whatever part of the spectrum is appropriate to the medium being used. The signal can be imposed on the carrier at one end, and retrieved from the carrier at the other end. This is known as modulation and demodulation. The important point to note is that a high-frequency carrier is able to carry many low-frequency signals. Thus radio-frequency carriers (as used over some cable systems) can carry hundreds of voice channels), and light-frequency carriers (as used on FOCs) can carry tens of thousands of voice channels. This is the fundamental reason why higher-frequency transmission, and particularly optical transmission, are so important.

So far we have considered guided, or cable transmission. Free-space or radio transmission is not guided in this way. There are both advantages and disadvantages, but radio transmission is the only viable technique for communication to mobile users in vehicles, ships and aircraft. Radio waves travel in straight lines, and this presents a practical problem: how to

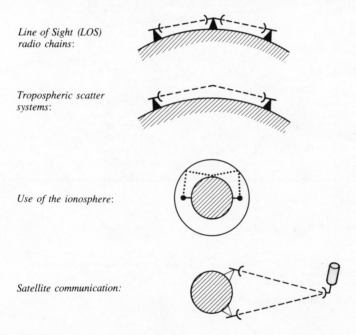

Line of Sight (LOS) radio chains:

Tropospheric scatter systems:

Use of the ionosphere:

Satellite communication:

Figure 5.7 Relay techniques

communicate between users who do not have straight-line visibility between them? Some solutions are illustrated in Fig. 5.7.

Line of Sight (LOS) radio chains can be used to carry microwave radio signals beyond the horizon, and are the basis for many countries' transmission systems, with radio towers sited on hilltops and each visible to the next in the chain. LOS equipment can now be very small (pole-mounted) and can give hundreds of Mbit/sec. capacity, to carry hundreds of voice channels for example. Tropospheric-scatter (or tropo) systems bounce the radio waves off turbulence in the atmosphere. This gives communication over some hundreds of miles, but requires large fixed equipment at each end. It is a useful method of transmission to offshore oil-rigs. The third technique is to use the ionosphere. This is a layer of the earth's atmosphere which is made electrically active by the sun's rays each day. Radio waves of certain frequencies will bounce off the underside of the ionosphere, and

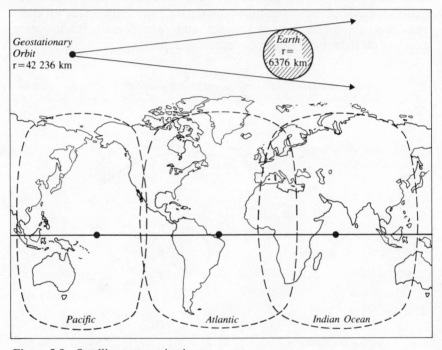

Figure 5.8 Satellite communications

then off the earth, and so travel right round the globe. This is the principle of long-range short-wave communication. It is simple, but rather unreliable, and is of decreasing importance for civil communication.

Today, the most important solution to the long-range radio communication problem is to use geostationary satellites. Figure 5.8 shows the principle of the so-called geostationary orbit. Looking down on the North Pole, the Earth rotates anti-clockwise (that is why the sun rises in the east). A satellite going round the earth is in a state of balance: the gravitational pull to the earth is just enough to make a satellite travelling at a certain speed follow an orbit at the selected height. Satellites appear to go round the earth more slowly the higher the orbit into which they are placed. A low-orbit satellite goes round the earth every 90 minutes. Eventually, at an altitude of 22 300 miles, the satellite will complete an orbit once every 24 hours. Thus if a satellite is placed at that height over the equator, going in the same direction as the earth rotates, it will appear fixed relative to the earth. This makes it very convenient for communication purposes, and the geostationary orbit is in some danger of congestion as a result. Because a geostationary satellite is so high, it can be seen from nearly half the earth's surface. In fact three such satellites, stationed over the major oceans, as shown in Fig. 5.8, can cover nearly all the inhabited globe. Many satellites for international communication use these three positions. However, it is an unfortunate fact that a geostationary satellite will not just stay where it was put; it has to be held on station using thruster-jets controlled from the ground.

The satellite can have a variety of aerials covering different parts of the earth's surface. A broad beam gives wide coverage; a narrow-beam could be used for local communication within a country. It is not possible to prevent the signals spilling over into adjacent areas, and this has important consequences for television broadcast.

In the 1970s it was thought that satellite communication (satcom) would largely replace submarine cables for international communication. However, the development of fibre-optic cables has led to a new generation of submarine cables: a UK–Belgium FOC was laid in 1987 and increased communications capacity by 12 000 voice circuits, or about 50 per cent. Transatlantic FOCs are now in use. Thus submarine cables and satellite communication (satcom) should now be seen as complementary. Satcom is still important for international traffic and this aspect is coordinated by the INTELSAT organization. The INTELSAT VI satellites will carry about 40 000 voice channels plus two TV channels. However, there is an increasing trend for satcom to be used for internal communications over difficult terrain, for example to remote islands, or across arctic or desert areas. Higher powered satellites mean that smaller dish terminals can be used on the ground. Thus it is now possible to have satcom terminals in aircraft, on small ships, or large vehicles like lorries. Often, the functions of communication and navigational aid are combined in a single system, for example the INMARSAT system for maritime use.

Thus communications transmission is using a wide range of technologies, both guided and unguided. Digital technology means that higher capacities can be used effectively. Fibre-optic cable (FOC) is emerging as the most important fixed method of transmission, while satcom is finding an increasing role for communication to remote or mobile terminals.

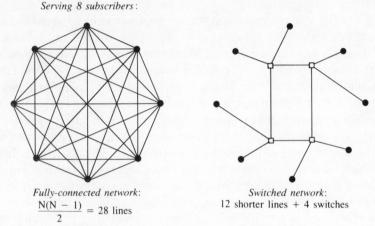

Serving 8 subscribers:

Fully-connected network:
$$\frac{N(N-1)}{2} = 28 \text{ lines}$$

Switched network:
12 shorter lines + 4 switches

Figure 5.9   Switched networks

5.5 Switched communication systems

Having reviewed signals and transmission, we turn now to the last component of a communication system – switching. Figure 5.9 shows why switching is necessary.

If we have a number of users, each of whom must be able to talk to any of the others, then we could meet the requirement by providing a transmission path between all pairs of users. For 8 users, 28 2-way paths would be needed. As the number of users increases, this approach becomes quite impractical. The solution is to provide a communication network, where each subscriber is connected to a switch, and the switches are linked together by higher-capacity transmission systems. When one user wishes to speak to another, he instructs the switch accordingly. The switches establish a path through the network so that the connection is made. There are no easy rules for determining the optimum configuration of the network; it is a balance between transmission cost, switch costs, and many other factors. However, switching is essential for all practical networks.

Automatic telephone switching started with an undertaker in the USA called Strowger. He thought that human telephone operators were diverting calls for his business to a rival. He therefore designed an automatic exchange, controlled by signals dialled by the user. Many electro-mechanical telephone exchanges based on Strowger's are still in service, but gradually the technology has become more electrical and less mechanical. Today's 'stored program control' telephone switches are based on computer technology and handle signals in digital form. Converting the world's telephone systems to digital operation is a slow process. It is relatively easy to make the inner part of the network digital, but 70 per cent of the capital investment

1 Overlay:

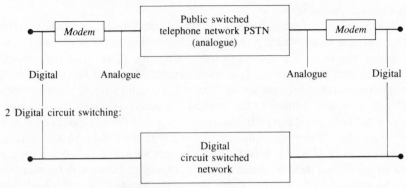

Figure 5.10   Digital transmission

lies in the cables and analogue telephone instruments round the edges of the network. This analogue interface with most users is likely to remain for many years; it presents a serious barrier to passing digital information.

There are several solutions to the problem of passing digital signals (for example between a computer and its terminals) over a communication system dominated by the analogue telephone network. The first is called Digital Overlay and is shown at the top of Fig. 5.10. Devices called modems (MODulator/DEModulator) are used to convert the signals from digital to analogue form so that they can be passed over the telephone network. Speeds are limited to a few Kbits/sec, but this is adequate for low-speed terminals such as those used in viewdata systems for example. A second method is shown at the bottom of Fig. 5.10. It provides a separate, wholly digital, version of the telephone network so that digital calls can be made as required. This approach has been adopted in some countries of the world, but it has disadvantages. It requires both ends of the connection to work at the same time, and at the same speed. A more successful method is called packet switching. This technique emerged in the late-sixties, and will support a wide range of types of data-user. The principle is shown in Fig. 5.11.

All digital data traffic is split up into standard-length 'packets' of about 1000 bits which go through the network independently and are re-assembled at the far end. This prevents big users swamping out small users, and allows different types of equipment to interwork. The interleaving of packets on the network is illustrated on the various links of the network in Fig. 5.11. More than 40 countries of the world now have packet switched data networks, operating to an internationally agreed standard.

It has therefore been possible to connect these networks together to provide an international packet switched service analogous to the international telephone service.

There are several other types of switched communication network. The first is cellular radio, which provides reliable communication to vehicles, or people on the move. Figure 5.12 shows how it works. The area to be covered is split up into small 'cells' a few miles across, which can be covered by a single low-power radio transmitter. The cellular radio terminal in the vehicle will automatically connect to the nearest, or strongest, radio transmission. Once a call is made, it can continue even though the vehicle moves from one cell to another. The system interfaces directly to the Public Switched Telephone Network (PSTN); it is intended mainly for voice calls but data can now be carried as well. Because the cells are so local, the radio frequencies can be re-used (avoiding the same frequency in adjacent cells) and thus national coverage built up based on only a few frequencies. Like the PSTN and packet-switched data networks, cellular radio can therefore be a Wide Area Network (WAN) covering a region, a country, or a group of countries.

'Cable' is a term which has come to mean a network, based on co-axial or fibre-optic cable, which serves a few hundred or few thousand subscribers in a limited area or town. This is sometimes called a Metropolitan Area Network (MAN). Such networks can be used as a broadcast medium, to bring large numbers of television channels into the home, or as the basis for two-way information services. The latter has potentially the greater impact, but requires a more complex form of the technology. Cable systems are now

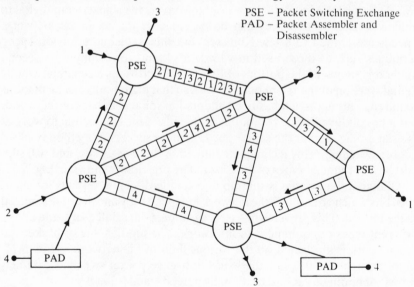

Figure 5.11 Packet switching

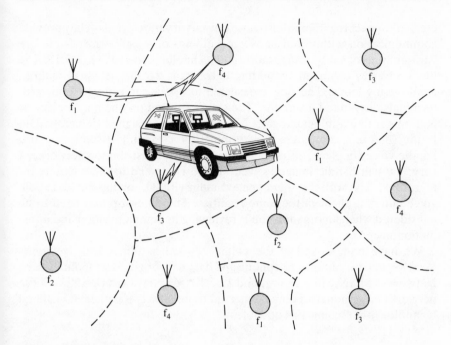

Figure 5.12 Cellular radio

well-established in developed countries, based mainly on distribution of television channels. Unlike conventional telephone connections into the home, they offer a very high capacity to support image and other services.

Finally, Local Area Networks (LANs) have a more limited coverage still. They are used on a single site (campus, factory premises, office complex,

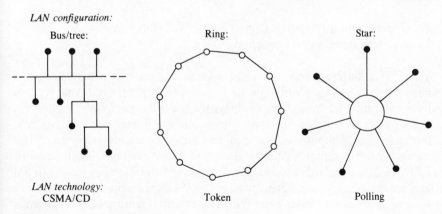

Figure 5.13 Local Area Networks

etc.) to connect together information devices of various kinds. They provide communication within and between buildings of a single site. There are various kinds of LAN configuration and technology, shown in Fig. 5.13. The bus or tree is extended by adding extra 'tails' to the network, without creating any loops. The ring is designed to operate in a single loop, with terminals distributed around it. The star is centred on one major piece of equipment like a minicomputer. Most LANs are designed to handle data traffic (between computers and terminals, for example); some will also handle voice (in place of the traditional telephone distribution network); a very few will handle image as well. There is a trend towards closely integrating LANs with the telephone exchange (PABX) on the site, to handle voice and data through the same facilities. These new options need to be considered when an organization is reviewing its communication and information needs.

We have now looked at the switching used in Wide Area Networks (WANs, like the national telephone and data networks), Metropolitan Area Networks (MANs, like cable), and Local Area Networks (LANs). These networks are gradually being connected more closely together; it is digital technology that makes this possible.

5.6 Two initiatives for the future

It is clear that the historical legacy of the analogue telephone system, and the recent emergence of digital technology and communications traffic, have led to many types of incompatible networks and equipment. The aim for the future must be towards interworking of equipment across digital communication systems. There are two major initiatives towards this of which the manager should be aware.

1. The Integrated Services Digital Network (ISDN), and
2. Open Systems Interconnection (OSI).

The first initiative comes from the telecommunications community, and aims to define a standard type of digital network service. Any type of information (text, data, voice or image), once it has been represented in a digital form, is suitable for transmission across a digital network. Speech, facsimile, and computer data can all be carried on a common system. The name for the common system is the Integrated Services Digital Network (ISDN). The standards for the ISDN are being formulated by international agreement. Meanwhile, early forms of the ISDN are being implemented in several countries, including the UK. The essential feature of this system is shown in Fig. 5.14

Each user has a direct digital interface which can be used for voice- and data-calls, independently and at the same time. Each channel will work at up to 64kbit/sec. As we saw in Sec. 4.4, that is the standard speed for digital voice communications, and for data it is a much higher speed than can be achieved by modems using the telephone network. The ISDN is now becoming available to the business community, and will make an important contribution to the support of new information services.

The second initiative comes from the International Organisation for Standardisation (ISO). It seeks to define a set of standards for computers from different manufacturers to work together effectively over communication systems of various types. This is known as Open Systems Interconnection (OSI). It is an ambitious target, and the problem is complex. However, all the functions necessary for computers to communicate and interwork have been arranged in a hierarchy of seven 'layers'. The layers are shown in Fig. 5.15. Each layer contains a group of related functions, and standard protocols can be defined to achieve these functions. Very briefly, the 'physical' layer is concerned with plugs and wires; the 'data link' layer with transfer of bits of data between two points; and the 'network' layer with switching within a network of links. Thus layers 1–3 are concerned with the communications function, and layers 4–7 are concerned with the computing function. The 'transport' layer establishes a data-transfer facility between the two computers, using the underlying communication facilities; the 'ses-

ISDN – Integrated Services Digital Network
    – All signals in digital form
    – Fully-digital connections, for voice and/or data

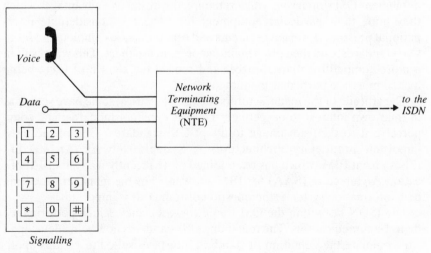

Figure 5.14   ISDN

OSI – Open Systems Interconnection
   – International standards for computer-communication
   – 7 Layers: 3 for communications, 4 for computers

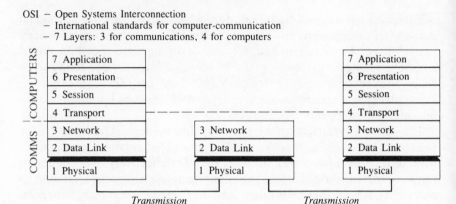

Figure 5.15   OSI standards

sion' layer deals with the exchange of data over that facility; the 'presentation' layer is concerned with the format of the data (for example as a letter or facsimile image); and the 'application' layer deals with the processing of the data, under the control of the user.

Standards for layers 1–4 are now well established. For certain types of application, there is a complete set of standards up to level seven. For text messages, and for the interconnection of certain kinds of computer integrated manufacturing systems complete standards exist. It is important to realize that OSI standards are for interfaces between equipment, and do not constrain how equipment operates internally. Individual manufacturers can implement OSI standards, whilst retaining the distinctive advantages which they hope their particular equipment has. There is considerable international pressure, from governments and other users, to complete the set of OSI standards, and then press manufacturers to use them. This will result in a more competitive market-place, and reduce the chance of users being locked in to one particular manufacturer.

The attitude of the manufacturers themselves varies; some have seen it as in their own interest to perpetuate their own unique standards, and some perceive it to their advantage to adopt OSI standards. One of the most important proprietary architectures is Systems Network Architecture (SNA) from IBM, which has been joined more recently by Systems Application Architecture (SAA) for IBM software. For the manager procuring new information systems, the question of standards is important.

The ISDN fits within the OSI framework; it achieves high performance digital communications. The remaining OSI standards now being developed will complete the definition of standard interfaces suited to various applications. ISDN and OSI together represent an ambitious target, but one which is essential if the present proliferation of networks and equipment standards is to be halted.

5.7 The legal and regulatory position

After this review of the technical developments in the communications field, we need to consider the legal framework within which information systems operate. There have been recent and important changes in the way telecommunications is provided in some countries, and in how data relating to living individuals is protected.

In most countries, telecommunications has traditionally been regarded as the natural monopoly of the State, rather like the postal system. However, there has been a recent move away from this view in some countries. The liberalization of the communications scene started in the USA, happened very quickly in the UK and then Japan, and seems to be setting the trend for the rest of Europe and some other developed countries. The UK case can be taken as an example, because it was watched very carefully by other countries considering liberalization of telecommunications. The history of the legislation is summarized in Table 5.1.

In 1863 the Telegraph Act was passed, to prevent a commercial monopoly of the growing electric telegraph service. Six years later the telegraph was seen as so important that it was made the monopoly of the State, represented by the General Post Office. After Bell's 1876 patent, the telephone became the most important system. A legal judgement in 1880 confirmed that the Post Office's monopoly extended to the telephone system as well. This meant that for over 100 years telecommunications in the UK were a state monopoly. In 1969 the Post Office Corporation was formed, and in 1981 British Telecom (BT) was split off from the Post Office. At the same time, BT's monopoly position was weakened and a certain amount of competition introduced. This process was completed by the 1984 Telecommunications

Table 5.1   Telecommunication legislation

The history in the UK:
  1863 – Act to prevent commercial monopoly of telegraph
  1869 – State monopoly of telegraphy, through GPO
  1876 – Bell's patent of the telephone
  1880 – Legal judgement confirms GPO monopoly of telephone
  1969 – Post Office Corporation (POC) formed
  1981 – British Telecom (BT) separated from the POC, and its monopoly position removed
  1984 – Telecommunications Act: Director–General and OFTEL; licensing of all Public Telecommunication Operators (PTOs); establishment of BT plc.
  1989 – PTOs' duopoly for bearer services due to end

Act, which provided for the privatization of BT, to become a public limited company. A large share-issue was made in 1984. An Office of Telecommunications (OFTEL) was set up with a Director–General whose task is to ensure fair competition in the telecommunications field. The UK Government issues the licences for telecommunications operators, and OFTEL polices their implementation. Until 1990, only two national Public Telecommunications Operators (PTOs) are licensed in the UK. These are BT, and its new rival Mercury Communications Ltd (a subsidiary of Cable & Wireless). In an important series of cases Mercury has established its right to operate international services as well as national ones. The equipment which uses the PTOs' networks (such as telephone instruments, facsimile machines, answering machines, etc.) has to conform to standards set by an independent body, the British Approvals Board for Telecommunications (BABT); in this sector of the market there is now almost unlimited competition.

The UK Government has issued several other important licences: for two competing cellular radio systems, for many Cable systems serving individual towns, and also General Licences for Private Automatic Branch Exchange (PABX) systems, and for VANS. VANS stands for Value-Added Network Services, and refers to the enhancement of the underlying communication service by the provision of additional computer-based facilities. Electronic mail and a computer bureau are examples of VANS. In the VANS area there is complete competition, and a very fast growth in the services offered. They will be considered in more detail in Chapter 6.

This rapid liberalization of the telecommunications scene has had a traumatic effect. Although examples of seeming duplication can be given, the overall effect has been to accelerate the modernization of telecommunication networks, and to provide a much wider range of services and equipment to exploit them. It is these effects which are desired by other nations moving towards a liberalized or deregulated position. In considering the UK experience in relation to other countries, it is important to distinguish between deregulation (which introduced competition into what was previously a monopoly situation), and privatization (which transferred BT from the public sector to the private sector). The issues should be kept distinct in any discussion of liberalization.

There is one other area of legislation which directly affects the use of information systems. This concerns the protection of data relating to living individual people. The increasing use of computers to store and process data about individuals, and now the ability of machines to communicate that information to other machines, has given rise to considerable concern. How can the individual ensure that the data kept about them are accurate and relevant? How can they ensure that the data are not used for some improper purpose?

Table 5.2   Data protection

Principles incorporated in 1984 Data Protection Act:
1 – Obtained fairly and lawfully
2 – Held only for the registered lawful purpose
3 – Used or disclosed only in accordance with registered purpose
4 – Adequate, relevant, and not excessive for registered purpose
5 – Accurate, and where necessary up-to-date
6 – Not kept longer than necessary for registered purpose
7 – Made available to data-subjects on request
8 – Properly protected against loss or disclosure

Gradually, nations have developed a number of principles for the safe-guarding of personal data. Those adopted by the Council of Europe, and reflected in the UK's 1984 Data Protection Act, are summarized in Table 5.2. The provisions of the Act took effect progressively. All data-users who store personal data on computers must be registered with the Data Protection Registrar; certain precautions to safeguard data are required; and data-subjects now have the right to inspect the data which is stored concerning them, and to require changes if it is inaccurate or is excessive for the registered purpose for which it is held.

The effect of these moves towards data protection has been that there is an emerging community of nations who apply such safeguards, and between whom data can be exchanged in a controlled manner. Those nations who have not introduced the necessary legislation are excluded from this. Data protection has important implications for management, to comply with the specific requirements of the law and in terms of what can be done with personal data. Any organization subject to data protection legislation should appoint an officer to oversee the implementation of its provisions and consider very carefully the balance between computer-based systems (which are subject to control) and paper-based systems (which are not).

5.8 Conclusion

In this chapter we have looked at recent technical developments in the area of telecommunications, and legal changes to the regulation of communication services and data protection. The key points covered are: the task of a communication system to serve people and machines; the elements of signals, transmission, and switching; analogue and digital operation; the analogue past, and the digital future; the major initiatives of ISDN and OSI; liberalization of telecommunications; and data protection for the individual.

6.
Current information systems

6.1 Introduction

In Chapters 4 and 5 we looked at technical developments which underlie modern information systems, and the effects of recent legislation. This chapter reviews some of the information systems which are currently available, using a format which links with the management guidance given in Part 3 of the book.

6.2 Classification of current information systems

There are four modes of handling information: text, data, voice, and image. These modes need progressively more capacity, and provide a useful way of classifying systems. This is shown in Fig. 6.1, which forms an agenda for this chapter. Look first at the structure of the diagram, rather than the systems listed in it. The four vertical columns correspond to the four modes of operation. Down the left-hand side are headings for systems of increasing complexity. The first group is communication services, subdivided into transmission and switched services. Transmission is the transfer of information between predetermined points, and may be one-way or two-way. Switched services allow users to send the information to designated recipients and can usually operate two-way.

The centre part of the diagram shows the main communication networks which have been developed to support the services listed in the top part. There is an indication of how communication networks are likely to evolve in the future.

The lower part of the diagram shows more complex information systems: VANs (Value-Added Networks), and VAS (Value-Added Services).

VANs build upon the basic communication service by using computers to store and process the information. They also have password control of access, and arrangements to monitor usage and bill users. A VAN does not, in itself, provide any new data or information; the users only get out what they have collectively put in, although possibly in a modified form.

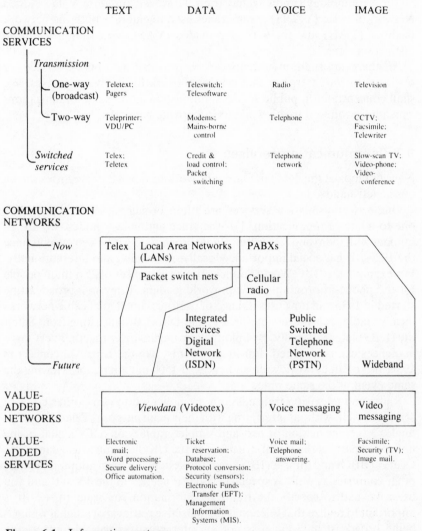

Figure 6.1 Information systems

A Value-Added Service (VAS) does provide new information for its users. The service uses the facilities of a VAN, but the value to the user lies in the data or information which is provided to him over the system. This information is assembled by a company in business for that purpose, called an Information Provider (IP). For example, IPs often sell financial market data, current news, and other facts whose value depends on speed.

This terminology is now widely used. However, the term Value-Added Network Service (VANS) is sometimes used to embrace both the network facilities (VAN) and the service provided (VAS). You should keep the distinction clear.

All these information systems can be provided as a public service, or operated by an enterprise as a private network for its own purposes. We shall concentrate on public services, but also mention some organizations which have found it worth while to run private networks.

6.3 Communication services

Now let's look at the detail of Fig. 6.1 by working down the categories shown on the left-hand side.

One-way transmission services are often broadcast services providing one-to-many communication. For the voice and image modes, we are all familiar with radio and television. Radio broadcasting has been around since the 1920s. It has social importance locally, nationally, and internationally. For example the BBC World Service attracts audiences of 25 million people for the phone-in programmes with world leaders. Television broadcasting started in 1936 and now uses a range of transmission media: cable networks locally, radio transmitters nationally, and Direct Broadcasting from Satellite (DBS) internationally. By linking these technologies together very large audiences can be reached. For major events, like the Live Aid concert in 1985, there can be worldwide audiences of 1500 million people viewing the same event at the same time.

Radio and television transmissions are now used to carry other types of service as well, without interfering with their main purpose. Teletext (with a final 't') is transmission of text and simple graphics on a TV signal, using unneeded parts of the signal structure. In the UK the commercial names are Ceefax (BBC) and Oracle (IBA), and the system has been adopted in many other countries as well. A special decoder is needed in the TV set, and you use a keypad to specify the frame of information you want to see. It is important to realize that teletext is just selective retrieval of a signal which is being broadcast anyway; it is not an interactive service. Moreover, the capacity is limited to a few hundred frames of general information, because of the limited space available within the TV signal. In the UK the number of teletext sets increased from 100 000 in 1980 to 2 million in 1985. Some people have stopped taking a daily newspaper, and rely instead on regular perusal of teletext. It is worth thinking about the advantages and limitations of this way of getting news.

Data signals can also be added to broadcast transmissions. A control signal on the BBC Radio 4 national transmission is used to switch electrical power loads on and off. This is called Teleswitch and allows the electricity authorities to manage their resources better. It is a useful by-product of a system provided for a quite different purpose. Software for home computers can be sent as audible tones during radio programmes, or as a flashing pattern in the corner of a TV picture (Telesoftware).

Paging is a broadcast service which uses its own small transmitters. People carry small receivers ('bleepers') which can be activated by ringing a certain number. Some systems allow simple messages to be received and displayed. There are about 500 000 pagers in the UK.

The next level of communication service is two-way transmission between predetermined points. A fixed link of this kind usually meets a very specific need within an organization. Telephone sets, closed circuit television (CCTV), facsimile, and teleprinters can all be used on fixed links. More recent are telewriters (which transmit handwritten pen-movements), and the linking of personal computers and other computer terminals. Mains-borne control is where signals are passed over the electrical power (mains) wiring without interfering with power transmission. This enables loads to be controlled from, and meter readings fed back to, the authority providing the electricity, gas or water supply.

Fixed links can use cables within or between buildings of a site. For longer distances you rent private circuits from the Public Telecommunications Operator (PTO). The agreement usually involves an initial capital charge, followed by a rental for an agreed number of years. These charges must be paid irrespective of how much you have used the private circuit.

The PTOs operate very large transmission networks to support the switched public systems. In the UK the only national PTOs at present are BT and Mercury. The inner part of the BT network is largely digital for both transmission and switching. Since 1985, BT has installed only Fibre-Optic Cable (FOC) on its trunk network, so that about half the total capacity is now provided by fibre, Mercury started from a very different position. Licensed from 1981 to compete with what had been a monopoly network, Mercury had to deploy digital facilities from the outset. Initially digital radio was used between major business centres. Then an agreement was reached with British Rail, under which Mercury could lay FOC beside railway tracks.

Mercury won a series of legal cases which means that it is a recognized international carrier and can operate its own satellite communication terminals. Initially the Mercury system provided only private circuits, but since 1987 switched services have also been available. To avoid duplication in the provision of local networks to individual users, the Government has insisted on the interconnection of the BT and Mercury networks, so that users on one network can connect to users on the other.

Private circuits are fine when the user knows what the level of communication traffic will be, and exactly where it has to go. This is not always the case, and then it is better to use a switched network. For data the most flexible arrangement is to use modems to transmit over dialled telephone connections (see Sec. 5.5). The speed of transmission is limited to about 2.4 kbit/sec. There are many types of communication terminal which have a built-in modem and dialling facilities for this purpose. A good example is facsimile (fax), where the technical standards have been internationally agreed and terminals from different manufacturers can therefore interwork over the telephone network. In the UK, facsimile is the fastest expanding method of communication, with about 200 000 terminals in use. The current (Group 3) equipment takes less than one minute to transmit an A4 page. The equipment achieves this by automatically skipping over any large areas of white, and concentrating on the black parts.

Switched services have important advantages of flexibility and convenience. Besides facsimile, there are several other examples to mention. For the text mode, telex is a network of teleprinters operating at low speed (about 50–100 bits/sec). Its advantage is that it is a well-established system for which most businesses throughout the world have a terminal. However, it is limited in speed and in the range of text characters it can transmit. It uses only upper case (capital) letters and can deal with only basic punctuation. The modern version of telex is called teletex (with no final 't'). This gives direct transmission between the memories of word-processing systems, and operates over the telephone system using a built-in modem, at 2.4kbit/sec, and is considerably cheaper than postage. There are international standards for teletex, which allow a much wider range of characters in the message than telex. Teletex is an example of a service which relies on the international agreement of technical standards, so that equipment can then be made by different manufacturers. The role of the PTO is often merely to publicize the service, and to publish a directory of users; the PTO is not necessarily itself a provider of the terminal equipment. Some users prefer to stick to telex, albeit with more modern terminal equipment. One way which the PTOs use to encourage users to adopt new services is to provide 'gateways' between the old services and the new. Thus a teletex terminal can transfer messages to and from the telex network (accepting the limitations of the telex system), and use data networks for transmission as well as the telephone network.

An example of using modems is the credit and load control systems by which electricity authorities can send control data over a telephone connection into the home, to switch loads on and off without the domestic user being aware. It gives a much more precise adjustment of consumption than the teleswitch system mentioned earlier (which uses a radio signal to control large groups of users), and is less complex than the mains-borne system. More generally, there is a growing need for users to send computer data of various types to a large number of possible destinations. Packet switching is the best technology for this (see Sec. 5.5). There is now an international packet-switched service linking more than 40 countries. Data transmission is possible at speeds up to 48 or 64 kbit/sec, which is much faster than with modems.

Telephone networks are essential because despite the growth of data and other traffic in most organizations voice is more than 90 per cent of the communication requirement. Some people believe that it would be useful to have a picture of the speaker transmitted along with the voice. However, transmission of moving pictures requires much higher capacity than the voice signal. One way round this problem is slow-scan TV, which updates or 'refreshes' the picture every few seconds. Such pictures can be sent at the relatively low average data-rate of 64 kbit/sec. Slow-scan TV is useful for applications like security surveillance. A security guard can watch say 30 screens, each of whose pictures is refreshed every few seconds and is covering a different part of the building, and thus keep an effective look-out for intruders or other unusual events.

Another major development is video-conferencing. This is designed to allow remote meetings between groups of people at various sites. For moving pictures, high data-rates are necessary (2 Mbit/sec). The transmission facility has to be ordered on a private circuit, and is not yet available as a switched service. You have terminal equipment in your own conference room. Several TV screens display the participants at the remote location, and a separate camera is available to transmit images needed during the discusions. Video-conferencing can be very effective for regular meetings between people who know each other, and for a well-understood agenda of business. For example, it was used to progress the merger between the Royal Bank of Scotland (based in Edinburgh) and Williams & Glyns Bank (based in London), and avoided much expensive and time-consuming travel. Video-conferencing involves a large front-end cost (for the terminal equipment and the private circuit facility), but can break even if used regularly.

6.4 Communication networks

The middle part of Fig. 6.1 shows some of the networks which support the services just mentioned. Remember that voice is much the largest requirement, and is likely to remain so for many years, so the Public Switched

Telephone Network (PSTN), will continue to dominate the scene. The PSTN is also affectionately (or unaffectionately) known as the Plain Old Telephone Service (POTS). It is said to be the most complex man-made device on earth; more than 700 million telephones in the world can be connected to each other. Telephones are very unevenly distributed, and give a good measure of economic development. There are more telephones in the city of Tokyo than in the whole of Africa. In the UK the BT network serves more than 20 million users (reaching all businesses and 85 per cent of homes), and Mercury also offers a switched telephone service. The two networks are connected together as well as each having international connections. There is a demand for more complex types of service which can only be provided by modern digital telephone exchanges. Such features include call diversion, priority interrupt, call-back-when-free and short-code dialling. Until recently such features could only be provided by a Private Automatic Branch Exchange (PABX) serving the business location. PABXs are now available in a wide range of sizes, and the market is very competitive. As the Public Telecommunication Operators (PTOs) install digital exchanges it may be possible to offer such features from the network. This is called Centrex, and is an important market in the US. In the UK Mercury offer it, and BT hope to.

The PSTN offers fixed telephone communication. Many users want to extend this service to mobile users, and this is behind the rapid growth in cellular radio systems. The technology was discussed in Sec. 5.5. Cellular networks are well-established in the US and are growing fast in Europe. In the UK two systems are licensed (Cellnet and Vodafone). They started operation in 1985 and they now reach more than 90 per cent of the UK population. The growth of cellular radio has exceeded market forecasts, and by 1988 there were about 200 000 users. Cellular radio is quite expensive both for the terminal and for calls, but is getting cheaper. It is now reaching people who spend a lot of time on the move and who need to keep in touch with their company. The current cellular systems can carry data traffic, so it is possible to have a computer or other data terminal in a vehicle. For example, British Gas use voice and data communication to technicians in vans, and the Automobile Association uses special data terminals to control their mobile patrol vehicles. A pan-European system of cellular radio is planned which will be wholly digital. Besides cellular radio, various Private Mobile Radio (PMR) systems are available. Frequencies are now being released from military and other use to extend the number of such radio networks available for commercial use. Radio systems now provide links to telephones on trains, ships and aircraft.

The latest mobile radio-phone technology uses low-power transmitters and receivers which will be situated on street corners. Users of fairly cheap mobile 'phones, like the domestic cordless ones, will be able to call into the public network as long as they are within about 50 metres of the base-station.

For the text mode, the switched telex network serves about 1.5 million users worldwide, of whom about 120 000 are in the UK. The system has an assured future, although not increasing in comparison with other systems. The network is being modernized, and is likely to remain the most pervasive international form of text-mode communication for many years yet.

For data transmission, the growth of packet-switched Wide Area Networks (WANs) has already been mentioned. Local Area Networks (LANs; see Sec. 5.5) are very important for extending the communication facilities around a building or group of buildings on a single site. Voice and text/data systems are often integrated in the LAN. A few can carry image signals as well.

The Integrated Services Digital Network (ISDN) was explained in Sec. 5.5. The idea is to provide reliable digital communication which can support a wide range of services. Initially there was some scepticism about whether this was really needed (ISDN was called 'Integration Subscribers Don't Need'). But with several countries now having ISDN networks serving the business community the outlook is more promising (and suppliers say 'I Smell Dollars Now'). The standards for ISDNs have been agreed internationally, and are accepted as a long-term goal. Several countries have ISDNs working to slightly different standards but intended to evolve to a standard which provides two 64 kbit/sec channels to each user. In the UK, BT markets ISDN under the name Integrated Digital Access (IDA) and it is becoming available in most business centres throughout the country.

Looking to the future, the PSTN will remain the mainstay communication network, albeit modernized, digital, and with a wider range of features available to the user. The ISDN will certainly grow, and become important for the business community. Access to special facilities like packet-switching will probably be via the ISDN. Telex will continue at its present level internationally, but with reduced importance within some countries. Wideband (high capacity) services include digital services at more than 64 kbit/sec, needed to support video-conferencing and other image services. They are likely to increase significantly. An example is the deployment of 'cable' systems which provide high-capacity communication into the home, with the possibility of interactive services. Such systems are usually funded by the entertainment market, because they can carry many channels of television simultaneously. However, Direct Broadcast from Satellite (DBS) systems has emerged as a competitor to cable systems for this domestic entertainment market.

The communications infrastructure is a matter of national importance. Some governments still exercise a monopoly, while others introduce market forces to speed up development and give competition. The experience in the US, UK, France, and Japan are all different in this respect.

6.5 Value-Added Networks (VANs)

So much for communication systems which simply transfer information or data from one point to another without significant change. Let us now look at Value-Added Networks (VANs) which enhance those basic communication services by providing message storage, processing, or other additional features. VANs in turn are the basis for provision of Value-Added Services (VASs), which can be sold as an information service in the market.

The exact scope of VANs is difficult to define. At the simpler end, there are Managed Data Networks (MDNs) which provide network control, management, security, and traffic analysis to meet a particular user's needs. Such a service can be used by a business to avoid these specialist tasks, which would be necessary if it ran its own private network. Beyond this, there are three main types of VAN shown in Fig. 6.1.

The most important is viewdata, or videotex. This uses for a terminal a combination of a TV set and a telephone line. A simple keypad is used to send requests for data to the viewdata computer, over a dialled-up PSTN call. The computer then sends the required data, at higher speed, to the terminal over the same PSTN connection. The data transmission, each way, uses built-in modems. The advantage of viewdata is that it uses a cheap terminal based on widely-available equipment, and is simple to operate. It is similar in operation to the teletext system. However, with teletext only a limited amount of information, already being transmitted within the TV signal, is accessible. With viewdata a very much larger amount of information is accessible on request. Viewdata is therefore an interactive service.

Viewdata technology was pioneered by BT and a service called Prestel was established in the UK in 1979. Since then many other countries have adopted the technology for their own systems. In the early days it was thought that there would be a large market among domestic users, who would be attracted by new information services for the home. In fact, home users did not find enough useful information on the system to justify the cost. The marketing of viewdata was therefore redirected towards the business community, with greater success. Travel agents were an example of a business community which found viewdata very useful. Once established in the business market, viewdata began to penetrate the domestic market. By 1987 Prestel had about 70 000 users, with nearly half in the domestic sector, and more than 300 Information Providers (IPs) offering some 300 000 frames of information. Viewdata will handle text, simple graphics, and modest amounts of computer data. It is possible to pay for goods or services ordered over the system by quoting a credit card number, to exchange messages with other users, or even to play computer games on the system.

In the UK less than one home in 500 has viewdata. In contrast, the French system Minitel/Teletel is much more pervasive. The initial idea was to provide a small terminal which would sit beside the telephone set and allow the user to access a computer database of all French telephone numbers. This would remove the need for printing and distribution of bulky paper telephone directories. The terminals were issued free or at very low cost. By 1987 three million were in use, and this number was expected to double within a few years. In turn, this widely available VAN has led to a growth of information services which can reach large numbers of homes. This is a good example of investment in communications infrastructure opening up a new market.

More recently voice messaging systems have been introduced which offer storage and retrieval for voice signals. They are usually associated with the Private Automatic Branch Exchange (PABX) of an organization and can be considered as a communal answering machine. Anyone ringing into the organization and finding that the wanted person is not available can record a message. When the intended recipient returns to the office and starts to use the phone, the system advises them that a voice message is waiting. Such systems avoid many of the frustrations of the basic telephone service, such as those revealed in a recent survey:

- Only 25 per cent of telephone calls reach the intended recipient;
- More than 50 per cent of telephone calls are used to convey information only one way;
- About 60 per cent of telephone calls are less important than the work they interrupt.

The telephone can be intrusive and time-wasting, but we cannot do without it. Voice messaging systems can make the telephone more acceptable, and the market is increasing. Besides PABX-based systems, it is possible for service companies to offer a 'front office' for telephone calls at a remote location, giving an initial response to callers and transferring calls which require access to the client organization itself.

The next logical extension of VANs is to image (video) messaging. However, the transmission capacity required (2 Mbit/sec for moving pictures) makes widespread switched networks impractical at present. For today's purposes, therefore, viewdata is the most important and widespread VAN. In the UK, as a result of liberalization legislation, several competing viewdata systems are available besides the Prestel one run by BT.

6.6 Value-Added Services (VASs)

VANs are the basis for Value-Added Services (VASs). In the UK this is a very competitive market and since 1984 it has expanded rapidly. The most commonly offered services are electronic mail, computer protocol conversion, and database services. Electronic mail, or E-mail, is the first and most important example. It enables users to exchange text communications via a computer-based 'mailbox'. The user's terminal may be a viewdata terminal fitted with an alphanumeric keyboard, or a personal computer with the necessary software and modem to allow communication over a PSTN connection. In this case, electronic mail becomes integrated with the other facilities available on the PC. For example, text can be produced in a word processing package and then despatched as an electronic mail message. The advantages of electronic mail are:

– The ease and speed with which the information can be entered into and retrieved from the system;
– The fact that the sender and the recipient do not both have to be available at the same time (the recipient can retrieve waiting messages from his mailbox at his own convenience);
– The system may allow messages to be sent to many recipients easily.

In terms of formality, E-mail lies somewhere between the ephemeral telephone call and the formal letter. Many organizations using electronic mail systems have found that information flows much more freely and effectively than before. This can, however, have implications for the structure of the organization itself. Although access standards for electronic mail exist, several separate and competing systems are available. This can cause difficulties of deciding the best 'club' to join. In the UK there are about five competing E-mail systems, of which the largest is BT'S Telecom Gold. There are moves to provide gateways between the various systems, because the providers recognize that incompatible networks will be a barrier to market growth. An international standard for messaging systems (called X400) is the basis for achieving this interlinking.

The use of viewdata by the travel industry has already been mentioned. The cheap terminals which could be deployed in even small travel agents' premises were particularly attractive. Financial and reservation systems are dominant in the data-VAS market. A recent offering is home banking, where a cheap viewdata terminal in the home enables the customer to control his financial affairs in comfort and at times convenient to himself.

There are several examples of companies (some mentioned in Part 1) which have used viewdata or E-mail technology to achieve competitive advantage. An early example is the American Hospital Supply Company in the US. From 1978 they provided their customers (hospitals) with data terminals which could be used to place orders. Because of the convenience to customers, the number of items per order more than doubled, the company was able to manage its stock more effectively and so become more competitive. Customers became locked-in to the system, and the company's competitors had to take retaliatory action. Another US example is American Airlines which was early into the market with air ticket reservation systems. Their system came to dominate the market, and by 1987 the Airline was making more money from its reservation system than from flying its aircraft.

In the UK the car manufacturer British Leyland set up information systems for its own purposes and then found that there was a market for these services elsewhere in the industry and for the public at large. Their subsidiary ISTEL has become a major provider of VASs in the UK. The Friends Provident life assurance company introduced a viewdata system to serve its branch offices. This proved so successful that they widened the scheme to allow brokers to obtain insurance quotations, and compare them with offerings from other companies. The holiday company Thomson replaced a system of 16 telephone booking centres by a viewdata system called TOPS. The travel agents could then make direct enquiries and reservations; this enabled Thomson to save 200 staff, improve their service, and maintain a market lead. For all these companies, the strategic use of IT has been important for continuing business success.

Viewdata can be used to support management activity. An example is to link people concerned with a particular project or activity. The system can then store data which is relevant to all of them, such as project milestones and deadlines, and provide a rapid and convenient method of communication between members of the team. Such services are marketed as private viewdata systems, or may take the form of Closed User-Groups (CUGs) within a public network. A CUG means that non-members of the group cannot gain access to the system or its data.

Another type of MIS which is growing in importance is the On-Line Data Base (OLDB). This enables the user to search for, and retrieve, information on subjects of interest. Commercial databases can provide company accounts, details of market opportunities, and statistics about business performance. They can give specialist advice on financial and other matters. The price of such information is determined by market forces; the provider of the information sets his own price level, and the provider of the underlying VAN will normally get a fixed part of that charge. Some OLDBs are based on abstracts of current literature. They may be searched by keyword, or by combinations of keywords, so that the user can rapidly find those abstracts which are of direct interest to him. For some publications, such as the *Financial Times* and other quality newspapers and journals, the full text is held on the database and may be retrieved electronically and then read in detail.

An important new type of VAS is called Electronic Document Interchange (EDI). This is concerned with replacing the paperwork systems used in various sectors of business. For example, an EDI system called Tradanet in the UK links wholesalers and retailers, and has reduced the delays associated with the old paper-based ordering systems.

Compared with viewdata systems, voice VASs are in their infancy. There are bureaux which undertake telephone answering services (with complex, computer-prompted responses to queries), systematic telephone marketing, and the provision of 'front-office' facilities. More recently, 'premium' telephone services have emerged, where calls to designated numbers on the PSTN give pre-recorded messages about the current state of financial markets or other items of current interest; such bulletins can be abstracted automatically from the Information Providers' own computing systems and sold as a primary product or as a by-product. Voice-based home banking systems are also being introduced in some countries. They rely on either a small tone generator with which the user signals numerical data, or on a voice recognition system which will deal with a limited range of words (like the numerals definining an account number).

Image-VASs are not yet generally available. However, they may be used on a limited scale for a company's own operations. For example the use of remote slow-scan TV can enable a security company to provide a surveillance service for a client's premises.

Overall, then, the VAS market is highly competitive and fast-moving. Some services are offered by companies set up solely for that purpose. In several other cases, the specialist information-service divisions of large companies have developed their own systems for internal use, and then found that there was a wider market among others in the same industry. They have therefore set up subsidiaries to sell the services to the industry-sector or to the public.

6.7 Private networks

All the systems discussed so far are public in the sense that they are available for individual or corporate use. We mentioned that it is sometimes worth while for a large enterprise to set up its own private network instead.

There are many options open. Private Automatic Branch Exchanges (PABXs) may be used to provide internal telephone services at a site, and provide access to the PSTN. Modern digital PABXs offer more complex features than the public network, can handle data, and may interface with Local Area Networks linking computers and other equipment. Private networks may be constructed by interconnecting PABXs at several different sites, using transmission rented from the Public Telecommunications Operator (PTO). This avoids the call-charges of the PSTN for calls between the sites. The financial appraisal of this option must compare PSTN call-charges with capital investment and running costs of the private network. Private data networks may be set up to carry computer traffic within the organization, or the company can subscribe to a managed data network (see Sec. 6.5). In this section we look briefly at some examples of privately-run information systems. The examples are drawn from the UK, but are representative of what happens elsewhere.

Central Government is the largest user of IT in the UK, with a large proportion on telecommunications goods and services. In 1987 expenditure on IT was running at £1.6 billion per year, with an existing investment worth £5–6 billion supported by 20 000 staff. The Central Computer and Telecommunications Agency (CCTA) in the Treasury is responsible for the IT infrastructure in Whitehall, and for advising and coordinating some 50 Government Departments. It runs a Government Telecommunications Network linking 600 offices, and gives strong support to the adoption of Open Systems Interconnection (OSI) standards. The Department of Trade and Industry sponsored office automation pilot projects in many parts of the public sector; they yielded valuable lessons about how to plan and introduce new office technology in large organizations. Government, with such a large requirement, is able to exert considerable influence in the development of the IT market and achieve considerable economy of scale in running its own networks.

The clearing banks handle so many financial transactions that they must fully exploit developing technology, both in communications and computing. The finance sector of the economy was discussed in Chapter 3. Internationally, banks operate a network called SWIFT; within the UK the clearing banks use a system called CHAPS for same-day payments, and many billions of pounds are transferred each day. The main high-street banks operate their own computer systems, linked to communication networks serving their branches throughout the country. In many cases banks and building societies have found it more effective to share the development of Wide Area Networks rather than incur the whole cost themselves. Together, the banks and the building societies operate perhaps the largest private networks outside Government.

In industry many large companies operate private networks for voice and data, and computer systems supporting a variety of services. There are examples of very large companies which invested early in analogue telephone networks, and as a result suffer the same difficulties as the public network operators in converting to digital operation. Most private networks, however, are now based on digital technology from the outset. We have seen that private networks can prove so successful that they become a profitable enterprise in their own right, by selling services either to the public or to other companies in the same sector of industry. In other cases, such as Unilever, the specialist data network has been sold to a professional communications company to run as a service. There then needs to be a precise agreement dealing with such issues as quality of service, backup arrangements, and any use by third parties.

In these and other sectors of industry, the operation of private networks has proved worth while, and given the company the opportunity to use new technology ahead of its general introduction into public networks. The balance of advantage, though, is now shifting.

6.8 Trends for the future

The choice between running a private network and subscribing to public systems is complex. A private network requires confidence about current and future requirements, specialist expertise either in-house or hired, a large initial capital investment, a danger that technology will become outmoded, and a readiness to accept responsibility for operations which can be crucial to the conduct of business. Use of public systems involves lower initial investment, has greater flexibility when requirements change, can more easily use new technology when it is introduced into the public networks, but does rely on a service essentially outside the user's control. The financial analysis depends on the tariffing policies of the Public Telecommunications Operators (PTOs). In a liberalized environment like the UK these can change quickly. The likely trend, though, is away from private networks and towards the use of large shared networks provided by the PTOs. This is more efficient from a technical viewpoint, and is likely to take full advantage of the accelerated modernization of the public networks.

6.9 Conclusion

In this chapter we have presented a method of classifying information systems and reviewed the systems currently available. We have looked at:

– Communication services, both transmission and switched;
– Public communication networks, and their development;
– Value-Added Networks (VANs);
– Value-Added Services (VASs);
– Private networks; and
– The likely trends for the future.

7.
The future of
information technology

7.1 Introduction

So far we have considered what IT can do today. We now look at some developments which will affect us in the future.

In the 20 000 years humans have been using tools to record and communicate information, most progress has been evolutionary rather than revolutionary. The major developments in communication include writing, printing, the telephone, microelectronics, and fibre-optics. Because there have been so few revolutions in the past, we should be cautious when people now speak of an 'information revolution' about to transform work and society. However, developments are now very rapid, and changes in a person's working lifetime are much greater than ever before.

We shall look at three aspects of the future of IT: the development of Fifth Generation Computing Systems; the emergence of expert systems which store and apply human knowledge; and the security measures which help combat the increasing abuse of information systems.

7.2 Fifth Generation Computing Systems (FGCS)

In Sec. 4.6 we saw how the generations of computers have developed in step with electronic technology. Today's hardware is often called 'third generation'. When the software enables users to develope their own applications with only limited help from experts, we call it 'fourth generation' (or 4th Generation Language, 4GL). The 'fifth generation' of computers is now coming. An ambitious research programme directed towards Fifth Generation Computing Systems (FGCS) started with a conference called by the Japanese in Tokyo in 1981. They invited representatives from the West, and announced a 10-year programme of research directed towards what they called FGCS, the features of which are summarized in Fig. 7.1.

There are three main aspects: hardware, software, and the human interface. FGCS needs very much more powerful hardware: integrated cir-

103

cuits with Ultra Large Scale Integration (ULSI) rather than VLSI. Such hardware will support new and more complex kinds of software. Today's computers operate step-by-step, following a procedural program (see Sec. 4.9). They are good at solving problems using a fixed sequence of steps. Many problems, especially those encountered in management, are simply not like that. The manager solves most problems by musing over the facts, bringing relevant experience and knowledge to bear, consulting with other people, finding out more facts, and then arriving at a reasoned judgement. This broader kind of problem solving is not possible with today's computers. We need systems which can solve real-life problems rather than just carry out fixed instructions, so the words in the centre of Fig. 7.1 emphasize knowledge (skill) rather than data (facts), the ability to relate data in different ways, and problem solving. With these features, computers could in a sense be called intelligent. The term Artificial Intelligence (AI) is controversial, but there is less difficulty if we define AI as behaviour by a machine which in a human we would call intelligent. In that sense some machines already seem intelligent.

Finally we need a more convenient interface between the machine and the human user. This should be based on the way people communicate with each other, using natural language, speech and pictures. With these features, computers would be much easier for us to use and would be able to tackle more complex types of problem.

To achieve these goals, Japan aimed for:

- Microchips with ten million components (a hundred-fold increase);
- 90 per cent accuracy in translating 100 000 words between Japanese and English (a twenty-fold increase in the complexity of knowledge based systems);
- The ability to perform real-time translation of speech (a ten-thousand-fold increase in speed).

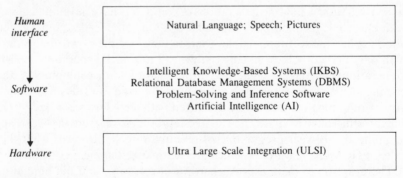

Figure 7.1 Fifth Generation Computing Systems (FGCS)

This was very ambitious. Although Japan formally proposed cooperative work with the West, the West interpreted FGCS as a challenge and started their own research programmes with similar aims. In the UK the 'Alvey Programme' ran betwen 1983 and 1988; it was the largest coordinated research programme ever mounted in the UK, worth £350 million. Since 1988 the UK government has reduced official funding, and placed greater emphasis on participation in the European Community's ESPRIT programme. IT is now the fastest growing sector of world industry, expanding at 15 per cent per year. The world software market alone is worth $22 billion per year, and the UK has only 2 per cent of this. In 1986 the UK production of IT was worth £5 billion, but imports were £1.5 billion greater than exports. As the use of IT increases, this deficit could get worse. By 1988 the UK's deficit reached £2.5 billion. Countries like the UK must therefore decide whether they should try to be in the forefront of all IT developments, or seek cooperative development and niche markets.

Well, what are these FGCS programmes achieving? Starting with hardware, there are two approaches to getting more components onto chips. First, the level of detail can be made smaller. There is research into 'sub-micron technology', where the individual conductors etched onto the silicon are narrower than one micron. A micron is one-millionth of a metre, so that 25 microns make 1/1000 of an inch, or $\frac{1}{3}$ the diameter of the human hair. Today's chips rely on a photographic process to etch the pattern of conductors; sub-micron technology uses X-rays or electron beams to achieve even finer levels of detail. Already it is possible to store one Mbit of data on a single chip, and there is considerable effort to get one-micron and then sub-micron techniques into industrial production. The second approach is to make chips from larger slices of silicon. Instead of making a few hundred small ICs on a slice 10cm in diameter, the idea is to make one very complex circuit. To do this the process has to be very reliable and the circuit has to have some redundancy, so that damaged parts of the circuit can be by-passed. This so-called Wafer Scale Integration (WSI) is becoming practical, and could increase the power of chips 1000-fold.

Traditional computer architecture, where each step is done sequentially by a single processor, is a barrier to increased speed. Figure 4.4 shows that the processor is the heart of the system and forms a bottleneck. Jobs like pattern-recognition (needed for recognition of speech or images) needs lots of processing. One approach is to have arrays of say 64 similar VLSI-based processors, working in parallel on different parts of the problem, and thus increasing the effective speed. The idea is simple but it is difficult to coordinate what the individual processors are doing. However, it seems that arrays can be more flexible, and perform well on tasks like image-processing. One processor designed to work in arrays is called the Transputer. It was developed by Inmos in the UK, and uses a special language called Occam with a limited number of commands. There is a general move towards this Reduced Instruction-Set Computer (RISC) technology, to improve overall speed.

Parallel processing with Transputer arrays is now available. A practical example is encoding a fingerprint image. If a fingerprint is stored as an unprocessed image it needs 2.5 Mbytes. If it is processed by a Transputer, so that a description of the fingerprint is recorded rather than the whole image, then this is reduced by a factor of several thousand. This makes possible storage of large numbers of fingerprints in databases, as part of police records or to form an identity check system for a bank. Transputer arrays are now the basis for several commercial 'supercomputers', and parallel processing will continue to be an important aspect of FGCS work.

The third main aspect of FGCS is the way people (the users) interact with machines. This is the Man-Machine Interface (MMI). We want natural language, speech and pictures for this. The difficulties of speech and language for today's computers were described in Sec. 4.7: individual differences of pronunciation, and the illogical structure of languages like English. However, steady progress is being made, so that devices such as speech-activated word processors are becoming feasible. Because of the importance of images for conveying information to human users, there is research into new types of visual displays (large, flat, and in colour), as well as machine-recognition of images so that they can be processed along with other modes in an integrated system. The image mode needs very much higher capacity for both processing and storage. Parallel processing may solve the first problem, and new optical storage technologies may solve the second.

Optical technology is becoming very important in IT. We have seen the huge capacity of digital optical recording and of Fibre-Optic Cable (FOC). There is immense potential for future expansion. Today, a single 30cm optical disk can store the images of 60 000 A4 sheets of text or diagrams, equivalent to ten filing cabinets full of paper. Potentially, an optical storage device one cubic foot in size could store about 400 Gbytes of data, equivalent to 200 million pages of text, 1.6 years of continuous speech, or 5 days of continuous TV images. In the longer term optical processing may also become important, so that storage, transmission and processing can be done with pulses of light rather than pulses of electricity. Optical computers could in principle work one thousand times as fast as electrical machines.

Important advances are being made towards FGCS. Japan believes that leadership in the information age will be vital to its survival; other countries think likewise and are responding to the challenge.

7.3 Expert systems

Expert systems are at the leading-edge of today's technology, and are examples of the knowledge-based systems we shall see with FGCS. It is important to distinguish between data, information, knowledge, and wisdom (see Fig. 2.7). Today's computers handle data, and make it appear as information relevant to the manager's task. The result should be more useful, but it is still factual. Knowledge, in contrast, includes human experience and the ability to relate information to it. It includes working rules and guidelines built up over years of experience. How can knowledge, in this sense, be placed on a computer? When we think, we do not operate like sequential computers. We operate in a more complex way, often relating ideas which seem to have no formal connection. This is the basis of lateral thinking, and a feature of human originality. To put knowledge onto a computer we must get away from the traditional step-by-step following of a program. Expert systems are beginning to do this. A block diagram is shown in Fig. 7.2.

Compare Fig. 7.2 with Fig. 4.4, the block diagram of today's computers. Three of the elements are the same: input, output, and software control. As before, the software controls the operation of the whole machine. The 'store' (memory) has become a knowledge base into which are put the 'rules' which constitute the human knowledge. The 'processor' has become an 'inference engine', which makes logical inferences (deductions) by applying the rules to the data fed into the machine. The performance of a traditional computer is often measured in millions of instructions per second (Mips) achieved by its central processor; today's machines reach several hundred

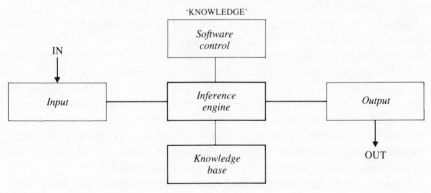

Figure 7.2 Expert system

Mips. The performance of an expert system is measured in logical inferences per second (Lips). Each logical inference, if performed on a conventional machine, may take 10–100 steps of a sequential program. Overall, today's expert systems operate at about 100 000 Lips.

The knowledge base is the foundation of the expert system. It is a record of the knowledge of one or more human experts, in a particular field or 'domain', expressed in a form which can be used by the inference engine. Special software languages exist for this, for example LISP and PROLOG. They use the form IF ... THEN ... to express the rules. For example, in the medical field a simple (but inadequate) rule might be 'IF the patient has red spots and a temperature THEN the patient has measles'. Typical expert systems have a knowledge base with a few hundred rules in this form. It is not easy for human experts to express their knowledge in this way, but it often leads to a more logical formulation. Sometimes a person called a knowledge engineer is used to help the expert formulate his knowledge; he acts as a bridge between the expert and the detailed programmers.

To use the expert system, the facts about a particular case are fed in, for example 'the patient has red spots'. The inference engine then searches the knowledge base to see which rules apply in the present case, and what deductions can be made from those rules. In the simple example, it might ask the user 'does the patient also have a temperature?'. If the user responds 'yes', then the machine determines that the rule in the knowledge base applies, and pronounces 'the patient has measles'.

Such an expert system, if used to advise a doctor, would not last long. Soon, a case would be found for which the rules were not adequately expressed. For example, a patient with chicken pox would have the same symptoms, and the diagnosis would be wrong. An additional rule, for example distinguishing the appearance of the spots in more detail, would need to be formulated by the doctor and fed into the knowledge base. Gradually the expert system is 'taught' by the human user and its performance thereby improves. A key feature of an expert system to assist this is the ability to explain its 'reasoning' when challenged to do so. Thus if the human expert disagrees with the expert system, he must be able to challenge it, and the machine must list the set of rules which it applied in reaching its conclusion. The human expert can then see where the flaw in the argument was, and formulate a new rule to avoid that mistake in future. Eventually the machine may, within a particular field of knowledge, be more expert than the humans who taught it. This raises important issues: would you entrust medical diagnosis or financial advice to an expert system?

Expert systems have been around since the mid-sixties. There have been successful applications in the fields of molecular structures (Dendral), medical diagnosis (Mycin), the interpretation of geological survey data (Prospector), the analysis of faults in telephone exchanges (Tracker), the analysis of computer crash-dumps (Apres), the application of complex legislation, and the application of social security rules. There are different motives behind these practical expert systems. One motive is to pool all available human knowledge in a difficult specialist area. Another is to encapsulate the expertise of a particular key individual. Another is to make possible automatic advice-systems which can be used by the general public. For business and management, it is perhaps the last two motives which are strongest.

Expert systems can run on Personal Computers (PCs), and packages are commercially available. You can buy expert system 'shells' which implement all the mechanisms of an expert system but contain no knowledge base. In this case, the user must individually formulate all the rules and build up the knowledge base from scratch. In other cases, the expert system is supplied with a knowledge base which covers the basics of the particular field, and it is intended that the user will develop it to suit his special needs and to exploit his particular knowledge. The part-filled shell is attractive to managers, and there are systems available in the areas of financial management, personnel management, and engineering design.

Managers need to watch this technology carefully, and consider whether special knowledge within their organizations could be recorded on expert systems and then applied by less-skilled people. This can reduce the organization's dependence on human experts and reduce training costs. This would apply for example in the implementation of complex administrative or legal rules. In the UK the Department of Health and Social Security is developing an expert system to advise on individuals' eligibility for benefit payments. By distributing the software to the many DHSS offices, consistent expert advice is available to the public without the need for continual training of staff. Moreover, when the benefit rules change only the software needs to be changed.

Expert systems can present a human dilemma. Should experts divulge their hard-won knowledge to a machine, and thereby make themselves less essential? Or is it a way for the human expert to enshrine his knowledge in a permanent form, and thus achieve some form of immortality? Expert systems, and other knowledge-based systems, will challenge some of the traditional areas of professional monopoly.

Expert systems are a practical tool of modern management, and we can expect substantial advances as the FGCS programme develops. A 1987 survey of UK firms showed that about 25 per cent believed expert systems would be vital to the future of their organizations, and of these 60 per cent believed that this would happen before 1990.

7.4 The security of information

Finally we turn to a different problem: how to protect information which is stored and processed in computer-based systems. In many countries the law requires us to protect information relating to living, indentifiable individuals. This was discussed in Sec. 5.7. However, industrial espionage and financial fraud are usually stronger motives for attempting to breach corporate security of information. The size of the problem is difficult to assess, because organizations are naturally reluctant to say how much computer fraud they have suffered. However, some notable cases have been reported, involving millions of pounds or dollars. Some statistics for computer fraud were quoted in Chapter 3, when considering the finance sector of UK business. Surveys of computer crimes show that most are perpetrated by manipulation of data, and most exploit weak administrative procedures within the organization. The main targets for computer crime are:

- personal data, for curiosity or blackmail;
- corporate data, for competitive advantage;
- money, for personal gain.

The extent to which individuals or organizations will try to get illicit data, or penetrate information systems, depends on the potential advantages they see. Here are some of the methods used:

- eavesdropping;
- illicit access to data;
- denial of service to the legitimate user;
- spoofing and forgery.

These methods are in ascending order of technical complexity. Eavesdropping relates mainly to the interception of communications traffic, with the aim of picking up interesting information without the legitimate user being aware. By definition, successful eavesdropping means that the user is unaware of the fact. Illicit access, often by so-called hackers, is a more active process and seeks to gain entry to information systems by posing as a legitimate user. The intruder can then manipulate data files or retrieve information of interest to him. An extension of this is denial of service, where the intruder upsets the system so that it does not perform the legitimate user's tasks properly. For example, communication systems can be disrupted or swamped with dummy traffic, or 'logic bombs' can be introduced to upset the operation of a computer system. Finally, spoofing is the active exploitation of the system by injecting messages or data which seem to be legitimate but actually have a malicious aim. Financial fraud based on illicit electronic transfer of money comes into this category.

The threat to the security of electronic information is therefore considerable, and managers need to be aware of the available countermeasures. Here are some relevant to commercial systems:

- electromagnetic screening
- enciphering, or encryption
- authentication
- computer security
- audit and control
- personnel security.

Electromagnetic screening is often overlooked. All electrical equipment radiates energy in the form of radio waves. This can sometimes be picked up at a distance and used to reconstruct the information content of computer and communication systems. Commercial word-processors have been interpreted in this way at distances of several hundred feet, and VDUs (computer screens) at distances of one kilometre. Thus covert interception may be possible without gaining access either to the building or its immediate vicinity. The electrical radiation can be reduced by screening of the electronic devices and wiring, and filtering the mains supplies. This is fairly cheap at the installation, but more expensive retrospectively. Special versions of some equipment can be bought with very low levels of radiation; they are called TEMPEST-proofed. An organization must decide which equipments are handling sensitive information, and whether they should be screened in this way. If a lot of computer equipment is working close together it is more difficult to reconstruct the information on any one screen, and this gives some measure of protection. A greater risk may be the isolated terminal in the chief executive's suite, which is easier to pick up and also is likely to carry the most sensitive data.

Enciphering or encryption produces a 'scrambled' version of a signal which is meaningless to a person who intercepts it, but can be decoded by the legitimate recipient. For effective encipherment, signals need to be in digital form, and this is a limitation for voice, where most current systems use analogue technology. Let's look at the principles, and some important developments.

To protect information sent over telecommunication systems which may be subject to monitoring or interception, the traditional solution is shown in Fig. 7.3. A Sender, A, wishes to send information ('plain text') to a legitimate Receiver, B. The message might be 'Hello'. To protect the message against interception while it is in transmission (and therefore outside the physical control of both A and B), it is enciphered or encrypted. This is done by using a key, which must be kept secret, to jumble up the message. It is then safe for transmission; anyone intercepting the message (now in 'cipher text') cannot make sense of it without the key. The intended recipient, B, has the key and is able to reverse the enciphering procedure and thus retrieve the message. It is analogous to having a padlock to secure a box of valuables sent through the post. There need to be two keys: one held by the sender and one held by the receiver. If a key is lost or copied, the security is lost.

Commercial equipment working on this principle is widely used. For example, it is the basis for communication security in the banking networks SWIFT and CHAPS. There is a Data Encryption Standard (DES) for the protection of information which is approved by the US authorities, and is available on a microchip. It uses a 64-bit electronic key, which gives a level of security adequate for commercial purposes: it might take a $100 000 computer 20 000 years to crack the code by systematic search.

A major disadvantage of traditional encryption is the need to generate and distribute the secret key. If the key is lost, an interceptor can, in principle, recover the plain text of the messages. It is like losing the key of the lock used to secure goods in transit. In about 1977 a novel solution to this problem was suggested. It is known as Public Key Cipher (PKC), and is shown in Fig. 7.4. PKC has the advantage that the secret part of the process is wholly under the control of the person receiving the information. In the diagram, B uses a 'seed' key to generate two related but different keys: the public key which can be notified to the world at large, and the secret key which is kept private to B. Anyone wishing to send a message securely to B enciphers it with B's public key. Only B, with his secret key, is able to decipher the message. There is no need for transmission of the secret key to

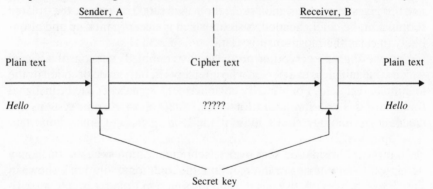

Figure 7.3 Encipherment

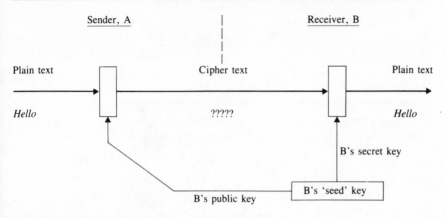

Figure 7.4 Public key cipher

anyone else, and so it is less likely to be lost. The lock analogy is again useful. PKC is like having a lock which requires one key to lock it, and a different key to unlock it. It is clearly possible to make such a mechanical lock (some locks need no key at all to lock them!). It does not matter if anyone makes a copy of the locking-key, provided this does not reveal the shape of the unlocking-key.

PKC seems paradoxical. It relies on pairs of keys such that the secret key cannot be deduced from the public key. Mathematicians have argued about how secure the system is, but it seems practical for commercial systems and could have a major impact.

PKC raises another problem, however. Even though it is not possible to decipher messages, it is very easy to forge them. Everyone has access to the public key, so a malicious person could forge a message and make it appear to be from someone else. We need a system of authentication; this is the third countermeasure on the list. In the paper-based information world we authenticate by using headed notepaper and manual signatures by responsible officials. The signature is taken, for practical purposes, to be unforgeable. There is now an electronic equivalent of this. It is called digital signature and is shown in Fig. 7.5. The Sender, A, uses his own secret key to encipher a message confirming that he is the originator. The enciphered message can now be deciphered by anyone, using A's public key. Anyone can read the message (including B), but no-one can forge it, because that requires A's secret key. This system, then, sends messages which can be read but not forged. The basic PKC system sends messages which can be forged but not read by an interceptor. It is possible to combine the two systems to give protection against both forgery and interception. This is necessary if we are going to move from paper to electronic systems without losing security.

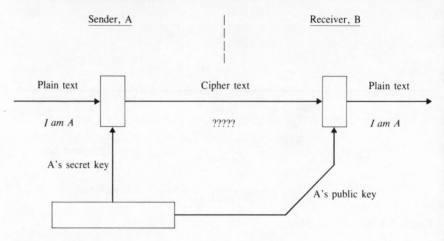

Figure 7.5 Digital signature

Of course authentication need not be high-tech. A simple precaution with the telephone is to ring back the alleged caller's number. Several authentication techniques are used in computer systems. The most common is the use of passwords to control access to the system or to particular categories of information within it. There are two options in running a password system. Either users are allowed to choose their own passwords and enter them into the system without support from the IS staff, or passwords are selected by the IS staff and users are told. Users often prefer the first method, but the fact is that they are likely to choose obvious passwords such as first name, room number, birthday, or car registration number. They also tend not to change passwords as often as they should. This makes it easier for hackers to guess the password and thus penetrate a system by pretending to be that user. However, if the second option is used then it is important that the IS staff choose passwords which are fairly easy to remember, otherwise users will write them down in accessible places like the corners of calendars, and the security is undermined in that way. Password systems have to be carefully managed if they are to be effective.

Other methods of authentication are becoming possible. Measurement of some physical characteristic like the size of the hand or the fingerprint pattern is feasible, and image-recognition has now reached the point where it can recognize faces and thus control a security gate into sensitive areas. The pattern of blood vessels on the retina of the eye is as unique as a fingerprint, and can be observed with an optical device. However, this is less popular with users than more benign devices such as those which observe the dynamics of the user making his signature with an electronic pen.

Besides authentication, there are other aspects of computer security. One has been mentioned already: the need to compartment information so that only those users with a genuine need to access information (as opposed to a casual curiosity about it) are allowed to see it. In shared systems based on networks and databases, it is usually necessary to draw up an access control matrix to decide who should have access to what. An example is in Fig. 7.6.

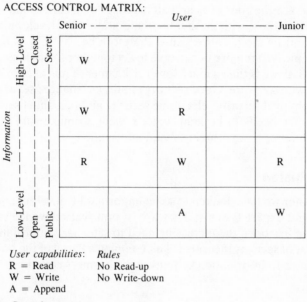

ACCESS CONTROL MATRIX:

User capabilities: Rules
R = Read   No Read-up
W = Write   No Write-down
A = Append

Figure 7.6   Security access

Several categories of information are defined, ranging from public (or open) to secret (or closed). For each user of the information system the level of access is decided, in relation to the job that person has to do. Often, each user is allowed to see information only up to a specified level. It is necessary to distinguish between authority to read what is already in a data file, to append new data to what is already there, and to write over what is already there. Each data file should have someone responsible for its accuracy who must agree who can write and append to his files. Within the system the security policy must then be implemented. For example, besides preventing individuals from seeing information to which they are not entitled ('no read up'), it must prevent users from reading data out of a sensitive file and then writing it electronically into an open file ('no write down').

It is difficult to have complete confidence that a computer system will always implement a defined security policy. The development of rigorous software which can be relied on is difficult and expensive. Sometimes, therefore, it is better to keep sensitive information on a physically separate computer system, and only allow transfers of data under strictly controlled conditions.

The remaining security measures involve the way computers are used by people, including the staff professionally involved. For most systems, this is much the greatest threat, and good audit and control procedures are essential. People are the root of nearly all breaches of security, and those with most access are those with the greatest temptation. The development of vital software, and its modification, must therefore be carefully controlled. A good principle is to require two people to act together to implement important changes; there is then a much lower risk either of mistakes or deliberate tampering with software. Good security requires a balanced set of measures, involving physical security, electronic security and personnel security. The security policy needs to be kept under review, to make sure it is still an adequate defence to any threat to vital information.

7.5 Conclusion

In this chapter we have looked at some important IT developments related to FGCS and expert systems. They are of practical relevance today. The other theme has been the increasing need to safeguard information with a balanced set of security measures. This completes Part 2 of the book, and in Part 3 we turn to information systems in the business context.

PART THREE
THE SOLUTION

8.
Business systems and information

8.1 Introduction

'A place for everything, and everything in its place'

For some people neatness and tidiness are a natural way of life. The rest of us can only marvel at the discipline that enables such people to arrange and keep appointments, never to miss meetings, to find files, meet deadlines, and still to appear relaxed and happy! Helping less fortunate managers to organize their business lives, to be neat and methodical, is a growing and fertile field for consultants. People want to be organized: all that is needed is some kind of systematic approach to the problem.

Business enterprises are often referred to as 'organizations', implying that there is a formal structure, a systematic approach, giving a sense of order and purpose. This chapter will show how the concepts of organizational structure and purpose may also be applied to the information within that structure and how information may be organized into systems designed for specific purposes. It is important to note that the term 'information system' does not apply exclusively to electronic or computer-based systems, although this book is mainly concerned with such. An information system may consist of paper flows, verbal communications or electronic devices. What is significant is the way these things are arranged into effective processes for the transmission and reception of business information.

8.2   Evolution of information systems

No study of business information systems would be complete without some examination of the way in which organizations are structured to achieve their objectives and of the way in which information can be created and used in those organizations. Organizational systems are no accident: they are constructed or they grow to meet a business need. In the same way, information systems should not simply evolve or grow out of some chaotic state;

they should instead be seen as part of business strategy and organizational development.

Later in this chapter we will be considering business organizations as 'systems' in the engineering sense, but first it is useful at this stage to look back at the way business and business information has evolved from being simply a way of achieving the transfer of basic goods and services to a way of mobilizing huge amounts of resources, money and people in the achievement of long-term objectives.

The reason for looking at the past is to demonstrate that several consistent themes have always influenced the growth and development of business information systems; themes that we should be able to identify in working to solve today's problems with today's resources. If we understand the interaction of the internal and external forces that influence organizations then we can pick out the more likely directions for future long-term development and discard temporary diversions. As with clothes, information systems have fashions; some will last, others, like last year's Ascot hats, will soon be forgotten.

Business information systems have developed over time because of ordinary economic pressures and the dynamics of business enterprise, especially under competitive conditions. The business that had accurate and timely information was the business that survived and grew. Information technology, first seen simply as a means of office automation, had introduced another dimension, allowing managers more choice of action and the freedom to experiment by using information systems to simulate business behaviour. Airlines no longer waste expensive flying hours in precious aircraft on training. Simulators are now available that can reproduce with considerable realism all the aspects of flight in the most complex of aircraft. Each new generation of computers and information systems offers managers the ability to plan and to simulate with more and more complex models. Information technology is now so cheap and so powerful that it is tempting for managers to buy the latest computing and communications equipment for their status value alone. We must never forget, however, that commercial pressures still apply and that, to earn their keep, information systems must be able to enhance the performance of the enterprise, to give it that elusive competitive edge over all its rivals. This issue will be examined in more detail later when we come to consider the information needs of business managers and ways in which that information can be used for decision making.

8.3 Where it started

Business organization has a long history and it is difficult to imagine a time when there was no structure or bureaucracy in business. It is easy to imagine how the need for organizing things and people and for having organizational structures came about.

The concept of organization for a purpose is a very ancient one. We tend to think of former civilizations as being simple and unsophisticated, but to do so is to ignore the amazing achievements of the Chinese, Greeks, Romans, Egyptians, Britons and others who, in ancient times, performed tasks of staggering technical and organizational complexity. One could say that civilization itself started when mankind first discovered the value of organization. Groups of people cooperated together to hunt, to build or to fight. Naturally there were the leaders and the followers. Soon there would be sharing or delegation of tasks, specialization and other familiar features of our modern business world. The building of the pyramids of Egypt, or of Stonehenge, would have been impossible without the organization and motivation of thousands of people. Monuments had to be designed and laid out to a high degree of precision. Materials had to be quarried and transported over long distances. Enormous masses of stone had to be cut, raised through great heights and fitted precisely together. This could only be the work of highly organized groups working to precise plans and very efficiently controlled.

It may be that those ancient organizations were created simply for the one purpose, only to be disbanded again when the work was finished. The concept of the multi-purpose permanent organization is a more modern one. However, to lose that sense of purpose, the pursuit of clear objectives, is to weaken the organization and the people in it. Worse still is the situation where an organization may appear to have no immediate objective, where things are done for their own sake and where individuals feel no sense of challenge or commitment. What is wrong in such cases? The missing ingredient may be *information*.

The ancient engineers and builders must have had plans, work-schedules, objectives and even the inevitable reports. All these were information which had to be communicated to different parts of the organization in order to be effective. Just as there was a physical organization to get the work done, so there was an organization of the essential information to define and control the work. Business organizations then may be seen as mechanisms, designed for some purpose but static and ineffective until information is provided to set the mechanism to work. Just as there may be a particularly appropriate form of organization for some business task, so there will be an appropriate form of information organization to support it.

The development of accurate methods of navigation, based on reliable information about time and the positions of the stars and the sun, opened up trade routes around the world. International trade led to the formation of international trading companies, such as the East India Company and the

Hudson's Bay Company. On the industrial side companies became established for extracting and processing raw materials, for manufacturing textiles and machines and for providing transport by railway and canals. By the end of the nineteenth century the scale, complexity and technical resources deployed by some business organizations had already become too large to be easily understood by any one person.

These industrial and commercial organizations and their resources possessed a momentum, almost a life of their own; the employee became no more than a small cog in a large machine. Because of the introduction of new technologies the pace of change increased dramatically, leading to misunderstanding, exploitation and unrest. We usually think of the problems of the Industrial Revolution in terms of its effect on the workers but it has always been difficult for managers at all levels to come to terms with new technologies. We have seen many examples to prove that the organization and its management who cannot be flexible and accept change will wither and die.

In early 20th century businesses simple interpersonal communication and hand-written records were no longer suitable forms of managerial control: relevant technologies had to be introduced to the organization. Printing technologies, the telegraph, then the telephone, the typewriter, the

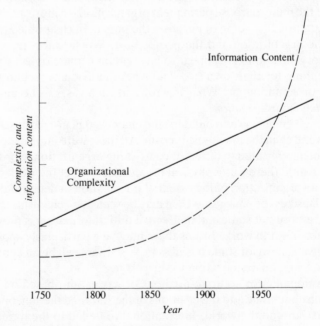

Figure 8.1 Organization and information

duplicator, were all forerunners of the IT revolution that was to come in the second half of the century. Information was beginning to take over as the chief determinant of business activity. Figure 8.1 represents the shift of emphasis in organizations from organizational complexity to information content.

8.4   Key factors

The following key factors were well established by the 1890s, and their relevance to information management today is indicated in each case.

The phase relationship

Industrially-manufactured goods were being produced in volume for mass markets both at home and overseas. The introduction of first the telegraph and then the telephone had allowed the communication of essential information relating to the ordering, sale and manufacture of the goods to become much more rapid than the cycle of production and delivery of the goods. The relationship between the speed with which physical business systems have been able to operate, as opposed to the information systems controlling them is called the 'phase relationship'. It is still an important factor in matching information systems to organizational needs and one that changes continually as the nature of business and of technology changes. The adoption by many industries of 'just in time' processes, whereby components and materials are not stocked in quantity but are ordered and delivered just in time for use in manufacture, depends entirely on efficient management of information and control of the phase relationship.

Managing the information

Continuous technological progress, as in the iron and steel industry, increased international specialization. Growth powered by innovation increased the importance of information of all kinds as a business resource but its significance was at times not recognized. At other times the means to produce the required information was not available. Several disasters, such as the collapse of the Tay Bridge, could be traced back to the lack of good information about processes, materials and conditions. The problem then, as today, was managerial rather than technical. The need for information continued to grow even faster than the businesses themselves. Technical means now existed to cope with industrial growth but the capability to manage information, and through it to control the industrial process effectively, was scarce. Modern managers need skills in handling all kinds of resources, especially information, if their businesses are to succeed.

Information themes

Themes to follow in this study of information systems therefore include the timing, appropriateness and management of information.

8.5 Information systems: Definitions

Before proceeding any further it is necessary to remind ourselves of what is meant by an 'information system' in a business environment. We have seen that a consequence of the growth of business complexity was a demand for more and more information. Not all of the data available to businesses is in the right form, nor is available at just the right time. It may need to be altered, added to, or simply stored for record purposes. It will certainly need to be turned into useful information. It will also need to be transmitted to different parts of the organization. So, we define an information system as:

> A collection of procedures, activities, people and technology set up for the *collection* of relevant data, its *storage* until it is required, its *processing* to help provide answers to a specific set of questions and the *communication* of the resulting information to the people who need to act upon it.

This definition enlarges on the ideas presented in Sec. 3.4. Note that four specific functions are identified:

Collection, Storage, Processing, Communication.

These functions are essential to any information system and are the basis on which systems may be designed, implemented, operated and controlled. They should be able to be identified in any business, no matter whether the information system is a modern electronic one or is paper-based.

Imagine the situation in a small shop, a newsagent's. Sales are recorded on the till roll as each item is sold. This is the data collection stage. Every evening the shopkeeper examines the till rolls, extracting details of sales of different items and recording stock and cash balances. That data is stored in ledgers, cash-books and stock lists. The data can remain in store indefinitely, but eventually the shopkeeper needs to complete VAT returns, to calculate revenue and expenditure, to forecast demand and to order new stock. The data must now be processed into useful information. The specific questions that the information answers may relate to taxation, stock levels, profitability and so on. Once the processing is complete the information can be communicated, perhaps by letter and forms to the tax and VAT authorities, by word of mouth to the employees, or by telephone to the suppliers. Many small businesses have now discovered the power of microcomputers to help with all these separate processes whereas large businesses may have automated everything from data capture (collection) through to stock control and payroll. It does not matter if the information is in the form of paper till rolls, or neat files in an office cabinet, or in magnetic signals on a tape or disk: the system that handles the information will have those four basic elements.

8.6 Information systems: Roles

Why do we need information systems? They may serve to speed up manual processes, or to simplify the tasks of record-keeping and information management. Information systems must be able to justify their existence.

As we have seen, from the earliest times businesses have been 'in business' to get things done: to make money, to produce, to buy and sell goods and to provide employment. Getting things done requires some deliberate action and in order to take action some decision has to be made. Unless the work of the organization and those in it results in *decisions* and *actions* nothing will be achieved.

The role of an effective information system within an organization structure is to assist and improve the decision-making process and to help to turn information and decisions into action.

That role can be exercised at all levels in the organization, although the nature of the information system may be different depending on whether the decisions to be made are simple or complex. Information is the life-blood of any organization, so it is instructive to study not only the structure of the organization, the 'body', but also its information processes, the 'circulatory system'.

8.7 Information and organizations

A mechanism for taking photographs used to be called a camera, nowadays it is likely to be called a 'photographic system', in the same way we can regard businesses and their information organizations as 'systems'. Careful study and understanding of the organization of our businesses will allow us to design and implement effective information systems, leading, it is to be hoped, to order and efficiency.

Organizational structures

Whatever kind of business we may work in we will know something about its organization. There may be organization charts in large concerns, or we may know all the members of the organization personally. Whatever the size or shape of the business there is almost certain to be some kind of hierarchy: there will be the managers and the managed, the Board of Directors and the administrators, the executives and the secretaries. All these persons com-

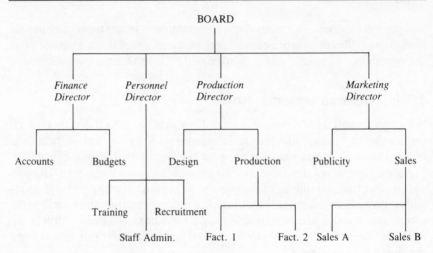

Figure 8.2   Basic organizational structure

municate in various ways up and down the layers of the organization. Information flows between departments, between functions and between supervisors and the supervised. The commonest form of organization structure is the tree, shown in Fig. 8.2, with a small number of senior staff at the top and with much larger numbers of junior or support staff at the bottom. The basic tree structure may contain functional units, such as Sales, Finance, Production and Personnel. There may be specialized departments serving several territorial or functional units, forming a matrix organization. Some organizations have many hierarchical levels, others are much 'flatter' with the top management more closely in touch with the shop-floor.

It must be realized that the shape of the organization chart does not fully describe the structure of a business. In fact the formal diagram may conceal a wealth of informal relationships, of systems, established either deliberately or accidentally to enable work to be done more effectively. Those systems depend on information for their success: they are the means by which orders are processed, people hired and fired, products designed and made and by which managers manage. The information systems in an organization may not be well defined or easily mapped out, but they are as essential as the people and functions that they serve.

> As with a body, the systems of an organization overlap and interlink the parts, the structure and the members. They are of a different logical order from the structure or the component pieces, for they are defined by their purpose and are concerned with flows or processes THROUGH the structure. They are in fact 'systems' – it remains the best, if the vaguest word, meaning at its broadest only an interdependent set of elements. (Handy, 1985)[1]

Why do we have hierarchical organizations? Perhaps it is for historical reasons. The founder of a business found it necessary to employ helpers, who themselves acquired assistants and so on. Gradually the pyramid is built up with the senior policy makers at the top and the makers and doers of things at the bottom. It seems sensible to suppose that the hierarchy is preserved because of the access to and understanding of different types and quantities of information at the different levels. The directors have their contacts in the City and their years of managerial experience to help them to make sense of the masses of information that are available to modern business people; policy and strategic matters are their particular concern. In the middle layers of the organization are the executives who must translate policy and strategy into action, using information given to them by both the senior managers and by the shop-floor. At the bottom of the organization information is needed about orders, money, people, materials and all the myriads of diverse elements that go to make up modern business.

The design of the structure is intended to assist the operation of the organization.

> Organizational design aims to devise appropriate structural arrangements. Organizational structure is a means for allocating responsibilities, providing a framework for operations and performance assessment, and furnishing mechanisms to process information and assist decision-making. Deficiencies in structure can give rise to serious problems. (Child, 1986)[2]

Information structures

All organization structures are complemented by some kind of information system. Different types of information are required at the different organizational levels. The nearer one is to the top of the organization the less detailed but the more strategically important is the required information. Towards the bottom of the organizational structure information is much more related to day-to-day activities, production levels, sales, performance, etc.

At the operational level the most appropriate type of information system may be the Transaction Processing System (TPS). At the middle-management levels one would expect to find IPS and DSS. At the top of the organization special forms of decision support systems may be required, able to cope with uncertainty, risk and long-term planning. Such systems are sometimes described as Executive Information Systems (EIS) or Strategic Decision Support Systems (SDSS).

Information flows around the organization in all directions. The main streams of information may, however, be classified as 'top-down' and 'bottom-up'. Figure 8.3 shows how information flows and decision-making processes in a business may be 'top-down', driven by overall strategic

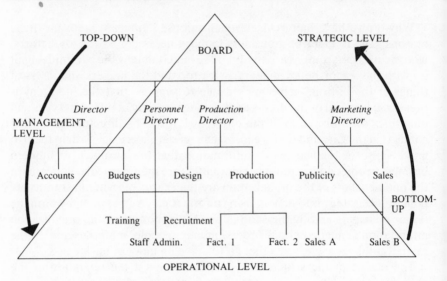

Figure 8.3 Organizational information flows

business objectives and policies, or they may be 'bottom-up', driven by practical, operational issues, market forces, etc. Those managers in the middle of the organization have to reconcile the often conflicting demands of the top-down and bottom-up processes. It is in these middle levels in the organization where most of the processing of the information goes on, for that reason it is at those levels that the impact of the introduction of modern information systems may be felt the most. That aspect will be dealt with in more detail in a later chapter.

In addition to the information flowing up and down an organization there will be substantial quantities of information entering and leaving it. A business operates in an external environment which may be national or international. The business reacts to external threats and opportunities, using information about the environment to establish its marketing and production plans, to allocate its resources and to plan its future.

Externally-generated information may enter the organization at any level by a wide variety of routes and ways must be found of directing it to the places where it is most needed. Similarly information within the organization flows out at various levels and some control over its content and destination will be required. Information systems therefore have three main functions:

1. to facilitate the flow of information within organizations,
2. to facilitate flows of information out of and into the organization, and
3. to provide facilities for the management of information.

Effective information is both the fuel and the lubricant for the business mechanism, without it the organization cannot function effectively. Just as the correct grades of petrol and oil must be chosen to give maximum performance in a car, so the most appropriate kinds of information must be found to maximize business performance.

Business information is therefore a valuable resource and must be carefully handled. Possession of the information is power whether it is in the hands of the managers or their competitors.

It is very important to realize that a formal organization chart may not actually represent what really happens in an organization. Whenever there is a business crisis there is a tendency to reorganize, in the hope that a new organizational structure may help to solve the current problems, but structure may not be the only answer. There will be informal links and flows of information across organizational boundaries; working groups may become established, drawing on personnel and resources from many different functions. People talking across desks and in dining rooms will pass on information often much more effectively than the 'official channels'. A formal system for collecting, storing, processing and communicating information for management decision making may actually distort or conceal the true nature of what is going on. An effective information system will interpret the strategic aims of the organization and will facilitate the top-down communication process while effectively using bottom-up information to monitor and to control the activities of the organization. Changes in information systems may be a more powerful tool for performance improvement than any amount of structural reorganization.

The information system should in some way mimic the underlying informal 'system' of the organization. However, the introduction of an information system which merely replicates and automates processes that existed before may deny an organization the real benefits of a new or revolutionary approach.

An effective information system cannot be constrained by the formal 'channels' of information flow: up the line of functional command to senior management and down another functional line. Rather, it will facilitate the establishment of a flexible 'matrix' organization, which is able to respond quickly to any change in the internal and external business environments.

8.8 The business environment

The enterprise, or business, however it is organized and for whatever purpose it exists, operates as an environment within an environment. The internal environment consists of data flows, information processes, physical processes, etc., all to do with the day-to-day running of the organization.

The external environment consists of economic, social, market, technological and other issues affecting the planning and operation of the organization in a competitive world. Internal data flows will consist of reports, statistics, memoranda, instructions, personnel data, financial data and so on. External data flows will include market research information, information about competitors, publicity, orders, accounts, specifications to suppliers, etc.

Figure 8.4 shows how these data flows interact to form a total business environment. Information systems are created to manage these flows of data and to turn them into useful information for the benefit of the enterprise and its management. Remember that data must first be turned into relevant information; then, to be of any use, that information must be converted into *decisions* and *actions*.

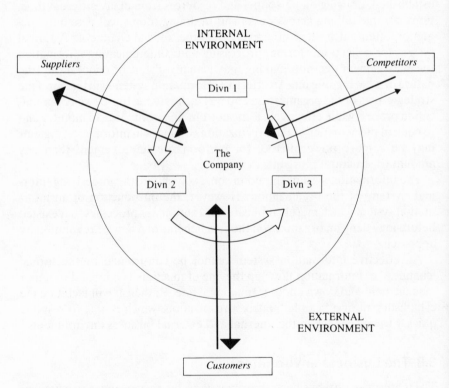

Figure 8.4 The business environment

8.9 The systems approach

Matching the information system to the business system is like matching parts of a hi-fi system together. We may want to link up a cassette recorder, a record turntable, a compact disc player, and perhaps an electronic keyboard to an amplifier. Unless the system is carefully designed with the right plugs and sockets carrying the right kinds of electrical signals there will be mismatches, incompatibilities, loss of quality and considerable frustration. If the information in such a system is not carefully monitored and controlled there may be instabilities which can actually destroy expensive equipment. Similarly in business inputs and outputs of information must be matched to the business processes. Information must be carefully monitored so that any deviations from normal may be detected and acted upon quickly before business performance suffers. Speed of response is an important factor: where business information is delayed, for example, because key management information is published only monthly, corrective action by managers may be too late. There may be over-reaction leading to instability and inefficiency.

In a hi-fi system there are control mechanisms in the amplifying chain that detect signal levels, feeding back unwanted errors or changes to correct the inputs. In this way noise, distortion and instability can be damped out before it becomes apparent. In a business context instabilities may be caused by unexpected events, by delays in supplies or by financial crises or any number of internal or external factors. A good information system should so match the operation of the business system that such deviations can be detected and corrected quickly.

It should be clear by now that in setting out to design an information system we have to remember that the information structure may not be the same as the organizational structure of a business. It is important to look at and then to understand the various components of the business and the real relationships and linkages between them, this may be done by treating the business itself as a system in the technical sense.

System behaviour

We all have some experience of domestic electrical and plumbing systems; perhaps we know about the fuel system of a car, or the human circulatory system. In each of these systems a number of components are linked together to perform one or more functions, the energy and motive force being provided by some fluid or current acting as a carrier. In considering the 'business system', linking components and functions of an organization, we will regard information as the carrier.

Using a small business as an example we see, in Fig. 8.5 and Table 8.1, that

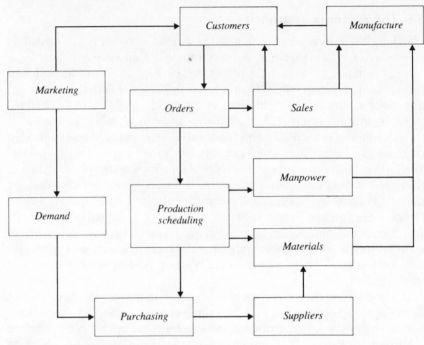

Figure 8.5   The business system

it has *content, structure, communications* and *decision-making*. All these elements will be present in any business. Each of the elements has particular information requirements and each component of the system is linked to others by information flows. An information system should match the business system, producing accurate and timely information, enabling efficient transfer and use of information leading to effective *decisions* and *actions*.

At each stage of the analysis of a business system we should look for the four processes of *collection, storage, processing* and *communication* of information in the contexts of the components of the system: *content, structure, communications* and *decision-making*.

A real benefit of treating businesses as systems is that, like electrical or hydraulic systems, their performance can be modelled. Relationships between elements of the business can thus be studied and understood and the behaviour of the business simulated in order to exploit future opportunities and to avoid unpleasant future shocks.

We can use an electrical analogy to represent a business organization. In a domestic hi-fi system information is communicated from the top level, the group or orchestra, via a storage device, the record or tape, to our ears through a complex electro-acoustic system. The information system, that is the amplifying chain, has built-in electronic control mechanisms to feed-back a portion of the output to the input, usually in a negative or out-of-phase sense. In this way noise, distortion and instability arising from components of the system or external interference can be cancelled out. In a business system the top-down and bottom-up approaches may be combined to produce an information system that effectively serves the strategic aims of the business while accurately monitoring and controlling the processes that achieve those aims.

All systems need to be effectively controlled to prevent instability or inefficient operation. A tap turned off too quickly may cause instability in the form of oscillations and banging in the water pipes; a constricted artery in our bodies may cause loss of function or even death. A key role of an efficient information system is to react to external and internal disturbances so as to damp out instabilities and inefficiencies in the business system. Such instabilities may be caused by internal or external step-changes: unforeseen events that impact on normal business operations. Inefficiencies may arise from blocked communications channels, thus delaying vital information.

Figure 8.6 shows how a business might respond to a sudden increase in demand. There may be over-correction, leading to surplus stocks, or an unstable situation may persist for some time because of a lack of relevant

Table 8.1   Business system components

Content	–	Work-sheets
	–	Schedules
	–	Materials
	–	Manpower
	–	Machines
Structure	–	Procedures
	–	Processes
	–	Organization
Communications	–	Publicity
	–	Orders
	–	Enquiries
	–	Invoices
	–	Designs
Decision-making	–	Scheduling
	–	Marketing
	–	Research and development
	–	Design
	–	Pricing
	–	Planning

information. The sales department realize that demand for some item has suddenly increased; it could be demand for ice-cream in summer. Messages go out to the production department to make more to meet the new levels of demand now anticipated. Inaccurate demand information, or delayed information may lead to over-production, so production is cut. Now the level is too low and so the cycle goes on.

Ideally appropriate and timely information should be made available to allow the system to respond quickly and smoothly, damping out any sudden change. Even better would be the situation where relevant information was made available to forecast the change in demand so that pre-emptive corrective action could be taken.

In machine systems, operational and control information flows are closely linked. Operational information, such as temperature, speed or load is measured and is then converted to control information according to predefined rules. Management systems on the other hand interpose human beings who interpret information flowing out of real business processes, make decisions and feed them back into the processes. Machine or process-control systems operate in a mostly predictable fashion. Management systems, other than simple Programmed Decision Support Systems (PDSS), are at the mercy of much less predictable humans.

It is important to be aware of some of the attributes of systems precisely because human beings act differently to pre-programmed machines. We live in a world where more and more control is being granted to machines while at the same time machine systems are increasingly capable of a kind of lateral thinking. Instead of merely making adjustments within an existing framework the machine may have an ability to devise a different system or structure as an alternative way of getting a desired result. Human intervention may still be needed to ensure that the limited 'intelligence' of such adaptable systems does not lead to chaos.

Modern machines are able to control complex processes far faster and more reliably than a human being. This means that, for example, aircraft can now be designed to be incapable of being flown by a human pilot acting alone. The aircraft is unstable, so computers are needed to monitor engine performance, altitude, loading, speed and direction. The pilot directs the aircraft to perform some manoeuvre and the computer gives the appropriate commands to the control surfaces. The benefit is that such aircraft can be more agile, role-adaptable or economical according to need. These attributes can be incorporated into the design once designers are freed from the basic constraint of ensuring that the product is inherently stable and capable of being operated by simple manual controls.

If we can see a problem as rooted in the structure and behaviour of some system, we may solve it by an appropriate change to the structure or function of the system. Recognizing the characteristics of the system is usually sufficient both to define the problem and shape the answer. Alternatively, it will occasionally be recognized that 'you can't get there from here!' But this too is a useful result: systems theory can demonstrate impossibility as well as opportunity.

Some short definitions can be offered to help identify the characteristics of a system and provide pointers to some of the ways of designing around problems thrown up by the way it functions.

Open or closed?

A system is open or closed according to whether its operation is affected by factors arising in the outside world. Most systems are not genuinely completely closed, being dependent upon or influenced by outside forces to some extent. A vivarium (a sealed vessel supporting small plants and creatures in a self-contained world) can be constructed, but it relies on energy from outside and an ambient temperature maintained within certain limits. A monopoly may act like a closed system, being little influenced by the normal external pressures of competition.

An indication of the management problems likely to arise from a business

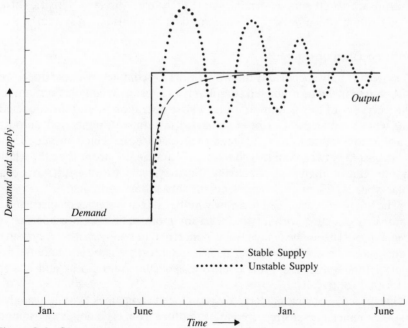

Figure 8.6   System response

system is given by testing the system for what is required to close it. That is, to identify those factors that must be completely under management's control for the system to function reliably within pre-defined tolerance limits. A good example is the operation of a whole company in the surrounding economy, or the operation of the economy of a whole country surrounded by shifting world trade and currency forces. The biggest headaches are caused by the exogenous factors which cannot easily be controlled, such as exchange rates or taxation changes. The best systems are those which cope with a wide range of disturbing factors.

Directed or undirected?

Most systems that we might set up will be directed or goal-seeking. Their efficiency and consumption of resources can be measured in terms of the purpose for which they were created. For example, the efficiency of a motor vehicle can easily be measured in terms of its fuel consumption in miles per gallon or its power-to-weight ratio. Where the interests of individual human beings are involved, as they are in business organizations, there is a strong tendency for notional external goals to be exchanged for internal ones connected merely with the survival of the organization and the people in it. If this happens the system becomes undirected. It may be very difficult for the outside observer to determine what are the true, directed, activities of an organization which need to be supported by an information system.

Fully specified or complex?

A system is fully specified if the way it works is completely understood and its behaviour can be predicted completely as a result. A complex system, for the purposes of this definition is one whose operation is not fully specified, but whose behaviour can be understood in terms of inputs and outputs. Certain combinations of inputs tend to produce the expected outputs. If the relationship between inputs and outputs is sufficiently strong then the whole system can be managed effectively. Such systems are often described as 'black boxes'. Figure 8.7 represents the 'black box' approach.

The analyst is concerned to know whether such a system is efficient and if control is effective without the need for more detailed knowledge of its operations. The analyst may also be concerned to know whether a system is being run as a black box because insufficient effort has gone into understanding its function and if gains could be expected from closer and better-informed control.

The practice of running large divisionalized companies by simply analysing the financial results received at head office from each unit is an example of the black box approach. The head office may have no real knowledge of

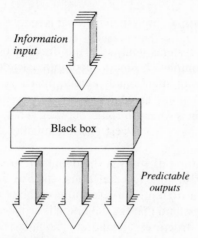

Information input

Black box

Predictable outputs

Figure 8.7 The black box approach

the processes that produced the results. A much more practical approach is to view the overall operation as an 'open box', represented in Fig. 8.8, where one can see and understand the processes and systems that are inside the 'box'.

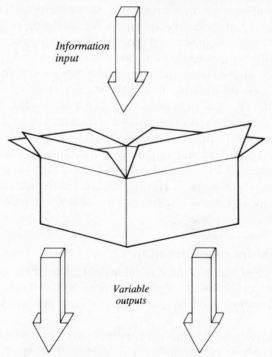

Information input

Variable outputs

Figure 8.8 The open box approach

Partial system or entity?

A real difficulty in systems analysis is the drawing of boundaries. Since all systems in a complex business feed into each other and overlap, problem solving can unintentionally extend over a far wider area than is practical. The ideal point at which to break a system into component sub-systems for study is where the links between sub-systems are easily and clearly defined and have the fewest possible number of information links between them.

One practical method of study is the definition of a business system in terms of a number of practical functions, such as sales, production or planning, rather than attempting a description of the system in its entirety. It is important to understand that the definition is artificial, however, since as with organization structures, temporary boundaries can come to be regarded as part of the natural order and may inhibit freedom of action later on.

For example, a small department may be set up to carry out some function which ought really to be part of another existing unit's function but for the purpose of easy startup, isolating any problems and so on, it is kept separate. Its members will soon see themselves as a separate entity and begin to collect further functions and communication links. Removing the original, artificial boundary may later become a real problem in its own right.

In considering business systems no distinction need be made between real flows of goods and services and information flows since all flows can be considered to be information flows. What matters is whether a flow is controlling the business operation or is being controlled. It is a useful exercise in systems analysis to construct a system map of your own organization or any part of it with which you are familiar. All of the issues discussed above may emerge and will require you to resolve them into a set of functions connected by real and control flows which best describes the overall system as you know it. Having constructed the system diagram you will then be in a position to proceed to assess the requirements for an effective information system.

8.10 The nature of information

Having looked at the historical development of business systems and at the structure and content of their information systems we can now look at information itself to assess its role and importance in modern business.

Good management information is particularly vital in large, diversified organizations where responsibility is delegated at all levels. Information provides the essential coordinating function and allows top management to monitor and to control business functions that may otherwise be too complex, too technical or too remote. It may seem obvious that key information should flow down through an organization, translating ideas into products and services and ultimately into money, but it is often the case that most information flows up the organization, in the form of 'management statistics' on all aspects of company performance. There are important lessons to be learned about the accuracy and reliability of business information and about managers' attitudes towards it.

8.11 The use of information

By the end of the 19th century improvements in communications had reduced the previous isolation of countries. Telegraph cables spanned the developed world, although the telephone was still in its infancy. Because of the comparative ease of transporting business information from one centre to another, and because of the establishment of world markets for industrial products, a common language of business created a common pool of business information. The process of sharing information has become so universal in recent years that we now see world business being conducted on a 24-hour basis, the action switching from one financial centre to another as the Earth rolls on.

This development has produced today's phenomenon of large numbers of similar organizations in many countries reacting to the same information at the same time, as if each organization were one of only a small group of actors on the scene. Decision-makers appear to react to accepted wisdom, artificial information and opinions collected from among themselves as a basis for decision making. Little account seems to be taken of the 'real' world. Worse still, important decisions may be entrusted to PDSS whose underlying assumptions may be very suspect.

As with the role of human intervention in the operation of systems this behaviour illustrates a problem in the mediation of responses to information, as well as a problem of determining what is valid information for decision-making purposes. We have seen recent dramatic examples of dubious decision making, where the computer and computer-processed information have played major roles. It is said that recent stock-market 'crashes' around the world have been precipitated by computers exchanging information with one another and generating 'sell' decisions without human mediation of any kind.

The number of people engaged in administering business, and in providing and using information for that purpose, was growing rapidly by the end of the 19th century. In time, the numbers of people involved in information processing had grown large enough to render the cost of their employment a significant proportion of companies' overheads, and to justify the development of productivity improvements to reduce this cost. The development of what we now call 'management services', together with the related developments of techniques for 'scientific management', eventually gave rise to specialist business information functions. The arrival of the commercial computer in the 1950s and 1960s led to the creation of data processing departments. These were mainly responsible for installing and operating the batch-processing mainframe computers of the first generation. With the increased emphasis on local computing the data processing personnel could have become information consultants. Unfortunately, such specialist functions are still regarded as luxuries and are often the first to suffer when, as now, there are pressing needs to reduce manpower and costs in all kinds of business operations.

Much business planning is confounded by failure to predict which key factors and circumstances will in the end determine the success or failure of a specific enterprise. In the context of information management this means that information systems planners have to relate all the factors – systems, equipment, communication media and so on – to the likely business requirements, to the competitive pressures facing the organization and to the general economic climate. Failure to recognize wider, long-term trends outside the information processing field and to relate them to probable technical developments can lead to costly mistakes in the choice of system. Such mistakes will deny business planners the vital information that they need.

The best remedy is possibly to have a sense of history, an awareness that a relationship between events through time is often more important than the events themselves. Effective business information must therefore describe historical situations, the relationships between significant business variables, present performance and future trends. Information management is an essential service to business management and its raw material, information, must be the best obtainable.

8.12 The value of information

The availability of cheap and attractive information technology has diverted attention away from information itself and towards what can be done with it in a purely manipulative sense. Information systems may be sold on the basis of the number of colours on a screen, the size of a display or the shape of a keyboard. Potential users should remember the old adage 'Garbage In – Garbage Out' and be as much concerned with the quality and source of information as with the system that manipulates it. When buying an expensive suit we should perhaps be concerned first with the quality of the cloth rather than with details of its colour or its width.

Computers and the cruel world outside are both indifferent to what is done with raw data. If inappropriate decisions are taken on the basis of 'information' which does not stand up to scrutiny, then nature will take its course, just as if no information had been used at all. The results might well be worse in fact, since known ignorance induces caution: illusory knowledge may well bolster up the manager's confidence.

Scientists, engineers and statisticians recognize information as having a number of clearly-defined characteristics. It is, however, possible to suggest a number of concepts for business managers and others who have to deal with the soft and ill-defined material of everyday life. These simple guidelines can be used to identify the nature and probable truth-value of much information, thus allowing data to be collected and decisions to be made on a consistent and effective basis.

Stocks and flows

All business and economic data describe either an existing static entity, having a value at one point in time, or the results of a flow of information, summing to a value over time. It is important to retain the distinction, since all flows derive from stocks (the static entities) in one way or another.

Since stocks in general determine flows, information about them is more reliable for forecasting purposes than the flows themselves. On the other hand, information about stocks is often hard to get and has to be inferred from the flows. Available markets – a stock variable – ultimately determine sales; but often the size of markets is hard to estimate and future sales can only be forecast on the trend revealed by past sales, which are a flow variable.

An example of the difference between stocks and flows may be seen in the case of a large airline.

Information systems were in place to monitor and control stocks, while other systems were concerned with flows, the consumption of spare parts, sales, orders, etc. When the auditors found large quantities of surplus stocks, including major items like aero engines, it was decided to sell off the surplus. The 'flow' systems coped well and the transactions went ahead. Unfortunately the 'stocks' system was not informed of these transactions. It detected a reduction in stock levels and immediately reordered equipment to restore them. In some cases the identical equipment was bought back from local traders, at an increased price. Clearly some integration of information systems was needed here before any realistic forecasts of requirements could be made.

Flows are very popular for management control purposes, being seen typically in tables of performance indicators and forecasts which are presented as 'management information'. The uncertainty and underlying trends of such figures make it very necessary to understand the long-term or secular trends and the stock variables on which they are based.

Residuals and aggregates

Residuals are the values that are left as balances between other variables which tend to cancel each other out. This is slightly different from the standard statistical concept of a residual being the bit of variation left in data after the other forces explaining its movement have been accounted for.

Because they are the product of different forces and often have a much smaller value than the values of the forces themselves, residuals may be both unreliable and unstable in the long run. However, because they summarize the other larger numbers very conveniently, they are often used as a proxy for them. A good example is the trade balance in a country's balance of payments. This is the difference between imports and exports; it does not represent the trend of either accurately, it is difficult to forecast and not particularly useful for determining future currency values, let alone its own future value in a complex economy.

Residuals often appear before managers as exception reports, management information that shows when a certain control variable has gone out of set limits. Decisions made on the basis of such information may be inappropriate, or too late since the process generating the residuals is a dynamic one with its own natural range of variability. An understanding of error, sensitivity, variability and other statistical measures is an essential part of the interpretation of such information.

Aggregates are more accommodating but carry a rather different risk. If two items of data are added together the result is an aggregate; but unless the original values are retained separately, information has been lost. Even more will be lost later when averages are calculated and other forms of summary prepared. Statisticians refer to this as loss of degrees of freedom. The term can be regarded as implying that there is also some loss of freedom in the kind of inferences and decisions that can be made using aggregates. In data processing it is often necessary and desirable to report aggregates, but the original data are often best stored away in disaggregated form for future analysis.

Aggregated data is useful for the generation of simple business models, but the manager must be aware of the assumptions made in the aggregation and must always check that basic underlying assumptions have not changed over time.

Hypothetical and actual information

Much hypothetical data comes to be regarded as actual, simply by being accorded that status in people's minds. This can happen to budgets which contain a large number of assumptions made some time before the period to which they apply, or to the results of operations to allocate overhead costs to departments. In the latter case the figures are purely a result of applying arbitrary rules. Often the 'information' derived from them changes because the rules, rather than any underlying reality, have changed. This distorts a basic concept of information as being a set of values which change in some way only when something real happens.

Knowables and unknowables

Much 'information' is created out of the desire to know something which cannot actually be known, but which, if it were known, would make decisions easier to take. It may be almost impossible to know the cost or the value of an item for example without resorting either to economic theory or to a complex calculation. Nevertheless, information may be classed as 'knowable' or 'unknowable' as if the distinction could be made reliably and easily.

This is not as difficult a problem as it may at first appear, however, since if we determine why we want to know the cost or the value of something – i.e. the nature of the decision that we wish to take, then on that basis something less than complete information will nearly always do. For instance, if a chief executive wants to know the impact of a cost change on a certain product, he need only consider that part of the cost which varies with the volume sold. It is not necessary to know the whole cost (indeed it may be unknowable), in order to take a volume-related decision.

Much time and energy can be wasted in the pursuit of 'perfect' information. Such perfection has a real cost and the manager now has access to techniques of decision making using imperfect information. These techniques allow quicker decisions to be made while at the same time providing an appreciation of the risks involved. Decision-making systems will be dealt with in more detail in Chapter 13.

Distortions and corrections

Raw data for the purpose of making decisions or reasoned assessments is often distorted. For instance, sales of column inches of advertising in a daily newspaper, reported on a monthly basis, can be distorted by up to 12 per cent due to the distribution of the number of publishing days in each month of the year. A simple calculation to put the figure on the basis of a monthly average per publishing day solves the problem.

On the other hand, correction can itself induce distortion; as when out-of-date seasonal correction factors are applied. The application or non-application of corrections is, therefore, an important decision to be taken by every information provider.

Precise or fuzzy information?

In the days before computing was quick and easy, large amounts of raw data simply could not be processed effectively or economically. Today enormous amounts of data can be processed without adding greatly to administrative burdens. Much of the data available to an organization may be imprecise or 'fuzzy'. Given the power of modern information systems there is no need to treat imprecise information as if it were precise, simply because the methods for handling fuzzy data are complex. The machine can handle that problem. Ranged data and ranged results can be extracted from the original data and the system can warn managers of the degree of imprecision in their decision making before any irrevocable decisions are made.

Techniques of qualitative analysis are now available which allow managers to handle complex and imprecise information in non-numerical form.

Stable or unstable measures?

Management information is often based on ratios and indices that themselves are founded on some 'standard' measurement. It may be a price, a quantity, or some performance indicator. The information so derived is valueless if the basic quantity is itself unstable. For example, if we were in the car manufacturing business we could measure the relative performance of car engines by simply comparing their fuel consumption. However, we should also take account of the costs of new engine technology, the need for new types of fuel and engine management systems and other factors. It is very difficult to identify truly 'standard' and stable measures for the assessment of business performance. The financial world tries to do it by relying on, say, gold as the absolute standard (or, as has been suggested, chocolate Mars Bars).

Management decisions, especially those affecting long-term issues, must often be made with uncertain data and 'fuzzy logic' where the manager's skill and intuition form important components of the decision process. Perfect information, perfect data, perfect forecasts may be unobtainable. The modelling of qualitative issues may be as important as the modelling of quantitative factors if all the relevant information is to be brought to bear on a decision.

8.13 What is information for?

Information may be differently treated depending on whether it is to be used for making a decision or not. The means of turning information into decisions will be dealt with later. At this stage it is important to recognize that information may be considered either as decision material or as intelligence or background data. If information is intended only to provide background data then its purpose is to feed the comparative processes which the human mind uses to reach all of its conclusions. In that sense all information is therefore ultimately for decision support. Background information may need to be stored and then presented in ways that stimulate thought and imagination, perhaps using graphic images rather than tables of statistics.

Information which is direct decision material needs to be valued differently according to whether the decision in question is a control decision – used to steer an ongoing process – or a resource allocation decision concerning a specific projected use of material, funds or human effort. Requirements for timeliness and accuracy will differ in these two applications. It will be useful to remember the organization and information structures of Figs 8.2 and 8.3 earlier in this chapter. The distinctions between information needed for long-term planning and strategic decision making and that needed for operational control need to be borne in mind in the design of all information systems.

8.14 The role of information technology

Having looked at the structures of organizations and the information structures and systems that support them it is worth while to take a quick look at the full impact of the information revolution. The introduction of information technology, including office automation, computers and communications devices, has transformed the world of business information. Unlike printed or written information, electronically-stored information can be processed, manipulated, reformatted, displayed or transmitted almost instantaneously. Business operations can be modelled and simulated using computer modelling techniques, accounts can be kept, documents produced or revised rapidly, even meetings can be replaced with remote teleconferences. Effective information systems can bring speed and efficiency to business operations, electronic systems in particular having the capacity to

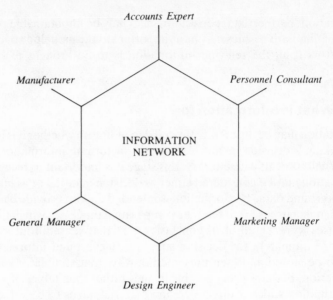

Figure 8.9 The virtual organization

bypass the bottle-necks and distortions that so often arise when information passes from level to level in an organization.

> Information technology extends the possibilities for management control in three main aspects. First, it provides faster and more precise knowledge of operating conditions and results. Second, it reduces the scope for indeterminacy in the behaviour of employees. Third, it unifies previously segmented control systems and thereby increases the potential for a comprehensive and balanced assessment of performance. (Child, 1986)[2]

Child also discusses the possible effects of information technology on business structures, identifying a dilemma. Will information systems encourage a swing back towards the centralization of decision making in diversified organizations where previously there was delegation? Or will the increased capability, knowledge and power of peripheral organizations, due to the use of information technology, lead to more effective delegation?

A particularly interesting consequence of introducing information technology into organizations has been the growth of 'networking'. This term, coined by the Xerox Corporation, describes a situation in which former full-time employees are engaged on contract to provide professional skills and services. By the use of modern communications and computing techniques these persons can work remotely, often from home. As long as they fulfil the terms of their contracts the rest of their time is their own; they keep in touch with their network employers through electronic mail or other computer networks. This development raises the prospect of the 'virtual organization', illustrated in Fig. 8.9, where a formal structure may not exist. All the activities of a business are represented by segments of an information system which links networked employees, brought into the system as and when their expertise is required.

Networking raises many difficult social and employment issues, some of which will be discussed in a later chapter, but it may become as common as the cottage industries of the 18th and 19th centuries.

Information systems are so important a feature of modern business that they cannot be left to chance: in the next chapter we will examine strategies for designing and implementing them.

8.15 Conclusion

We have seen how organization is a means of achieving strategic business aims and how information is required to make any organization work effectively. In designing information systems due account must be taken of the nature of the operations of the organization, especially where there may be time- or phase-relationships within the system. Information systems should enable managers to make better decisions, leading to actions which enhance the competiveness of the organization.

It is always useful to consider the organization as a 'system' of interlinked activities, and to study the flow of information between those activities. Managers must understand the nature of the information that the system handles, its timeliness, accuracy and appropriateness. It may be necessary to make decisions based on imperfect or 'fuzzy' information, but computers can help in the analysis and application of such information.

Information technology and systems should not be seen only as a means of automating office processes: they have a revolutionary potential.

References

1. Charles B. Handy, *Understanding Organizations*, Penguin, 1985, copyright © Charles B. Handy, 1976, 1981, 1985. Reproduced by permission of Penguin Books Ltd.
2. John Child, *Organization*, Paul Chapman Publishing Ltd, 1986.

9.
The design and introduction of information systems

9.1 Introduction

It has already been stated that this book is about the management of change, especially the change that results from the introduction of information technology and information systems into an organization. We have seen how information can flow round and through an organization and how it can be applied at different levels of management. The design of information systems should be part of an integrated approach to planning and business strategy because information is a necessary and expensive resource: it needs to be managed carefully, like any other resource. Information management aims to achieve that flow of information which will best enable the organization to achieve its goals.

Information which does not contribute to achieving the business aims is a costly irrelevance. Information management is concerned with the activities of the whole enterprise, so the organization needs an information system which is carefully designed with the aims and objectives of the organization in view, not one which just 'happens'. The task of the system designer is therefore to design and implement an information system embracing people, procedures and technology within the organization to enable it to achieve its goals most effectively.

The next two chapters of the book describe how to go about designing and implementing an information system. Few of us may ever be asked to do such work in the future; however, the structured approach to project design and management described here will be of use to managers in any discipline as they tackle the challenge of change. The treatment here is not exhaustive, it simply outlines a commonsense layperson's approach to the design and introduction of information systems.

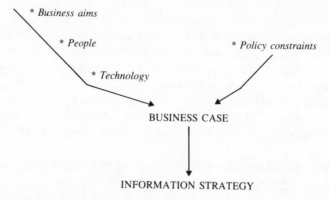

Figure 9.1 Creating an information strategy

9.2 The information strategy

Before any planning or design work can be undertaken it is important to have some form of information strategy which sets out the scope for information systems in achieving the organization's goals. A structured approach to generating such a strategy is illustrated in Fig. 9.1.

The policy constraints which might affect the technical solution need to be clearly stated. They might include a commitment to a particular vendor (because of satisfactory performance previously, or because of existing investment), the issue of standards (Open Systems Interconnection, OSI, or a proprietary standard like IBM's SNA). The organization may already have a private communications network in place, or it may wish to use the public networks. Longer-term factors relating to business strategy, such as proposals to expand or to build new premises, must be taken into account.

These proposals, even though still at a strategic and general level, must make sound business sense. They should therefore include a convincing business case. It might for example show why it was necessary to concentrate on particular functions (or business aims), groups of people, and technology options in order to improve performance or to withstand competition.

The whole process at this level leads to an information strategy document. It has to be documented because of its long-term importance, as a discipline to ensure logical thought, and so that it can be reviewed periodically. For most organizations the information strategy statement should look forward at a five-year timescale and might therefore be reviewed every 18 months or two years. In order to give it the necessary authority it must have the positive endorsement and support of senior management.

Once the overall information strategy has been established the organization can move on to the design and implementation of appropriate information systems.

Information systems and technology are specialist fields. There are many experts who would be much better suited to the tasks of system design and implementation than a busy general manager. However, the manager should be aware of the components of system design and of the risks that may be run if an important step is missed. Organizations may wish to employ consultants to handle all or part of an information systems project. What follows should enable managers to draw up suitable terms of reference or tender documents for consultants and to monitor progress of the project.

9.3 From problem identification to agreed outline solution

Tackling the problem

Let's assume that you have been asked to design and implement an information system for your organization, within the framework of the overall information strategy. One of the first things that you will be asked to do is to produce a report on the project. Management wants an information system, so a report is commissioned to tell them what is possible, what it will cost and what it will achieve.

How many reports are there lying in your bottom drawer or gathering dust on office shelves? It sometimes happens that management will call for a report on some situation and for recommendations as to what should be done but then the report, over which people have laboured hard and long, is shelved or only partially implemented. The aim of any information systems development project is not just to produce a set of proposals but to see the results implemented. Unfortunately a high proportion of projects in the information management field do not reach that stage. Information systems are likely to affect everyone in an organization. The more changes that the report proposes that affect the people who are responsible for implementing the proposals the more likely it is that your report will never go further than the bottom drawer. Issues of credibility, internal politics and fear of the unknown represent serious problems which must be tackled as a basic component of any assignment.

A typical management project proceeds through a set of steps, eventually presenting a detailed solution to a problem. If that solution is approved it is implemented. A subjective, unstructured approach will lead to numbers of conflicting objectives and proposed solutions. A neutral, objective and structured programme should ensure that problems are first systematically identified, then documented before proposals are finally made to introduce new methods. Since management commissioned the project, its members will presumably fall in behind a soundly reasoned set of proposals that address the problem that they originally specified.

Unfortunately, this may not always work! First, the real problem may not be the one originally specified. Second, even if investigation shows the problem to be exactly as foreseen, most people are not able to weigh the cost of the solution against the cost of the original problem. This is particularly true with information system projects because there is little understanding of their organizational implications. Solutions may be seen before the event as being costless but will later turn out to be very costly in time, equipment and money. The manager who said that there was a problem may individually become the problem when the cost of implementation is revealed.

The difficulties have to be recognized and allowed for in the design of the project. The aim of the project manager should be to turn every assignment into a strategy for the acceptance and implementation of its proposals. This implies very careful project design and control.

Resistance points

Resistance to change is a familiar problem. People involved in change in organizations may recognize their reluctance and try to compensate for it by discussing the proposed change and by appearing to agree to proposals that they may actually be reluctant to carry out. Part of the project manager's strategy must therefore be to commit the clients to action in ways that establish a timetable for change and encourage communication and liaison with others. Sharing problems in this way can be a powerful means of overcoming difficulties and of encouraging 'ownership' of problems and solutions. We can all be persuaded to adopt a scheme if we can be made to believe that it was our idea in the first place!

Many areas of information technology and management have had bad publicity. People are naturally fearful of the prowling 'efficiency expert' whose aim may actually be to increase efficiency and to improve working conditions. We hear many stories on the theme of 'the computer gets it wrong again', usually causing distress or disadvantage to some innocent party. More recently we have experienced growing concern about potential job losses and de-humanization through automation.

Resistance to change will be encountered in any complex project involving long-term entanglements with the forces of technology. Information system proposals should therefore be simple enough to convince their readers that all the implications have been considered, and that they can feel happy with the consequences.

The older established disciplines, like accountancy, the law or architecture can get away with a degree of obscurity and technical jargon; but such jargon is not yet respectable in the information management field. The aim of making information system proposals clear and simple faces another difficulty: the proposals will deal with aspects of running the business that are familiar to most people and if clearly written will seem to be very simple, even naive. People will feel that they truly understand the situation and will wish to add little details that they perceive the analyst has omitted. This temptation to interfere with, and to complicate proposals, is not easily resisted, but it can have dire results if a number of managers and user-departments are involved in a comprehensive scheme.

Few managers could check the stress calculations that went into the design of their building, but who would not have a go at improving a simple office procedure to suit themselves? The result of such interference, however well meant, could be chaotic and unworkable.

A new approach

These difficulties can be resolved by a consultative approach to the design of a project. Basically an additional step is added to the programme. It involves presenting the managers, who will be the 'clients' of any new system, with a restatement of the problem to be solved, together with an outline of the solution in principle at the earliest possible stage. The problem and the outline solution together with new information from the clients form new terms of reference for the rest of the project. Important elements of agreement are thus obtained before enough detailed work has been done to deter the willing and provide ammunition for the unwilling.

This new stage involves the production of detailed specifications, here called 'design requirements', in negotiation with the scheme's sponsors and potential users. The design requirements recognize the actual problem being tackled and the principles governing its solution; they will include a programme for the detailed working out of the methods and systems to be employed and a timetable for implementation. The project's sponsor is then asked for commitment to these detailed terms of reference which are the outcome of independent study of the problem as originally specified. The new terms may be substantially the same as the old ones, or they may reflect a new view entirely. The key feature of the design requirements is that they incorporate the aims and objectives of the client departments and of individual sponsors. Once again, convincing clients that they 'own' the problem and its solution may be more than half the battle.

9.4 Structuring the project

The objective of any effective information system must be to help managers and others to make better *decisions* leading to *actions* in support of the strategic objectives of the company. To achieve this, the designer must clearly understand the business system into which the information system is

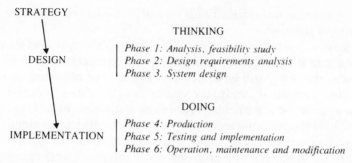

STRATEGY

THINKING

DESIGN

Phase 1: Analysis, feasibility study
Phase 2: Design requirements analysis
Phase 3. System design

DOING

IMPLEMENTATION

Phase 4: Production
Phase 5: Testing and implementation
Phase 6: Operation, maintenance and modification

Figure 9.2 Project life cycle

to fit. A plan of action must be devised, with clear and comprehensive terms of reference. Any attempt to rush quickly into the experimental or implementation stage may lead to disaster; time spent thinking about the problem and carefully planning for an effective system is time well spent. Risks cannot be entirely eliminated, but at least they can be minimized if a structured approach to information system design and implementation is followed.

An outline of a suitable strategy for the implementation of information systems is shown in Fig. 9.2, the *Project life cycle*.

Six phases are shown, but the model is not definitive. Any number of stages may be envisaged as long as the key elements of thinking, analysis, planning, design and implementation are present. The length of the 'project life cycle' obviously depends on the complexity of the project. The detailed content of each of the phases may alter. However, what is essential is that a structured approach with clearly defined goals must be followed.

Phase 1 – Initial analysis

No project can begin without some definition of what it is supposed to achieve. The first requirement therefore is to have some terms of reference. These are outline statements of requirements, usually from senior management, for the intended information system. The terms of reference should describe why an information system is required, what parts of the organization it is expected to serve and what major functions it is required to perform. Management may require the new system to interwork with some existing system, either a manual system or an electronic one. It may be necessary to replace the old system entirely. The terms of reference should indicate what overall budget, what personnel resources and roughly what timetable is to be allocated to the project. It is very helpful if the proposed project leader can be identified early on and then involved in the creation of the terms of reference.

The next step is to carry out a feasibility study. This study asks the simple question 'can it be done?' At this stage of the project there will be many unknowns, but there will be evidence available from published literature, from other companies and from consultants to indicate whether an information system for a particular application is feasible or not. It may be possible to visit other companies who have successfully implemented similar systems. Technology is wonderful, and it may be tempting to assume that there are no more technical problems to be solved. A little research into other people's experience may save much time, money and frustration later.

Note that at this stage it will not be possible to state a final cost for the project, so the feasibility study is really asking for approval in principle to proceed with the more detailed examination of the project which follows later.

At this early strategic stage of the information system development process it is essential to outline the intended role of the new information system and to compare it with any existing information systems in the organization. Existing systems may be paper-based, manual, or may rely entirely on the spoken word.

Management should decide whether the new information system is intended to be evolutionary in impact, meaning that it should gradually extend and improve the facilities of an existing system, or whether it should be revolutionary, meaning that it should completely replace an existing system with one that is radically different. If the approach is to be revolutionary then special attention must be paid to the organizational challenges and opportunities offered by new working methods.

The information system will have to handle all kinds of information, flowing up and down the organization. It is necessary to look at the organization from both ends. This means working upwards from the lowest level to the top, gathering information about systems and requirements and the expectations of personnel and the demands of processes at each level. Then one can work downwards from the most senior level, studying the communication of strategic information through the organization. Understanding of the scope for information systems and expectations of their effects may be markedly different when looked at in these two ways since different kinds of information flows are involved.

Because existing systems may be informal and may form part of some well-established office procedures, having grown up over periods of many years, they may be difficult to define. Users of such systems will often find it hard to say why they do a certain thing in a particular way. One approach to developing an understanding of such systems is to use *input–output* analysis.

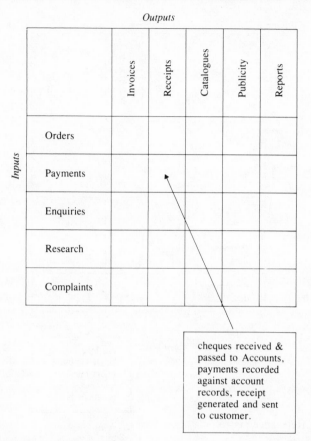

Figure 9.3 Input–output analysis

Figure 9.3 shows only a very simple example, but the principle is the same for all situations. The various inputs of information to the business operation are compared in a matrix with the different output processes and information requirements. Entries in the cells of the matrix represent processes converting input into output. In the example shown in the diagram the *input* process, 'payments', is linked to the *output* process, 'receipts', by a series of activities including the receipt and recording of cheques, entries in the accounts, correspondence, etc. Any of the other input and output processes may be linked in similar ways by activities within the business that can be identified and described.

With any established enterprise it may be found that there are significant gaps in the matrix: these may represent output processes for which insufficient information is available, or they may indicate expensive information-

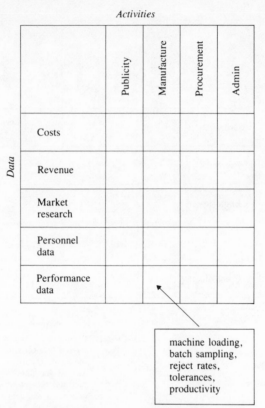

Figure 9.4 Relevance matrix

gathering activities with no clearly-defined purpose. The information system must eventually be designed to achieve the best match between input and output processes without wasteful duplication or significant gaps.

Another analytical tool is the *relevance matrix*, illustrated in Fig. 9.4. Here the various activities of the business are plotted against the types of information required to run those activities successfully. The example shown in the diagram is very simple but it shows how even a simple approach can identify significant flows and processing of information. In this case performance data, in the form of statistics about machines and products, is used by the manufacturing function. As with the input–output matrix, this analysis may show up gaps or surpluses of information.

By now the system analyst will have a good idea of the scope for information systems within the organization and can form some ideas about their design. Having adopted some initial terms of reference and carried out a feasibility study into the possibility either of extending an existing system or of introducing a totally new system, the analyst becomes a project leader and must now put some flesh on the bones of the project and examine it in detail.

Phase 2 – Detailed design requirements analysis

Now the responsibility for specifying the information system passes temporarily to the potential users; or at least it appears to. This is the important stage where users must become the 'owners' of the problems before solutions are proposed. In this way a high degree of commitment to implementation of the project can be gained at an early stage. The initial terms of reference and the report on the feasibility study should be discussed with the management and staff who will be affected by the information system. This is done partly to refine the requirements of the new system and partly to reassure personnel who may feel threatened in a variety of ways by the introduction of it.

Once user requirements have been satisfactorily identified the terms of reference can be finalized and *design requirements* can be drawn up and agreed by the project's sponsors. These more detailed terms of reference list not only the outline objectives of the project but also key elements of the system design, indications of the technology to be employed, timing of stages in the project and indications of the costs and benefits to be expected from the project.

At this point it is important to discuss exactly what benefits may be expected from the project. Management will be looking for cost-effective solutions to business problems and may seek to cost-justify every step. Unfortunately the cost-benefits of new information systems are not at all easy to specify or to forecast. If the approach to designing the system has been evolutionary, that is, the system is simply to replace an existing process, then it may be possible to say how many people can be redeployed or removed from the payroll and how costs can be reduced. If, however, the impact of the new system is revolutionary then the cost-benefits can only be guessed at. It may be necessary to justify such projects on the basis of the additional capacity that they offer for information, or of the new procedures that they make possible. Commissioning such projects must in a sense be an act of faith. Only experience will show if the right decisions have been made.

The responsibility for accepting risks of this nature is a prerogative of senior management; their commitment to all aspects of the programme is vital.

As has already been outlined, the design requirements specify in detail what the information system is to achieve, what facilities it is to offer, what hardware and software is to be used and over what timescale it is to be implemented. Most importantly they represent the agreement of management to proceed with the project as defined.

Some key features of design requirements may be listed:

- They should clearly restate the original terms of reference, since there is no intention to change managers' minds for them. They should indicate where the feasibility study has shown a different diagnosis and should make proposals to direct the main effort of the project in that direction. The whole should constitute new and comprehensive terms of reference.
- They should offer an analysis of the nature of the principal problem recommended to be tackled and the architecture of the solution envisaged.
- Recognizing that internal company politics play a major role in any proposals for change, a separate section should give advance notice of proposals for significant organizational change at a later date, for example: 'We intend to propose the formation of a new department requiring a staff of between five and nine people, whose function will be . . .'

  Thus notice is given of the intention to make specific organizational proposals later. This will improve their chance of acceptance at the time, since the design requirements will by then have become part of the fabric of the project; it also allows room for manoeuvre in the meantime.
- The design requirements should go on to specify any activities which will be discontinued or replaced and the broad costs and benefits expected to flow from the project as a whole
- A project timetable should always be supplied. The project can then be managed more effectively and its progress reported on.

  The criticism is often advanced that dates, like costs and benefits, are unknowable in advance where new systems and technology are involved. This amounts to saying that decision-making managers should either supply their own estimates or make their decisions blindfold. It is better to quantify as early as possible, if only to identify clearly what sorts of quantities will be involved and then regard the rest of the project as a process of progressively refining the original understanding.

The design requirements document may be organized in the following sections:-

- *An executive summary:*
- *A system overview*: this section described the business functions which will be carried out by the system to be proposed. Linkages with existing systems should also be detailed.

- *The operating environment*: this section sets out the technical environment in which a new system will operate and must therefore include
  reference to likely changes and additions to existing equipment, communications links and so on, as well as to major items of operating
  software.
- *The system development approach*: this part of the document will describe
  the main performance standards to be achieved.
- *Products and criteria for delivery*: these are system functions to be supplied to specific users, they may include elements of hardware, software,
  networks, etc.
- *Major tasks in the project*: this section will specify the many tasks required
  to complete the project, assigning responsibility in each case. The list of
  tasks may be used to construct a control network (see Chapter 10) by
  which the project will be managed. If the project is somewhat complex, or
  if the sequence of events is not obvious, a network diagram, plus an
  explanation, may be included in this section.
- *Key project assumptions*: at this stage there may be a large number of
  assumptions to be made: they should be clearly stated and none left to be
  implied by the manager(s) sponsoring the project. Such assumptions may
  relate to organizational structure, business operations, financial climate,
  state-of-the-art, etc.
- *Global estimates of time and cost*: times and costs should be allocated to
  tasks. A distinction should be made between elapsed time (the time
  expected to be taken to complete each task) and the work content involved, in man-hours or man-weeks. The two may differ widely.
- *Procedures for approving and incorporating changes*: changes in this
  context are changes or additions to the system functions which will be
  delivered, as discussed earlier. Revisions to the project schedule itself are
  part of project management.
- *Project status reporting*: this section specifies the way in which project
  progress will be measured. It describes the documents used to report
  progress as well as the frequency of and planned attendance at progress
  meetings.
- *Financial justification*: this section will give a summary of the benefits of
  the system in terms of monetary savings or other measurable gains, plus a
  summary of the cost of developing and operating the system.

The 'products' to be delivered by the project, that is, user-requirements
for facilities, hardware and software, may be identified using the information systems matrix shown in Fig. 9.5.

The most appropriate type of information system for user-needs, in terms
of text, data, voice and image information can be specified. The functions of

INFORMATION MODE

	Text	Data	Voice	Image
Collect				
Store				
Process				
Communicate				
MIS: TPS				
MIS: IPS				
MIS: DSS				
MIS: PDS				
MIS: Expert System				
MIS: Database				
ORGANIZATION: Intra-site				
ORGANIZATION: Inter-site				
ORGANIZATION: External				
COMMS: Transmission				
COMMS: Switching				
COMMS: VAN				
COMMS: VAS				

Figure 9.5 Information systems matrix

the system, the utilities and facilities to be provided, the types of networks needed to interconnect parts of the system must all be listed as must communications facilities for connecting the system to other systems or to the external telecommunications network.

Phase 3 – System design

With all the preliminary work of defining the system completed it might be assumed that the design stage would be easy. However, technology is changing fast: components of the information system capable of meeting the requirements now may be obsolete or unobtainable by the time the system is due for commissioning.

At this stage, having completed the analysis of requirements, it may be appropriate to hand the practical aspects of the project over to a consultant or to a specialist technical team. Their knowledge of the capabilities of modern systems may enable them to devise quick and elegant solutions in terms of hardware or of software.

In the design stage a balance must be struck between having the best and most modern technology and the need for proven and lasting solutions. As the project proceeds more information about new developments in technology and systems will become available. There will be a natural temptation continually to modify the system design as the project proceeds, but this must be resisted. Any experimentation should be done in non-critical areas, away from the mainstream of the project activities. An essential feature of any design process is the testing and refinement of the design to meet project objectives, but the designer must eventually 'freeze' the design so that effective implementation can proceed.

Where user-requirements have been difficult to specify, or in a dynamic situation where requirements change rapidly, it may be necessary to adopt the technique of 'prototyping'.

A fairly simple system, or a number of specialized systems, is provided for users who have specified their own particular current requirements. The users are asked to gain experience with the prototype systems and to specify what changes are required. The system design can then be changed and the systems modified to meet the new requirements. In projects involving complex software systems, prototyping may be achieved with modules of the software. For example, an integrated suite of business software may combine financial analysis and communications into one package. For testing purposes those functions can be independently implemented and tried out in realistic situations. At some stage, however, the designer must decide not to allow further changes and must proceed to incorporate all the available prototype experience into the final systems design.

9.5 Conclusion

We have seen how time spent thinking about and planning a project is time well spent. Great care needs to be taken in identifying problems and in documenting them before any proposals for new systems are made. Involvement and commitment of all the interested parties in the specification and design of an information system is vital. System designers need to be aware of the revolutionary effect that information systems can have on the operations of an organization. Examination of the flows of information within an organization, between inputs and outputs, will facilitate the design of efficient information systems.

The next chapter looks at the completion stages of a project and how such projects can be effectively controlled.

10.
Completing the project

10.1 Introduction

In the previous chapter we saw how an information systems project might be initiated. The various stages of thinking about the project were described and it was emphasized that sponsors and potential users of the system should be involved in the specification and design stages. That involvement was a means of securing support for and commitment to the project.

Now we can move on to the implementation stages of the project. Once again it is important to involve the users of the system in its implementation, and, as we shall see, in the associated training programmes.

10.2 Implementation

The information system may be constructed from components, such as computers, printers, network cables, etc. bought from a supplier; or the system may be supplied as an entity by a systems house. In either case it will be necessary to establish some criteria for the selection of the system. The initial system studies should have indicated what volumes of information need to be handled and in what form that information is to be presented for use. Numbers of internal and external communications links will have been specified. These features may be used as the basis for deciding on the choice between competing systems. Performance standards can be set, such as the time needed to file or retrieve a number of information items, or the time taken to transfer files of information over communications links. The memory capacity of computers and their data storage capacity may also be criteria for choice.

Other criteria will include the capability and performance of the potential suppliers in the supply of similar systems. It is important to know if the system needs to be compatible with existing systems in terms of hardware and software or if special programs or devices are required to allow interworking of systems.

Once the components of the system have been selected the project moves into the practical implementation phases.

Phase 4 – Production

It is unlikely that anything other than a very simple system will be installed in one go. Parts of the system will be delivered before other parts, some users will be kept waiting for network cabling or special peripheral devices, or there will be delays due to unexpected snags and faulty components. Rather than expect the system to be provided as a 'going concern' it may be better to acknowledge the realities of the situation and to adopt a flexible approach to design and implementation.

Production of the system can be facilitated by a modular design. The system is split into its essential component functions such as computing, communications, and storage. It may then be possible to identify sub-systems which can be implemented step by step as the various system components become available. Equipment and networks can be ordered on this basis, accommodation prepared, and training sessions planned.

Potential users of the complete system can be made familiar with elements of the new equipment and networks working in 'local' mode, for example, before any local area or wide area network is completed. This piecemeal approach has the advantage that equipment or operational difficulties may be identified early on, before the system reaches an advanced state of completion and while remedial action can still be taken. The process of prototyping, described in Chapter 9, may be applied to hardware and software components of the system.

However the project is implemented, as a series of sub-systems or as a complete entity, the production phase needs to be carefully managed in terms of time, resources and performance. This phase and the following testing and implementation phase lend themselves especially to the application of some project control technique such as Critical Path Analysis (CPA) which will be described later in this chapter.

Phase 5 – Testing and implementation

The terms of reference and the design requirements lay down in detail what the system is intended to achieve. That specification has been agreed by sponsors, users and designers alike and expectations will be high. Before the system can be brought into use it must therefore be tested fully against the specifications, preferably with some involvement of the users. If the system is being implemented in a modular fashion it will be easy to test components of the system as they become available. However, testing cannot be complete until the full system is implemented, with all its terminals, peripherals, networks and software in place.

During the testing process any shortcomings of the system must be noted and details must be reported back to the design and implementation team so that corrective action can be taken quickly. A careful distinction must be drawn between those shortcomings which relate to specified performance and those which, perhaps due to the passage of time since the design requirements were agreed, stem from changed perceptions of the users. The knowledge that a new system is to be implemented will have raised awareness amongst its users so that they will be more knowledgeable and more critical when the system actually appears.

Tests of the information system may be made with 'live' data by running the new system in parallel with the old one to check performance. Parallel working may be seen to be wasteful in time and resources but it is a good way of instilling confidence into the users. If the new system is able to produce the same, or better results using the same data as the old system then there will be a natural move to adopt the new system. This approach is best used where the new system is replacing an existing system, perhaps adding new functions at the same time.

Where the new information system is revolutionary rather than evolutionary in its application it may be necessary to devise an artificial test programme or simulation to test the system. One approach is to nominate specific areas of company operations as test sites, with special allowances of manpower, time and money to cover the additional work of testing and reporting on the new system.

Adequate training must be provided for all users. This training could be provided on-site, using the organization's own training staff or training consultants from outside. Alternatively, it may be possible to offer external courses to staff or temporary attachments to other organizations where similar systems are in use. One possible approach is to identify those in the organization who are already familiar with information technology and to give them special responsibility for learning about the new systems and for training their colleagues.

Phase 6 – Operation, maintenance, modification

Even after formal training has been completed there will be considerable unease among users about the new systems and their ability to cope with them. It may be better, especially with a complex system, if the system is brought into operation in stages, with users who are more experienced assisting in the introductory and training processes for new users. Nothing succeeds like success and reluctant first-time users are much more likely to be convinced by successful colleagues than by 'experts' who may not be thought to have any knowledge of the special problems of the organization and its people.

Careful provision must be made for maintenance of the system, either by in-house staff or by a service organization. When any new and complex system, whether it be an information system or a car, is first brought into service there will be some early faults. These may be due to errors in the manufacturing or testing procedures or to failures of components from faulty batches. Figure 10.1 shows the typical 'bath-tub' graph of fault incidence for new equipment or components. Early in the life of the subject the fault rate is high. Once the initial faults have been rectified the equipment settles down to a quiet life with a low fault rate. Later on, as the components begin to age and to wear out, the fault rate rises again.

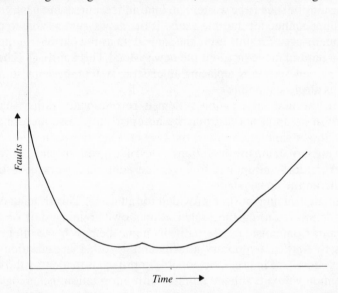

Figure 10.1 Bath-tub curve

The early faults period for information systems may be covered by a manufacturer's or supplier's guarantee, usually valid for a few weeks or months. It is important to know the conditions of these guarantees, especially if the information system consists of an assembly of equipment and networks from different suppliers, as it is very easy to invalidate a guarantee by some innocent action, such as making an adjustment or removing an equipment cover. Equipment manufacturers and suppliers keep teams of maintenance staff on call. For large installations they may be on 24-hour call. Most suppliers will offer at least next-day attention to a fault or a quicker response in return for some premium payment.

As the incidence of faults will be higher during the early life of the system it is important that all such faults should be reported quickly so that trends can be identified and faulty components changed. Many organizations have found it worth while to employ a maintenance person with responsibility for 'front-line' maintenance of their systems. Many faults in computer systems can be cured by exchanging plug-in units, cards, chips or other components. It is not necessary to have access to sophisticated testing equipment or to be fully trained in computer maintenance to provide a basic service. Faulty units can then be shipped off to the suppliers or to a specialist repair centre. Short training courses are available for non-experts, giving them the basic skills needed for front-line maintenance.

Users should be encouraged to report not only faults but also to report on shortcomings of the system. A programme of modification and refinement can thus be implemented, particularly if the implementation has been on a step-by-step basis. The project manager must, however, avoid the 'creeping features syndrome'. This arises when adjustments and modifications are continually made to a system with the intention of improving it. By this means costs may rise and overall system performance may suffer due to the continual tinkering that goes on. Any experimentation with the system should be kept to a minimum and should not be allowed to affect vital data. If some modification to the system or to a software package is proposed then it may be tried on a stand-alone machine or an experimental area of the system without running the danger of interfering with the working system.

An essential aspect of system design is security. This topic will be returned to in a later chapter. At this stage it is enough to emphasize that part of the regular 'maintenance' processes should be to ensure that back-up copies are made of all data and that the back-up copies are kept in a location away from the main computer installations and are stored in a secure manner.

10.3 Controlling the project

Any complex project involves a number of people, a variety of resources, a timetable and usually a host of unforeseen problems. The only thing that can be forecast accurately about an information systems project is that something will go wrong. Equipment, ordered well in advance of the required date, will not be delivered; there will be difficulties in linking parts of networks together; key personnel may be called away on other urgent business. Less serious, but often just as awkward, are those occasions when jobs are completed ahead of time, leaving expensive equipment and systems idle while the rest of the project catches up.

It is the responsibility of the project manager to cope with all these problems and to bring the project to a successful conclusion on time, and within budget. How can such complex situations be managed effectively? Small projects could perhaps be managed by one unaided person, keeping track of all the dates, times and costs in the mind or on paper. Very complex projects, however, involve numerous people and complex interlinked activities, situations too demanding for even the cleverest person to deal with alone.

The project manager needs to know just what is going on at any time so that the project can be effectively controlled and so that problems can be speedily dealt with. Attention must be drawn to those parts of the project that are in trouble, either through being late or through over-expenditure. Fortunately there are powerful techniques available to help the project manager with project control. In the early days of business computing these techniques were confined to the mainframe and minicomputer. Now that microcomputers are in common use there are many project control packages available for managers to use at their own desks. Two of the basic techniques will be described briefly here, the Gantt chart and the Critical Path diagram. Both of these techniques can be used manually for small projects, but the power of the computer is needed to analyse the data required for large projects.

The Gantt chart

The first step in this simple graphically-based process is for the project team to agree on the nature and likely duration of all the tasks that will go to make up the complete project. These tasks can be identified in discussion with the users and designers of the system. The level of detail required depends on the extent to which groups of activities can be successfully separated and delegated to members of the team. Start and desired finish dates are allocated to each of the project activities, the finish dates being simply the start dates plus the expected durations.

Table 10.1 illustrates a simple project, the repair of an electrical machine.

Table 10.1 Machine Repair

Activity	Duration (days)	Start (week.day)
Inspect machine	10	1.1
Dismantle machine	14	2.2
Transport	19	2.6
Order parts	12	1.6
Parts delivery	14	2.1
Repair	19	3.1
Test	22	3.4
Transport	10	5.3
Reassemble	10	5.7
Test on site	8	6.6
Commission	5	7.1

Each major activity in the project has been listed, together with the time that each activity is expected to take. A chart is now drawn, either physically, or by inputting information to a computer program, in which the time an activity should take is represented by a horizontal line or cell. The length of the line is made proportional to the duration of the activity so that the chart shows how much time is available for an activity. The current date is indicated by a date cursor, which may be moved physically or electronically across the chart, showing the extent to which the various activities have been completed.

Figure 10.2 shows the Gantt chart for the job described in Table 10.1. As work on each activity proceeds so the progress bar is extended to fill the appropriate cell. Note that incomplete bars to the left of the date cursor mean under-achievement, whilst those to the right mean over-achievement. The Gantt chart may be printed out and copied, then distributed to members of the project team, a master copy being kept on display at some central place. Regular project meetings should be held at which representatives of all the project functions are asked to report on progress. Activities at risk of delay can then be identified and corrective action taken before the item shows up on the chart.

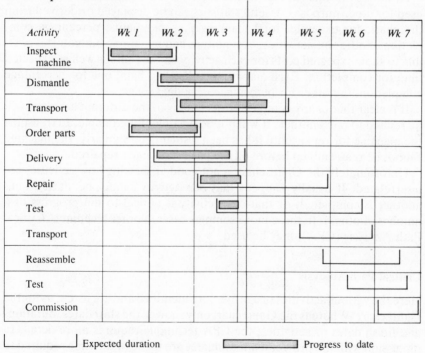

Figure 10.2   Gantt chart for machine repair

Table 10.2 Computer system activities

Activity		Duration	Earliest start	Earliest finish	Latest start	Latest finish	Total float
Select system	1–2	10	0	10	0	10	0
Agree facilities	2–3	14	10	24	19	33	9
Obtain finance	2–4	30	10	40	20	40	0
Order equipment	3–5	7	24	31	33	40	9
Appoint training staff	4–6	10	40	50	60	70	20
Buy software	4–8	5	40	45	65	70	25
Delivery	5–7	28	40	68	48	76	8
Set up training	5–6	30	40	70	40	70	0
Run courses	6–9	15	70	85	75	90	5
Install equipment	7–9	14	68	82	76	90	8
Prepare data	8–9	20	70	90	70	90	0
Test	9–10	14	90	104	90	104	0
Commission	10–11	7	104	111	104	111	0

Although the chart in Fig. 10.2 only shows activities and times, it may be used for other purposes. Useful statistics can be displayed or derived from the chart, for example, total manpower requirements, percentage completion of different activities, expenditure and remaining budget. It is possible to show expected costs for each activity on the chart as well as expected time for completion. Each activity then has two bars: one for percentage completion, the other for percentage of budget spent.

It is clear that in any complex project many of the different activities will be related to one another. It will not be possible, for example, to transport the machine for repair until it has been dismantled. Similarly, the machine cannot be reassembled before all the parts have been repaired.

Unfortunately the Gantt chart is not good at showing how activities are interrelated. It usually happens that one activity cannot be started until another is completed, or that one activity is critical to the progress of a number of others. In these more complex cases another technique, Critical Path Analysis (CPA), may be used.

Critical Path Analysis

Here the various activities of a project are identified and are listed, as for the Gantt chart. Whereas the Gantt chart only showed the start dates, durations and finish dates of activities, the CPA technique requires more detail. In discussion with the project team estimates are made of the time required to complete each activity together with the earliest and latest start times and the earliest and latest completion times. Activities are then represented on a diagram as lines linking nodes which represent the start and finish points of those activities.

You should note that there are two ways of drawing critical path diagrams. One is to show the activities as nodes in the diagram; the other way, used here, is to use the nodes to identify the start and finish points of activities, the links representing the time taken for each activity.

Critical path methods are based on the idea of dependency, the idea that one job depends on another finishing before it can be started. Not only does one job depend on another, the cost and duration of a project are entirely determined by the whole chain of dependencies that exists as one job follows another from start to finish. In any project it may be difficult to assess the consequence of some delay or difficulty that occurs early in the project. The critical path diagram is able to show those consequences and to indicate what action can be taken by the project team to overcome them. The diagram may also be used to identify tasks where time can be saved, or costs reduced, without prejudicing the rest of the project.

The setting up of a critical path diagram begins with the identification of the various activities, in this case an example is given of the design and installation of a computer system. Table 10.2 lists all the major activities involved. This table is more detailed than that used for the Gantt chart in that earliest and latest start and finish times are shown for each activity. The reasons for the numbering of the various activities, 1–2, 7–9, and so on will become clear when the diagram is drawn.

The diagram shown in Fig. 10.3 represents the activities listed in Table 10.2. The whole project is charted progressively from left to right as a set of lines and nodes. Each line represents a job to be done and shows the time allocated to that job. Each node represents the logical point at which the next activity can begin. It is clear that in this case installation of the equipment cannot begin until the equipment has been delivered by the supplier. Activity 7–9, 'install equipment' cannot therefore start until activity 5–7 'delivery' has been completed. Node 7 represents the completion of one activity and the beginning of another. Some nodes represent the end of one activity, some represent the beginning of other activities, other nodes have both functions. The links between the nodes are labelled with the name of the activity and its expected duration.

It will be seen that there are a number of different paths through the diagram linking node 1 to node 11. If a number of activities must be finished before the next can begin, then it is clear that the whole project cannot be completed in less time than it takes to follow the longest path in terms of time through the diagram.

Whichever route through the diagram to the last node is the *longest* in

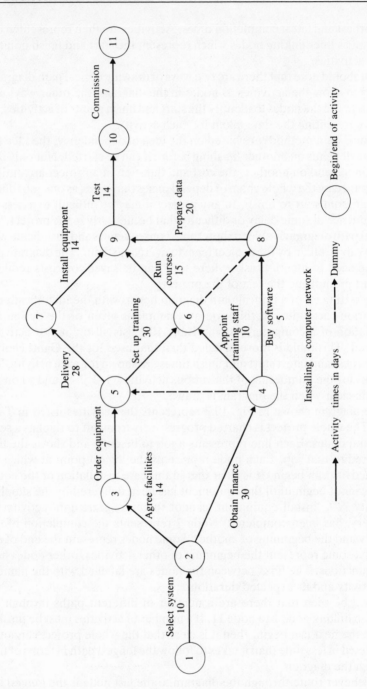

Figure 10.3 Outline CPA chart

Figure 10.4 Expanded CPA chart

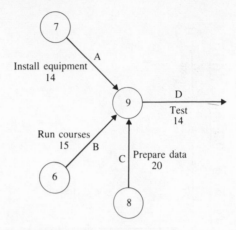

Figure 10.5 Multiple activities

time, that is the *shortest* time the project can possibly take to reach that point. As the project manager it would be a waste of time to concentrate special resources on a different path, shorter sequences of tasks, to reach the end point. They would be finished earlier of course, but the logic of the diagram is that we cannot move forward to the next task until every other sequence on which starting the new task depends has been finished. The convoy moves at the pace of its slowest member.

The diagram can now be developed by relating the durations of the activities to their earliest and latest start and finish times, shown in Table 10.2, and the 'float' can be calculated, that is:

(latest finish time – earliest start time) – duration = float

The float for each activity is the extent to which the activity can be allowed to slip in time without upsetting other related activities or the completion of the project as a whole. Figure 10.4 shows the project diagram with each activity having a duration, a latest finish time and an earliest start time.

Now that the diagram shows activities, durations, floats and relationships the project manager can trace all the paths through the network, calculating start and finish times and overall durations. Some activities will be found to have zero float, that is, they must start on the earliest start date and must be completed by the earliest finish date. These activities are 'critical' because any delay in their completion will delay the whole project. The path linking all those activities with zero float is called the 'critical path' and is the longest time path through the network, representing the shortest possible duration for the project as a whole.

Any required change to the overall duration of the project, either to shorten it or to lengthen it, must be made by first altering the duration of

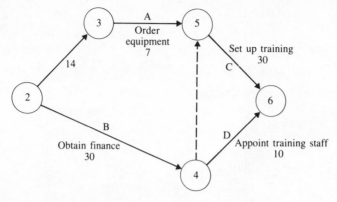

Figure 10.6 Dummy activity

activities that lie on the critical path. In monitoring the progress of a project it is vital to check that delays or early completions in the component activities of the project have not caused the critical path to change. This is where the computer is really useful: it can recalculate times and durations easily and can allow the project manager to explore alternative strategies.

There remain a few details to clear up before we can see how the critical path diagram can be used to control all the tasks appropriate to the computer system project.

First, whenever there is a node with more than one line, that is more than one task, coming into it, the logic of the network implies that *each* line coming out at the right depends on *all* lines going in at the left. The situation is shown in Fig. 10.5 where activities A, B and C must be completed before activity D can begin.

In the earlier critical path diagrams there were activities linking nodes, shown as solid lines and there were others shown as dotted lines. Consider the situation in Fig. 10.6. Here activities A and B must be completed before C can begin, but only B needs to be completed before D can begin. The link between B and C is shown by a dotted line, called a 'dummy activity'. This activity takes no time and consumes no resources: its function is to clarify the logic of the diagram. When computing the critical path, the duration of a dummy task is always taken as zero and has no other influence on the proceedings. A dummy activity can lie on the critical path however.

In the list of tasks for a major project, for example a systems development project, a number of activities will appear to have been split in half. Or rather, their completion has been regarded as a separate task from their commencement. This is a simple way of representing the fact that many activities can be started once certain elements of a preceding activity are in

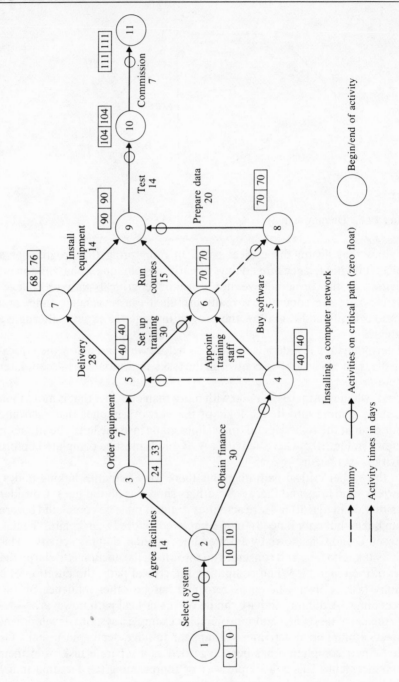

Figure 10.7 Completed CPA chart

place. They cannot be finished off altogether until the preceding activity or some other has been finalized.

In large projects this problem is tackled by breaking activities down into individual phases and linking them to the corresponding phases of the next-to-start activity. The process produces 'ladders' or mini-networks within the main network. This aspect of critical path networks needs no further explanation here but would be relevant to anyone involved in the detailed planning of rather large projects.

Figure 10.7 shows the completed critical path diagram or network for the computer network project and identifies the critical path.

10.4 Conclusion

This chapter has described how systems may be implemented in organizations and how the design and implementation project may be controlled. Special attention must be paid to the familiarization and training of all staff who will use the new systems and to the maintenance of those systems. Two project-control techniques were discussed, the Gantt chart and the critical path diagram. The Gantt chart shows progress by plotting activities as independent 'time-bars', while the critical path diagram uses linked nodes to represent start and finish points of interrelated activities. The critical path has zero float and represents the shortest possible duration for the whole project.

11.
Practical information systems

11.1 Introduction

This chapter is concerned with the bringing together of computing and communications technology to form information systems. Much of the technology has already been described in Part 2 of this book but some of the important features relating to the use of the technology in systems are repeated here. Cross-references to Part 2 are given to help you to refer to the detail if needed.

Computing and information systems have come a long way since the world's first electronic programmable computer, Colossus, was designed to crack German military codes in the early 1940s. After the war research laboratories in Britain and the USA designed and built experimental computers, some for research programmes, others for calculating and modelling for military purposes. Soon it was realized that computers could be applied to business problems, particularly those involving lots of tedious calculations such as payroll and accounting functions. The rapid development of computing was outlined in Sec. 4.6.

The earliest business machines were physically massive, occupying whole floors of buildings, consuming enormous quantities of electrical power and requiring constant attention for the replacement of faulty thermionic valves and other electronic components. In terms of storage and processing power they were equivalent to a pocket computer of today. These elementary machines were very costly and very complex, they were at the 'leading edge' of technology. Even so they could only respond to very simple commands. Operators had to feed in the instructions one-by-one in very simple or 'low-level' code. Only specially-trained experts could program and control these computers. Computer 'users' in business never saw the computer, they saw only its input and output documents.

Users would specify what data was to be processed and what computation was to be performed. This information was submitted to the computer

178

department in the form of written instructions, punched cards or paper tape. Hours, or even days later the results of the computer process would be delivered to the user as a pile of paper print-out.

Immensely powerful computers can now be put on the manager's desk. In a matter of only ten years office computers have evolved dramatically. The first office machines, still too big for the desk-top, contained only 32 or 64kByte of internal memory and used large 8-inch data storage disks. The screen and keyboard were often the same VDU (Visual Display Unit) as had been used as a dumb terminal for connection to a mainframe machine. Today's top-of-the-range personal computers occupy about the same space as a portable TV set, have integrated colour screens, Megabytes of internal memory and use miniature disks or even optical disks for data storage. The power and speed of the machines have grown hundreds of times while the costs have reduced by a factor of about ten.

The original low-level programming in machine code has given way to high-level languages like COBOL, PASCAL or 'C'. Although users can, if they wish, now prepare their own business programs in computer languages that approach plain English, there is no longer any need. Expert programmers are no longer required to operate the machines since packaged software can be bought for almost any business application.

There has been a simultaneous development of modern communications systems, bringing about a convergence of technologies, so that communications systems and computer systems look much alike. Both technologies are now firmly based on digital techniques and it is the development of digital computer systems combined with digital communications networks that is bringing about an information revolution in business.

Information systems contain the essential elements of computing, communications and information. In this chapter we will briefly examine developments in these areas and see how they can be brought together into practical systems.

11.2 Basic topology of information systems

Centralized or distributed?

For many companies 'computer' means 'mainframe computer'. The mainframe computer is a large, centralized machine capable of large storage capacities of hundreds of Megabytes (a Byte represents a single character or number) and of great processing power. Its great capacity for work makes it particularly suitable for 'batch' processing, where many jobs are prepared 'off-line' on data-entry machines and then are queued for sequential processing. Batch processing may take place at night when the computer is not being used by 'real-time' processes. If batch processing is done during normal working hours then the computer will have to allocate appropriate priorities to batch processes and to on-line users. Mainframe machines are used for the maintenance and operation of large databases such as personnel and payroll applications for large organizations and for running complex computational programs.

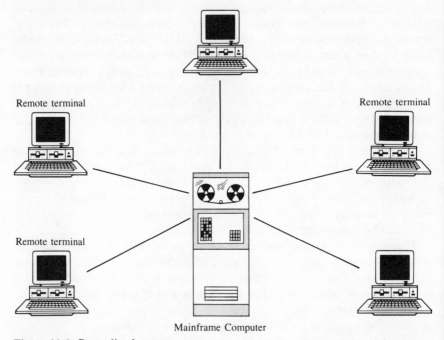

Remote terminal   Remote terminal

Remote terminal

Mainframe Computer

Figure 11.1 Centralized system

The mainframe may be driven by a number of simple remote VDU terminals, usually described as 'dumb terminals'. These terminals have no processing power of their own, they act simply as windows on the mainframe computer. VDUs have a screen, a keyboard and electronic components enabling them to be connected to a telephone line or to a direct link to the mainframe computer. The mainframe computer with its cluster of local or remote terminals forms a *centralized* system, illustrated in Fig. 11.1. The terminals are 'polled' or interrogated by the central computer to determine which are active and which should be given the computer's attention. Because the mainframe has to divide its time among a number of remote users and perhaps a series of batch processes it may not give instantaneous response to a remote terminal. Users are normally allocated priorities appropriate to the kinds of task that they are engaged in.

All software, storage, processing and input/output facilities are centralized in the mainframe. The remote terminals may be directly connected to the mainframe computer if they are in the same building, or may be linked to it from distant sites by public telephone line, private telephone circuit or direct line.

As users became more familiar with computing techniques and were accustomed to having computer terminals in their offices they became more demanding. The speed of response of centralized installations, as far as the remote users were concerned, was often poor and there was little choice of software. Strict rules were often imposed on users who had to conform to the protocols and data structures of the mainframe system.

The rapid development of computing and communications technologies, together with the raised expectations of users, have brought about radical changes in the topology of computing networks. Instead of being centralized the computing resources of a company may now be *distributed*.

In a distributed system the individual terminals may be powerful microcomputers, each capable of independent operation, but linked by a network so that computing resources, software, peripheral devices (printers, plotters, etc.) and external communications can be shared among the terminals. The network may also contain even more powerful minicomputers providing local database functions, specialized processing or communications access to the distant mainframe. The essential feature of distributed systems is that a number of physically separated computers are connected through communications facilities, often to a mainframe computer. Data and programs can be downloaded from the central machine for local processing in the 'intelligent terminals'. Figure 11.2 illustrates a distributed system.

A further definition is required for those situations where a local network of microcomputers, or a collection of stand-alone machines is used to provide a number of specialized local information services for an organization. In such cases software, databases, etc. are usually the property of individual users and the network, if any, is used for sharing peripheral devices, document transmission and for electronic mail. This kind of computing may be described as 'informal', whereas the computing processes offered by a system linked to a mainframe may be 'formal', We can therefore describe the small local network or group of stand-alone computers as an *informal distributed* system.

It is important to note that different authors use different terms to describe distributed, centralized, formal and informal systems. The essential difference between the types of system is the extent to which the users are dependent on any form of central computing facility provided by a mainframe.

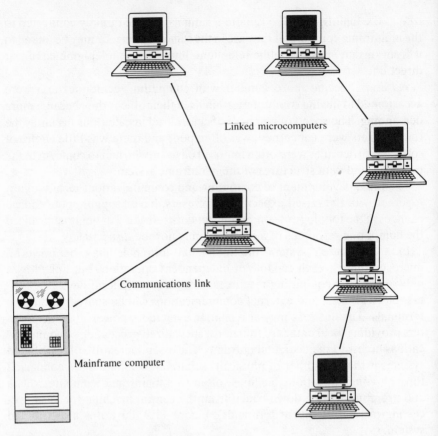

Linked microcomputers

Communications link

Mainframe computer

Figure 11.2 Distributed system

11.3 Network configurations

A network operating within one site of an organization is a Local Area Network (LAN). A network with terminals on a number of different sites, requiring telecommunications links to connect them, is a Wide Area Network (WAN). A third type of network may be found in a large city where a number of installations, of a company or an educational organization, are linked together. This is a Metropolitan Area Network (MAN). In large installations a number of LANs may be found. These may have been installed to meet different requirements over long periods of time and may therefore be of different types. 'Gateways' and 'bridges', consisting of special hardware and software, will have to be provided to link these LANs together if intercommunication is required.

Most modern microcomputers are equipped for external communications either by means of internal devices or by external equipment linked to telephone lines. Although they are not part of a permanent network, users of such devices may be regarded as being connected to a form of WAN. Services such as PRESTEL in the UK offer network facilities, electronic mail, information, databases and limited information processing to simple domestic and business computer terminals. The Public Switched Telephone Network (PSTN) or the Packet Switch Stream network (PSS) is used as the carrier. The latest cellular radio systems also offer facilities for data transmission from remote terminals.

Telephone systems all over the world are linked together by international circuits, carried by cables or satellite links. These form a universal network for voice transmission and for computer data, provided that a conversion from digital to analogue format is made at each end of the link. With the introduction of digital telephone networks nationally and worldwide it is possible to envisage a universal digital network, capable of interconnecting terminals, LANs and WANs of any kind and at any location. The so-called ISDN (Integrated Services Digital Network) now being developed and installed by telecommunications operators throughout the world, is intended to be a network of that type.

11.4 Basic technology of information systems

Whatever the configuration of the system, or the choice of terminals and network technology, the same basic functions must be provided to establish a workable system, those key functions are:

Collection, Storage, Processing, Communication.

Each of these may be performed in a variety of ways: this section reviews some of the techniques that make it possible.

Collection

The technology of computer input was discussed in Sec. 4.7, here we look at some of the practical applications of that technology. There is a wide variety of methods of data collection, or data capture, here are some examples.

- *Paper-based*: using forms, reports, returns, receipts, punched cards, till rolls, tickets, etc.
    Paper-based data input systems can be seen in operation in many retail establishments, restaurants, small shops, etc.
- *Voice-based*: by telephone, direct reporting, tape recordings, voice-bank systems, eventually by computerized voice-recognition systems.

If the booking office can be regarded as part of an information system then the telephone booking services offered by major theatres and concert halls can be described as voice-based systems. Experimental aircraft have been designed to be controlled by voice commands.

– *Telemetry*: readings from remote instruments, process control systems, data from spacecraft, reservoirs, radio tags on whales and other wild animals, radio pills inside patients, etc.

Keen fishermen will know that it is possible to ring automatic announcement machines connected to measuring devices in some major rivers. Details of water temperature and flow are given. Weather conditions in the upper atmosphere are transmitted from miniature weather stations carried by balloons. Under the oceans submarines can be detected by electronic listening devices.

– *Optical*: bar codes on merchandise, point of sale terminals, optical character recognition of printed text, pattern recognition, counting of objects, measurement by interferometry.

Bar code readers are now a familiar sight in supermarkets. Codes printed on the merchandise can be read, at high speed and in almost any position, by crossed light beams. Facsimile machines are becoming common in offices: these transmit data generated by a light beam which scans a document.

– *Manual coding*: input from keyboards, either at the desk or from portable terminals.

Portable keyboards are now used by some retail chains for stock control, details of shelf stocks are transmitted to a central computer which then arranges for new stocks to be delivered.

– *Magnetic*: bar codes, magnetic stripes, proximity measurement, counting.

Many shops and petrol stations use machines that read the magnetic stripes on credit cards, transmitting the information to an authorization centre. Bank cheques carry numerical information printed with magnetic ink. When the cheque is processed the ink is magnetized and the codes are then read by automatic sorting machines.

– *Electronic*: automatic monitoring of databases, scanning of messages, text-retrieval systems.

The monitoring in this case is done by computer software which is programmed to find keywords in text or messages. The so-called automatic trading systems in the world's stock markets use this technique to spot market trends.

You may like to think about methods of data collection in your own organization and to consider whether there is scope for using different technologies to accomplish the tasks. For example, an electricity or gas company needs to collect meter readings from its customers so that bills can be sent out. The usual method of doing this is to send a meter reader to the customer's premises to read the meter. Meter readings are recorded against the customer's name and account number and then sent to a central office where the information is used to prepare bills. An alternative method is to use a portable computer terminal, with a simple keyboard and internal memory. Meter readings can be taken and then fed into the company's information system via the portable terminals. This allows records to be updated and bills to be prepared quickly. The next step would be to connect the customer's meter to a telephone line so that the data can be sent directly to the utility's computer.

Data collection is an expensive business, especially if the data has to be handled and processed a number of times before it can be used. Collecting data at source for immediate entry into a computer system saves time and expense and allows the organization to make use of the information in a variety of different ways. Not only can customer accounts be prepared but information about the customer's pattern of usage may be useful for maintenance or for marketing purposes.

Storage

Information systems have two different requirements for the storage of data: one is for temporary storage of data and programs for use during a working session. As long as the computer is switched on or the system is active such data will be continually checked, refreshed, and ready for use. The second requirement is for long-term storage of data. This may be required for archive purposes, or for backup copies as security against system failure, or it may be the means of physically transferring data from one system to another. These two types of storage, and the technology available, were discussed in Sec. 4.8 and 4.9.

Information storage technologies have improved dramatically in recent years, bringing the cost of computers and information systems down by a factor of approximately 1000 since business computing began. Magnetic systems were and are the mainstay of data storage, but semiconductor and optical techniques are now challenging them. However, no sooner is there some breakthrough in new storage technology, like that of the optical disk, than the supporters of more conventional technology, like that of the floppy disk, fight back. New techniques of magnetic recording on conventional disks now offer capacities that may exceed even those of the optical disks.

Optical storage systems are particularly suited to large volumes of data and so may be used for archive purposes or for access to standard reference information. Agencies now exist for the conversion of company information to optical format.

Information can be stored in all of these devices for subsequent retrieval and processing. Information stored in a logical way forms a 'database' which can then be acted on by an external program to extract specific items of information. A 'relational database' permits the user to ask structured questions relating areas of the database to one another or relating different databases together, e.g. to find the records of all students with a first degree *and* with a professional qualification but *not* with wooden legs.

Many organizations have extensive collections of data, some of it arranged in formal databases, but much of it preserved in simple archives. Recent developments in hardware and software allow such collections of data to be searched very rapidly for any required piece of information. As will be seen in a later section, such techniques provide significant benefits for management decision-support systems.

Processing

The first mainframe machines took up whole floors of buildings and required kilowatts of power to drive them and their air-conditioning plants. The equivalent machine can now be slipped into a pocket. Business computing grew up round mainframe installations and batch processing and information systems expertise was concentrated in a small group of data processing personnel. Centralized computing, with numbers of 'dumb' terminals connected to a mainframe or minicomputer, was the next step.

As storage and processing costs came down so smaller and more powerful machines became available. Eventually the personal microcomputer, or small business computer, was small enough and cheap enough to be put on the user's desk. The personal computer user of today wants to be free to experiment, to buy and to develop software to solve individual problems. Traditional computing and information systems, and the organizations to support then, are no longer appropriate in an 'informal' computing environment.

After experimenting with 'stand-alone' PCs many managers are finding that distributed networks of linked microcomputers are the best way of implementing information systems. Networks may be served by one or more especially powerful machines providing bulk storage, central filing and some central processing facilities. Users can access central databases, downloading information for local processing on their own PCs.

The basic technology of processing and software was described in Sec. 4.10. The processing 'engine' of a computer is the Central Processing Unit (CPU). Business micro- and minicomputers have CPUs based on one of a number of standard microprocessor 'chips'. The most recent systems contain chips such as the 80286 or 80386 or the 68000 series. These allow 16- and 32-bit data words to be handled within the CPU and are capable of addressing enormous amounts of RAM. They provide computing power that would have been unimaginable only a few years ago. It has been said that the chips used in the latest versions of the IBM-PC have the ability to address 256kByte of memory for every man, woman and child in the United States!

Computers need a controlling program to make them work and to manage access to disk drives, screens, printers and communications devices. This program is known as the 'operating system'. As with microprocessors there are a variety of competing operating systems, each known by some acronym. Older business machines may use CP/M (Control Program for Microcomputers), the original IBM-PC family uses PC-DOS, a version of MS-DOS; DOS is the abbreviation for Disk Operating System. Other machines use UNIX, XENIX or similar systems. The latest IBM PS/2 machines use OS/2. It is not necessary to know much about these different operating systems, except that they may not be compatible with one another. An information system should ideally be based on one operating system so that data formats, file structures and communications protocols are common throughout the system. The operating system need not even be seen by the user who commonly works with specialized software packages but it is always active, handling keyboard input, screen output, filing and other essential functions.

Communication

Communications between machines on the same site may be provided by a Local Area Network (LAN). LANs, introduced in Sec. 5.5, may use ordinary twisted wires, coaxial cables, or optical fibres and may be arranged as rings, trees, or in star formation as shown in Fig. 11.3. The different network configurations have their own advantages and disadvantages, for example, the star network depends entirely on the central computer. If that machine fails then the network may be unusable. Ring networks can pass information between machines in either direction, so the network is resistant to failure of any one machine or network node.

LANs enable many machines to be connected together with shared resources such as printers, file servers and software libraries. Some way must therefore be found of allowing all the machines to have access to the network facilities without there being any interference or blocking of signals. Some networks allocate different signal frequencies to each machine, others

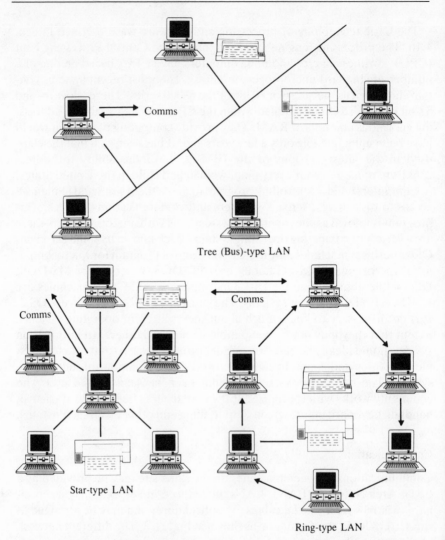

Figure 11.3 Local Area Network types

transmit blocks of data with identifying tokens. The management of the network and its peripheral equipment is usually performed by one special machine, this will have extended processing facilities and additional disk memory for software libraries and shared files. It will probably also control external communications, allowing the LAN machines to communicate with the telephone network, with other LANs or with a Wide Area Network (WAN). A WAN is a network linking computers and information systems on a number of different sites. WANs use the Public Switched Telephone Network (PSTN) or a network of private circuits to link different sites together. Organizations may have information networks that link systems in different countries, in which case the WAN will contain links carried by submarine telephone cables or by communications satellites.

Public telephone networks are mainly designed for carrying voice signals and the majority still use analogue technology. The analogue voice network may be used for data transmission provided that modems (MOdulator/DE-Modulators), are used to convert the computer's digital signals to analogue form (see Sec. 5.4). Modems can provide a number of useful facilities, such as automatic dialling of distant numbers and automatic answering of incoming calls. Until recently the electrical characteristics of the PSTN restricted reliable data transmission between modems to speeds of between 75 and 2400 Baud (signal elements per second.) Modems now available claim to allow transmission over suitable circuits at speeds up to 9600 Baud. Higher speeds can only be achieved if special dedicated circuits are provided.

Modern digital systems such as PSS (Packet Switched Stream, see Sec. 5.4) allow direct interconnection of computers through a public network. Stand-alone computers or LANs are connected to a PAD (Packet Assembler/Disassembler), which in turn is connected to the digital network. Data from the computer or LAN is formed into 'packets', each containing a standard number of Bytes and each equipped with a header carrying address information, just as an addressed envelope contains a letter. Packets from many sources are injected into the network and travel around it until the addressed packets are detected by the appropriate destination computer. The international standard governing the way in which digital signals are handled by a packet switched network is called X25 and any computer or system having an X25 interface will be able to be connected to the PSS.

Eventually the construction of integrated digital networks will allow information of all kinds, text, data, voice and image, to be transmitted over public telecommunications facilities. The term now used to describe such an all-purpose network is the Integrated Services Digital Network (ISDN). Parts of that network are already in place in many countries, especially for inter-city links. Local communications links, from local telephone exchanges (central offices) to users' premises are normally provided with conventional copper wires in underground cables. This kind of equipment is not suitable for the reliable transmission of high-speed data signals. It is possible to provide special equipment to convert some local lines to digital working, but it will be many years before digital systems are available to the majority of telephone users. Alternative networks, like the cellular telephone network, or a cable TV network, may provide high-speed digital links before the conventional local network can be converted. This threat poses interesting strategic problems for the national telecommunications authorities.

The key to all computer communications is *compatibility*, either between machines within a network or between networks. To achieve compatibility any information system should ideally conform to international standards for interconnection. These standards are established by international bodies, such as the CCITT and CEPT representing the communications and computing operating agencies and manufacturers. The Open Systems Interconnection (OSI) architecture should enable machines of all kinds to be interconnected. The IBM standard Systems Network Architecture (SNA) is widely used to interconnect installations of IBM machines. All system suppliers are aware of the need to offer compatible machines and networks, so that IBM now offer OSI-compatible systems while other suppliers offer SNA facilities.

11.5 Putting it together

The information system designer is faced with a huge range of options. There are many competing and essentially similar types of computer, a variety of LAN technologies is available, the choice must be made between public or private communications networks.

The key factors in choosing hardware and software for an information system are:

- *Capability* of the machines to do all that is asked of them;
- *Capacity* in terms of storage and processing power;
- *Speed* of processing, of input and output;
- *Accessibility*, ease of use and convenience of location;
- *Security* of data, software, and hardware;
- *Compatibility* of data formats, software, communications;
- *Cost*.

At all times the requirements of the intended information system, that is, the users' needs as set out in the design requirements, must be matched by the equipment selected. The information system should not only be capable of satisfying present needs but should also be capable of expansion and development in future.

11.6 Towards the virtual network

Telecommunications administrations throughout the world are installing digital systems for the transmission and switching of telephone and data traffic, the ISDN has already been described. Once those digital systems can be connected direct to LANs and stand-alone systems a virtual network can be provided, nationally or internationally. No permanent links need to be provided between computers, LANs or WANs, the network can be set up on demand at any time using public facilities. Very powerful computers could be provided within the public network, offering advanced information storage and processing facilities. Those computers could facilitate the interconnection of individual machines or networks or could act as central information resources.

Where should the 'intelligence' in an information system be? In a small, local machine or concentrated in the centre of a vast network? The history of information systems has been that there has been a swing away from centralized systems towards distributed and informal systems. This has been partly a matter of economics and partly of performance. With reductions in the real cost of communications and the enormous increases in the power and speed of large computers we may see a swing back towards more centralized systems.

The success of the 'virtual network' depends on the level of investment that telecommunications authorities are prepared to put into new local and inter-city networks. Optical systems are being provided by both BT and Mercury in the UK for inter-city links. Mercury and BT are connecting up offices in the City of London with optical fibres. Negotiations are going on between the public network providers and the operators of cable TV systems, since such systems may be the first, and possibly the only wide-band communications links into small business and domestic premises.

Other means of bypassing the conventional wired network are by cellular radio, now capable of carrying digital data, and by satellite. Simple satellite terminals, designed originally for ships, are now available for land-mobile and aeronautical use. One of the first applications of this technology will be to provide simple electronic message facilities for long-distance lorries travelling in remote places overseas.

The 'in-car phone' is the latest status symbol. It cannot be long before the 'in-car computer terminal' takes its place.

11.7 Conclusion

In this chapter we have seen how the basic information system functions of *collection, storage, processing* and *communication* can be achieved, and how networks of computers can be created to provide systems. The distinction was drawn between centralized and distributed systems. The reader was invited to consider his own organization and to try to relate its activities to those attributed here to information systems. The very rapid developments in technology and the emphasis on Open Systems Interconnection (OSI) make it possible to imagine highly distributed virtual networks of computers, analagous to public telephone systems. At the same time, the enormous power and speed of the latest generation of mainframe computers almost guarantees them a place at the centre of such networks.

12.
Practical information systems management

12.1 Introduction

In the earlier chapters of this book we looked at the background to organizations, and the information systems that serve them, mainly from a technical point of view. All managers know that there is more to business life than hardware and software, systems and procedures. These are only things to be used by the people in the organization. People are perhaps the most valuable business resource: they are flexible, imaginative and cooperative, but only if treated properly. Any plan to introduce an information system into an organization will fail unless it takes account of the human element. The expectations, fears, misunderstandings and enthusiasms of people must be considered in designing for effective information management.

So, the project manager and the general managers who have specified the information system are faced with a much wider range of problems than simply technical ones. We must now look at some of those general management problems of implementation. Some of the most difficult problems in business are those to do with the people employed there and with matters of internal politics. The project manager must be something of a diplomat to deal with them.

12.2 Implementation issues

We have already seen how the early emphasis on centralized, mainframe-based systems has swung towards decentralized systems. At the present time the trend is strongly towards decentralized, or distributed informal systems. This follows a period of near anarchy in some organizations when managers and others wishing to experiment with the new information technology, and perhaps frustrated by poor service from an overworked or unsuitable mainframe installation, simply went out and bought office computer equipment and software for themselves. However, buying a desk-top computer is one thing, making effective use of it is another. Many managers must now be regretting that they don't have the time or the skill to use their fancy new machines properly. Desk-top microcomputers have their advantages, but each of these may become a disadvantage unless the user is skilled at getting the best from the system.

Advantages of informal systems

The advantages of informal systems, that is systems consisting of stand-alone or LAN-linked microcomputers, each with its own software, may be classified under five headings: organizational, technological, operational, financial, and personal.

ORGANIZATIONAL

The use of microcomputers, either as stand-alone machines or linked to a LAN, can increase the efficiency of everyone in the office. Initially the introduction of new technology may be a means of automating the office, the evolutionary approach. As people become more familiar with software packages such as word-processors, spreadsheets and databases they will be encouraged to experiment with new applications. Eventually that experimentation may encourage the introduction of wholly new business techniques; the revolutionary approach.

TECHNOLOGICAL

Informal distributed systems are a way of introducing IT to the office with low risk. With powerful microcomputers, now approaching mainframe capability, being available for a few thousand pounds the cost of entry to the technology is low. The latest technology can be acquired and managers can experiment with a number of different machines or software packages until the most satisfactory solution to a problem is found.

OPERATIONAL

The ease with which business micros can be bought, installed and made to work leads to the rapid acceptance of information systems and of new working methods. Managers more familiar with paper-based information systems come to expect the improved speed of response to enquiries that a good electronic filing system can offer. They will welcome the increased accuracy and timeliness of management information. The systems will offer easy access to local databases and even to external databases. Specialized software may be purchased or even written for specific local needs.

FINANCIAL

Only a small investment is needed to enter the world of IT with desk-top computers. Some organizations operate a system of financial control in which sums less than a certain figure can be spent from an office budget, without the necessity for formal allocations of funds or competitive tenders. Because a number of machines of different types may be purchased for different offices the financial risk may be spread over a number of departments. Office equipment, which now includes microcomputers, is depreciated over short periods, say, two years, so an unsatisfactory purchase can be disposed of and replaced fairly quickly.

PERSONAL

The screen and keyboard on the desk is a sign of the up and coming manager. To have a personal computer, and to be seen to use it, enhances personal status and provides job-enrichment. Watchers of television commercials will know how desirable it is to have a computer that can produce better written reports and graphics than anyone else can.

Disadvantages of informal systems

Just as every action has an equal and opposite reaction, so almost every advantage listed above can also be seen as a disadvantage! Those disadvantages can be listed under the same five headings.

ORGANIZATIONAL

As has already been explained, the development of new patterns of information flow may cut across traditional work and organizational boundaries. The introduction of personal computers may give rise to *ad hoc* office systems and informal information flows. Jobs may be undertaken by people who have no formal responsibility for them, they just happen to be the people who can process the data effectively, or produce the clever reports. This becomes a real disadvantage if the efficient functioning of the organization still depends on formal lines of reporting and responsibility and on the disciplined handling of information of clearly defined types and formats.

TECHNOLOGICAL

There are so many different computers, microprocessors and operating systems that any one new machine may be incompatible with other machines. The incompatibility can simply be due to different floppy disk sizes or formats or to some more esoteric problem. Even in the apparently standard world of IBM microcomputer products there are now three different colour screen 'standards', three microprocessors and two different operating systems. Some machines may be incapable of networking and of performing external communications functions (unless internal modifications are carried out). The proliferation of types makes maintenance and support difficult. It also makes it difficult to transfer data between machines.

OPERATIONAL

When efficiently used the desk-top computer can offer productivity improvements. If its users are unfamiliar with its operation, or if there is any incompatibility with other office machines, bottlenecks and delays will occur. Programs and data held in storage on hard disks in individual machines may not be backed-up or may become inaccessible if the machine becomes faulty. Computers are great time-wasters, sometimes becoming a kind of 'executive toy': managers, like anyone else, welcome a challenge and will try to master the machine, often without the aid of the instruction manual. Businesses cannot afford to waste the time of senior staff in this way.

FINANCIAL

If direct purchases by managers of machines and consumable supplies (disks, paper, etc.) are made using office equipment budgets then IT costs will not be controlled, so the real costs of introducing the technology will be hidden. Direct purchasing from dealers of single machines may not qualify for bulk discounts that would otherwise be available to corporate buyers. Such transactions are not easily audited. No proper records will exist for asset valuation or depreciation purposes.

PERSONAL

As will be described later, desk-top computers actually can cause stress and other health problems. They may become addictive, as any parent with children hooked on home microcomputers will know. Computers, especially when used by other managers, are often unwelcome agents of change.

Many of the disadvantages can be overcome with careful planning. Proper financial procedures will be needed so that costs and expenditure are kept under control while still allowing a certain degree of freedom of choice of equiment and systems. The dangers of incompatibility can be reduced if some new roles for formerly centralized data processing departments are established, such as the establishment of standards for database format, network operation, machine compatibility, etc. It is not necessary that all machines used by an organization should be identical, only that they should be compatible. In order to establish some central control over the purchasing of microcomputers and software, to secure compatibility and to take advantage of bulk purchase terms, it will be necessary to set up a supply procedure and organization for IT within a company.

12.3 People issues

All new technologies are seen as threatening by those with more traditional skills who are expected to work with them. The industrial revolution of the eighteenth and nineteenth centuries gave rise to whole movements devoted to the prevention of technological progress. New machines were smashed and factories burned. There were strikes and lockouts, marches and even riots. People were afraid of the new technologies which deafened the formerly rural world with their noise and blackened it with their smoke. Even today the older industries, such as coal-mining and steel-making, contain traditionally-minded workers who are resistant to new technologies and procedures. So, when the latest technological revolution, the information revolution, came along there was bound to be trouble.

Computers and information systems have for years been seen as threatening the job security of managers and staff alike. The new machines would, it was argued, sweep away mundane clerical tasks, typists and typing pools would be replaced by word-processors, management decisions would be made by computerized decision systems, robots would take over the production lines. Although we see some of this happening today, the computer and robotic age has always been just round the corner, but it never seems to have arrived. However, the threats perceived by workers are often real, computers *will* take over mundane clerical and administrative tasks. But there are compensations too, computers offer revolutionary ways of organizing and completing business tasks, freeing managers for more creative work and offering new kinds of information-based employment. The shift of the economy away from traditional industries and towards information-based service industries has been described in Part 1, Chapter 1.

It is no good attempting to minimize the threats, both real and imaginary. People are intelligent and perceptive beings and will soon see through any attempt to persuade them with half truths. The introduction of computers and information systems to an existing organization requires careful preparation in order to reassure staff and to secure their acceptance of the proposals and their commitment to the project.

Some of the perceived threats are:

- *To jobs*: Computers may take over clerical, administrative and lower-level managerial tasks, leading to redundancies and unemployment for the less skilled and for older personnel. Interestingly, it is generally assumed that the major job losses will be at the lower levels of the organization. However, it is at the middle levels of an organization that most of the information is processed and communicated. Computers are therefore particularly suited for many middle-management tasks and it is at that level that a major impact of the information revolution is likely to be felt.
- *To status*: Centres of influence and power, established in organizations over many years, are likely to shift as the information systems take effect. In any organizational structure, the person controlling the information has the real power. Formerly that control might have been exercised by a senior clerk, or an office manager. Now the computer and its associated systems control the information causing the one-time 'king-pin' to lose face and status.
- *To confidence*: People who have worked in familiar surroundings and at familiar jobs become thoroughly set in their ways. The introduction of new technology and systems into the working environment will pose unwelcome intellectual challenges. The majority of the staff will not have been educated in information technology and will be unwilling to change the habits of a working lifetime. At the same time, they will not like to appear slow or incapable of mastering the intricacies of a machine. Those managers with higher educational qualifications and years of managerial experience are even more likely to face a crisis of confidence, leading to the well-known computer-phobia.
- *To the organization*: We have seen how information systems can alter patterns of responsibility in an office. Because of their revolutionary potential, information systems can threaten traditional organizational structures. Unless those structures are redefined, or some alternative form of organization adopted, traditional objectives, rules and procedures may cease to be relevant or may be ignored. Work appropriate to the new computers will tend to gravitate towards those users who are the most competent, not necessarily to those whose specific organizational responsibility it is to deal with the work.
- *To competence*: New systems will inevitably increase the pace of work and this increased pace will add to the actual workload for individuals.

Increased pressure will lead to work being delayed or badly handled which, in turn, will lead to a loss of confidence. Staff will feel incompetent to deal with the technology and with the increased pressures and performance will suffer as a result.

- *To health*: This is a very difficult area, and is often the subject of sensational headlines and earnest television debates. Although it is certain that some health problems are associated with the use of computers it is not clear that there are any real causal relationships. Back trouble can certainly arise from poor posture at the keyboard. Eye problems and headaches will arise from vision uncorrected for the 'VDU distance'. Less certainly, VDU screens are said to emit dangerous X-rays which are a particular danger to women, especially pregnant women. Stress, headaches and other ailments, which can arise from any number of causes, will all be attributed to the effects of the computer or VDU screen.

If these 'threats' are seen as real by employees then they must be treated seriously and adequately dealt with before any information systems project can be completed. Several steps can be taken to minimize fears:

- *Consultation*: People must be told, well in advance, about the intention to introduce an information system. Their views must be sought and reflected in the design requirements.

  This process of consultation is not simply a one-way process. Certainly the project manager will have a story to tell about the intentions behind the new systems and about the technology to be employed. The users, too, will have their story to tell. It is at this early stage that the careful listener will pick up a great deal of useful information about the organization and the people in it. Some of the informal systems will be revealed and people may feel able to discuss the 'unofficial' ways in which things really get done in the organization. Such inside knowledge is an essential input to the specification and design process.

- *Negotiation*: Terms and conditions of employment must be negotiated with the staff or with their appointed representatives. Any threats of redundancies or of redeployment must be dealt with at an early stage and satisfactory procedures devised.

  It is too easy for the manager to assume that the unions representing the employees will be against new technology and information systems in principle. In fact, many of the unions have tried for many years to devise and implement new technology agreements. Unfortunately they are often caught in a dilemma; on the one hand they must seek to protect and preserve the jobs of their existing members, while on the other hand

seeking to establish new employment opportunities in the future. Consultation before negotiation can help to expose issues and problems.
- *Familiarization*: Demonstration sessions and 'hands-on' experience should be provided for those who will be using the systems, possibly employing a simulation of business processes. It may be possible for potential users to visit similar installations elsewhere.

Hands-on experience of using information technology in a relaxed and informal environment is a very succesful method of familiarization. After an initial introduction to software and systems users can be left to experiment on their own with demonstration packages and data. A little guidance from time to time and assistance with the interpretation of instruction manuals is all the expert input that is needed.
- *Training*: A comprehensive programme of formal training for all affected staff and management must be devised. The programme should be designed so as to make adequate numbers of trained personnel available when the systems are first commissioned.

Training courses are often specified as part of any contract for new equipment and systems. The supplier may initially run such courses on their own premises. It is better if the training can be given to users 'in-house' in familiar surroundings. One way to set up a training programme is to identify the enthusiasts and those with some computing experience. These people can be trained first and can then act as a team of trainers to assist their colleagues.
- *Support*: Once the systems are working, continual support should be given to users by the specialists (possibly the former data processing staff).

The creation of a users' group or forum for the exchange of views, suggestions, complaints, etc. may secure the cooperation and commitment of staff. This subject is further developed in the next section.
- *Environment*: Careful attention paid to the siting of computers and peripheral equipment will pay dividends. Properly designed desks, tables and chairs should be used.

Many of the health problems listed above can be avoided by providing a good working environment. Computer screens should be at the correct height in relation to the desk-top and keyboard so that users do not have to stoop or peer at the screen. The keyboards themselves should come readily to hand with the operator sitting in a relaxed and comfortable position. Glare, due to reflections from the VDU screen can be minimized by careful positioning, or by the provision of a diffuser or polarizing screen. One of the more annoying features of modern offices, static electricity caused by friction with carpets and furnishings, can damage computers. Electric shocks and damage can be avoided by providing anti-static mats adjacent to computer terminals.

The 'human factors' aspects of computer installations are described in detail by David J. Oborne in his book *Computers at Work* (1985).[1]

12.4 System support

The question of support and maintenance of systems was briefly discussed in Chapter 10 as part of the project life cycle. Once the initial project is over, the commitment to support the system remains and may be a significant cost to the organization. Faulty equipment will have to be repaired or replaced, new hardware and software will be introduced as the system grows and develops in complexity and capability.

No system, however well designed and implemented, is going to operate for any length of time without expert attention. In Chapter 10 it was explained that it is a characteristic of machines and equipment of all kinds that numerous faults, often quite minor in nature, will occur in the early life of the system. Thereafter there will be a long period of fairly stable operation, followed by a decline in performance as the system components begin to wear out. Expert maintenance attention must therefore be provided, especially at the beginning of the system's operation.

The users of the system will change too. New personnel will take over the jobs of experienced users. Even experienced users may require retraining from time to time, while introductory training programmes will be required for new staff. As new facilities, hardware and software, are introduced into the system there will be requirements for familiarization training.

A less formal kind of training support can be provided by skilled users of systems and software packages who can be called on to help their colleagues when problems arise.

System support can be provided by experts within each unit of the organization, or by a specialist function. Where the growth of distributed systems and informal computing has reduced the load on a data processing department it should be possible to use the resources of that department to provide training and other support throughout the organization.

Maintenance of computer and communication systems requires a high level of technical skill. It is unlikely that such skills will already exist in companies other than those in the high-technology area, so outside help must be sought. Computer system suppliers and equipment dealers normally offer a guarantee period with their equipment, so that early faults are dealt with under that guarantee.

Customers are often invited to subscribe to an extended guarantee that will ensure rapid attention should faults occur outside the original guarantee period. Users of large systems often pay for 24-hour attention because of the risks of a system 'going down' for even a short time.

Dealers and other suppliers often offer a maintenance service which is in fact delegated to a specialist organization. The system managers should ensure that the level of maintenance cover, especially in emergency situations, is adequate for their purpose.

12.5 System security

Some aspects of systems security were dealt with in Chapters 2 and 7 where issues relating to the cost of computer fraud and ways of encrypting information to protect it against unauthorized access were discussed. The effective implementation of security measures is not just a matter for the system designer, it is the responsibility of the organization as a whole and of each individual user.

Effective security measures form an essential part of the design requirements for any system. Company information is a strategic resource; money, time, even markets can be lost if that information is lost, corrupted or even temporarily inaccessible.

Mainframe security

Because they are usually operated by professionally trained staff, mainframe computer systems are managed and operated in such a way that security is good. Each day's activities are continuously logged and records may be kept of the transactions performed by individual users. Back-up copies are made of all the data and programs in the computer on a regular basis. Users can often specify the degree of protection to be afforded to their files of information and the frequency with which it should be archived.

Archive tapes or demountable disks are kept safely stored away from the main computer installation, preferably in fireproof cabinets or specially-protected rooms. Any disaster at the computer centre will then only lose a day's transactions.

Computer centres themselves should be protected against fire, flood and unauthorized access. It is common practice to install computers in rooms with raised floors, under which pass all the control and communication cables. Those under-floor spaces can be a fire hazard. Special equipment for fighting electrical fires should be provided so that if a fire should occur the computer room can be flooded with a gas that will extinguish the fire. The gas will not remove all danger, however, since the heat that caused the fire may still be there. A fire can re-ignite if the source is not found and dealt with quickly. The fire brigade will use water because it puts out fires by removing heat, but it does no good to computer and communications equipment.

It may be possible to duplicate all the units of a computer or a part of the installation so that service is not lost in the event of a component or unit failure. Some computer systems consist of two machines running effectively in parallel, so that the overall system becomes fault tolerant. If one part of the system breaks down the other goes on working. A message is then sent to the operator to report the failure. Another technique is to keep a second machine on 'hot stand-by', that is, fully equipped and switched on, so that it can take over from a faulty machine.

Failure of the electrical mains supply need not be as disastrous as it sounds. Computer systems can be provided with battery-driven emergency power supplies. These will probably not have enough capacity to run the system for more than a few minutes, but that time is long enough for working programs to be saved onto disk or tape. Large installations will have emergency power supplies driven by a diesel generator which starts automatically when the mains fail. Very large installations will have 'no-break' power supplies which are capable of providing an uninterrupted supply.

Some organizations subscribe to disaster recovery services who operate computer centres, either fixed or mobile, to replace those lost by fire, major failure or any other disaster. It may be possible for an organization to rent capacity on a similar computer system operated by another organization. If the main system fails then data can be transferred to the second computer. If an organization has a computer network, either a LAN or a WAN, then computer facilities can be duplicated in the network, allowing the transfer of files and processes to another part of the network if there is a failure of one node.

Distributed systems security

Distributed and informal computing systems introduce a whole range of new security problems. Because each of the terminals in the system has its own processing power and storage media the security problems are multiplied. Instead of system security being the responsibility of experts in the data processing department it may now be the responsibility of relatively unskilled office workers.

Whereas mainframe computers enjoy carefully protected, air-conditioned environments office computers normally operate in unprotected environments: in offices where there may be dust, movement, electrical interference, smoke and other enemies of the computer. The author has seen computers in City dealer rooms being used as dining tables for snack meals! Microcomputers are fairly robust, but they will not resist tea or coffee. Heat is another problem. Microcomputer components, especially the microprocessor chips, will only work satisfactorily below a certain temperature. If the office is centrally heated then the temperatures inside the casing of the computer can approach danger levels. Great care must be taken to allow good ventilation of computers and their VDUs. Ventilation slots must not be obstructed by papers. Desk-top computers compete for space with all the other bits and pieces of office life, telephones, books, documents, and so on. The temptation to regard the computer as a convenient surface on which to pile things must be resisted.

The floppy disks used in modern systems are particularly vulnerable to damage, especially the 5.25 inch ones in cardboard cases. They are frequently left lying on desks, exposed to dust, physical or magnetic damage and to bright sunlight. Even if the disks are protected, as are the latest ones in plastic cartridges, they may simply be mislaid or stolen. Unless especial precautions are taken even the internal storage mechanisms of the computer, the hard disk and ROM storage, can be attacked and data may be corrupted, stolen, or simply deleted.

Security is now the responsibility of every user. Programs and data should be copied regularly onto backup disks or tapes. Those backups should then be stored, preferably in fireproof and locked cabinets, well away from the computer. Users should consider keeping the backup material in another building. Some users of personal computers keep a set of backup disks at home. It is, of course, essential that the backup process should be carried out rigorously and regularly, so that there is never a danger of losing a significant amount of information. It was reported in 1987 that a fire at the Open University Computer Centre in Milton Keynes had destroyed both the computer and large amounts of irreplacable research data. The data had been backed up, but many of the backups were stored in the same (wooden) building as the computer. Fortunately many of the staff using the computer had their own personal backup copies of important data in offices, briefcases and at home.

Apart from backups on disks and tapes it is possible to 'dump' the contents of files and databases onto paper print-out, which can then be safely stored. The print-out can itself be reduced to microfilm or microfiche format, or, using the latest technology, to CD-ROM.

One backup method is to use three sets of disks or tapes. This is the 'grandfather-father-son' technique. Each day a backup copy of current data is taken, this is the 'son' copy. On the next day a new backup is made, becoming the 'son', the original 'son' becomes the 'father'. On the third day the 'father' becomes the 'grandfather', the 'son' becomes the 'father', and a new 'son' is added to the family. Thereafter the disks are used in rotation, the oldest becoming the new backup for the day. Each generation of disks should be kept safely, in physically different locations.

Unfortunately, the author's experience indicates that even this apparently foolproof technique is liable to failure! An experimental database had been established for teaching purposes and was available to numbers of users in a network of microcomputers. The database grew in a matter of months to contain over 2000 records. The database was regularly backed up onto floppy disks using the 'grandfather-father-son' technique. One day it became clear that the database on the network had been corrupted: an index file was split in two, making it impossible to retrieve records from the database. The most recent backup disks were used in an attempt to restore order, but it was found that the backups themselves were corrupted. The computer had allowed the damaged file to be transferred in its damaged state to the backup disks. The next set of backups proved to contain disks that were physically damaged. Again, the backup process had ignored the damage. The last set of disks, some three days old, actually worked! Thereafter every disk to be used as a backup was rigorously checked and formatted before being used.

Another security problem, common to both centralized and distributed systems, is the unattended office. Computer terminals or microcomputers are left in offices that are temporarily unoccupied. If those terminals are switched on, and even worse, logged in to the system, it requires only a few moments' work for some intruder to cause havoc with the system, or simply to copy data onto a floppy disk. Unattended terminals should be switched off, or at least logged-off, with their keyboards locked if possible, and all their floppy disks should be removed from sight.

There has been recent publicity given to the 'software virus'. This is a computer program capable of working invisibly within a computer to destroy active programmes and data stored on hard disks. The virus is injected into the computer when an apparently innocent program is run, usually from a floppy disk. Viruses may also be contained in programs downloaded from public 'bulletin boards' or databases. There is no easy cure for such a virus, only prevention works. Floppy disks and programs must be obtained only from reputable sources. As was the case with the database described above, floppy disks should be formatted before use, preferably using a computer utility that writes over any files already resident on the disk.

Distributed systems, and stand-alone PCs, are particularly vulnerable to power supply variations. In an office environment the computer will probably be plugged into the same electrical mains circuit as the photocopier, the electric kettle, and even the air-conditioning unit. As these devices are switched on and off electrical surges and 'spikes' are injected into the mains. These disturbances can cause corruption of data, or even system failure. A complete power failure, due to a blown fuse, will cause the loss of all work in progress on office computers and may damage disk files that may be open at the time.

Great care should be taken to isolate the supplies to microcomputers as much as possible, by connecting them to a dedicated circuit or by fitting them with devices to filter out mains spikes. Small battery-driven inverter units can be bought to supply power for a few minutes in the event of a complete power failure. This will be long enough for the computer operator to save essential data and to remove floppy disks from the machine.

People security

Only authorized users should be allowed access to information systems. Most networked systems and all mainframe installations require users to input details about themselves before access is given to programs or data. Users should have log-in identities and passwords. The identity code is usually issued to users by the system manager, the password is a matter of personal choice and often consists of a number of letters and numbers. Unfortunately, we all find it hard to remember codes, so the temptation is to choose a password that we can easily remember. We may use the registration number of our car, the name of a member of the family, our date of birth, or some similarly memorable code. What we find easy to remember will be easy for others to guess: there is in fact a published list of the most popular passwords!

Security can only be ensured if passwords are carefully chosen to be obscure and if they are frequently changed. Some computer systems require users to change passwords at regular intervals; if the code is not changed, the user will eventually be denied access to the system.

Microcomputer systems do not usually require users to enter passwords. However, many business software packages can be set up to require a password before the user can gain access to data. Special care needs to be taken where computers are linked to public communications networks by auto-dialling modems. The user may program the modem not only to dial up and connect to the remote service, but also to send the identity code and password. Any other person, given access to the computer, could easily perform the same operation.

Some computer operating systems contain facilities to make development work easier. This is done by simplifying the access arrangements and by providing special log-in facilities for demonstrations and casual users. Such access is often restricted to a small proportion of the computer's programs and data, but it could be enough to cause real trouble. The system manager must ensure that access to the system is not easily obtained by unauthorized users and log-in processes may have to be changed to achieve the necessary security. The question of security of information is dealt with in more detail in Sec. 7.4 of this book.

Data security

Much business information is commercially sensitive and must be protected for that reason; it may also relate to individuals. Users of confidential and personal information must be aware of the responsibility to guard such information. They should also be aware of the legal regulations relating to data and computer systems. The requirements of the Data Protection Act in the UK have been described in Sec. 5.7.

12.6 Management responsibilities

We have seen that the introduction of information systems into organizations can have very wide consequences, affecting every aspect of the organization and the people in it. Such change needs very careful management by managers who themselves may be affected by the change. Even the most traditional managers can learn to survive in the information age if they are sufficiently interested and flexible and if they are sympathetic to new ideas.

When an information system is being planned the project team should not forget the senior management of the organization, they need information, reassurance and training just as much as the middle and junior management levels. It is the senior levels of the business that should be able to use the power of the information system to make better decisions and it is they who will ensure that the system is used effectively throughout the organization.

Managers at all levels should be kept up-to-date with new system developments. This can be done by circulating relevant magazines and newspapers, or by arranging occasional briefing sessions. In one major UK company the information systems department has set up a computer shop, where management and staff can inspect the latest equipment and receive guidance in its use and where they may buy equipment for their offices. This has the dual effect of giving apparent freedom of choice while ensuring compatibility with other equipment and systems.

Information technology is changing rapidly: management must learn to change at the same rate.

12.7 Conclusion

We have seen how internal politics and people issues are as important as technical issues in designing and implementing information systems. Although informal distributed computing systems are now common, they have disadvantages as well as advantages and can cause problems for organizations unless carefully controlled. Staff have real fears about the introduction of new technologies and systems and must be reassured, through consultation, negotiation, familiarization, training and support. System security in distributed systems is now the responsibility of the individual user who must exercise great care in protecting and backing-up important data. Systems must be protected against interference and unauthorized access.

In the next chapter we will look at ways in which information can be used more effectively by managers.

Reference

1. David J. Oborne, *Computers at Work*, John Wiley & Sons, 1985.

13
Using the information

13.1 Introduction

Earlier in this book we have been reminded that the chief purpose of information systems in business is to aid *decisions* which then lead to *actions*. We have also seen how different types of information and decisions could be found at different levels in an organization. At the top of the organization where long-range strategic decisions are made there is a need for more externally-based and qualitative information. At the bottom of the organization the information will be used for and derived from operational processes and will consist largely of financial and performance data.

In Sec. 8.13 a distinction was drawn between information used for intelligence or background data and that used for decision making. A further distinction was made between information for operational, short-term decisions and that needed for longer-term strategic planning.

The information system designer and manager must find effective ways of handling information at all points in the system. Much effort will have gone into providing the most appropriate processing and storage facilities. Procedures will have been established for inputting information to the system by collecting it from within the organization or from external sources. What happens then? What use is actually made of all this information? There are, unfortunately, many cases where the provision of an information system has not materially affected the decision making in an organization because insufficient thought has been given to the extraction, communication and effective presentation of the information to managers.

13.2 What information?

One of the essential features of information systems is the *communication* of information to the people who need to act upon it. Communication of business information may be by means of the written or spoken word, or through telecommunications and computer-based information systems. There are two basic elements of such communication, the medium and the message. The medium, or practical means whereby the information is communicated, has been described in Chapter 5. In this chapter we are more concerned with the 'message'. All too often 'information' is thought to be the same as 'data', with the result that managers find themselves submerged in seas of paper and statistics. Many managers will be familiar with the situation in which the Board or Executive Committee of a company calls for monthly management information or management reports. These often consist simply of piles of computer print-out or endless tables of numbers; in more enlightened organizations there may be a few diagrams and graphs. The information so presented is often out-of-date, so that management decisions are based on statistics that have already been overtaken by events and are useless for efficient control of company operations. How is the busy manager to make sense of the data so that it can be used for the competitive advantage of the company? How can it be turned into *decisions* and then into *actions*?

13.3 Decision support

Businesses are faced with a variety of problems, some short-term, others long-term. Computer-based information management techniques and systems can offer help whatever the time-scale of the problem. The use of information for problem solving, planning and decision making is described by the term 'decision-support' and it is important to note that information systems are not seen as taking over the decision-making functions of the manager. Information technology and systems can provide powerful tools to enable the manager to work better and to make better decisions.

We have already seen that at the lower levels of an organization information is of an operational nature, often serving a Transaction Processing System (TPS). Basic facts and figures relating to company operations, customers, materials, etc., are required to be communicated and processed in well-defined ways. At the middle and upper levels of the organization, however, information needs to be interpreted and assessed for its relevance and importance in particular situations and for particular problems; only then can it be supplied to Decision Support Systems (DSS). Communication of the information to the decision-makers must therefore allow for alternative ways of accessing and presenting it so that information is in the most appropriate form. The information needs to be packaged or formatted to suit the special requirements of the manager or management group that is using it.

Computer models may be constructed, to be fed with data from the company database or from outside sources. Sensitivity analysis of key business forecasts will be carried out, 'what-if' questions will be asked. The information system should communicate with the users in a simple and supportive way, encouraging exploration and experimentation.

Short-term decisions

Short-term decisions will be those concerned with such matters as transaction processing, inventory control, book-keeping and invoicing. The kinds of decisions to be made will include how much of a product or service to make or sell, and at what price. Orders and stock levels are controlled, bills and receipts are prepared and the accounts are kept. Managers will be able to make better decisions on these matters if they have rapid and easy access to the latest information. Simple business models, to calculate business ratios, stock levels, income and expenditure can be used. Such models can easily be constructed using familiar spreadsheet packages like LOTUS 1-2-3 or SUPERCALC. Figure 13.1[1] illustrates a simple LOTUS model of the cash-flow forecast for a small company.

Decisions about what sales must be achieved to give a certain return or profit, or the timing of capital investment, can be made with the assistance of this model. New values for sales figures, or for capital investment are entered into the cells in the spreadsheet. The model is then recalculated and the new values of profit, return, etc. can be seen. The skilled user can write 'macros', short computer programs in the LOTUS language, that will automatically test different values of variables in the spreadsheet and present the results in tabular or graphical form. Those results will allow managers to experiment with a number of different options before making a decision about the preferred course of action.

As the manager looks further into the future, or as the decisions to be made involve more complex factors and relationships, so the difficulties of making realistic models increase. The spreadsheet user would have to ask a great number of 'what if' questions in order to explore the full range of possible outcomes for a project involving considerable risk or uncertainty. All forecasts of future events are, of course, largely guess-work. However, given sufficient information, the forecaster can make very intelligent guesses. Simple forecasting models can be built around the analysis of past trends, then those trends can be extrapolated into the future. Trend forecasting is based on the assumption that the past trend will continue: it would obviously be better to know something about the future itself.

Probabilistic methods

Facts about the future cannot be known with any certainty, but it is possible to make assumptions about the range of possible values or outcomes of any future variable or event. Statistical analysis can then indicate the probability of that event occurring. That technique is used in decision-support packages such as the BASICS (Battelle Scenarios in Corporate Strategy) program

MINT ALUMINIUM CASTINGS
PROJECT CASH FLOWS
IRR Calculation

	1986	1987	1988	1989	1990	1991	1992	1993	1994	1995	TOTAL
Sales	52.5	240	285	352.5	390	427.5	472.5	502.5	525	550	3797.5
Contribution @ 40%	21	96	114	141	156	171	189	201	210	220	1519
Deduct Directly identifiable fixed costs	68	58	63	68	73	77	81	86	90	95	759
Net Contribution (1)	−47	38	51	73	83	94	108	115	120	125	760
Deduct Tax Allowances	−135.2	−44.825	−34.918	−27.489	−21.917	−17.738	−14.603	−12.252	−10.49	−21.068	−340.5
Taxable Income	−182.2	−6.825	16.082	45.511	61.083	76.262	93.397	102.748	109.51	103.932	419.5
Tax(payable) Recoverable (2)		68.325	2.389	−5.629	−15.929	−21.379	−26.692	−32.689	−35.962	−60.39	−127.956
Capital Expenditure (3) *Startup	−382.35										
*Additional/ disposal	0	−87.25	−6.3	−9.45	−5.25	−5.25	−6.3	−4.2	−3.15	253.5 / 433.5	−256 / −76
After Tax Cash Inflow/ (Outflow) (1-2-3)	−429.35	19.075	47.089	57.921	61.821	67.371	75.008	78.111	80.888	318.11 / 498.11	376.044 / 556.044
Net Cash Flow (1)	−429.35	19.075	47.089	57.921	61.821	67.371	75.008	78.111	80.888	318.11	376.044
Net Cash Flow (2)	−429.35	19.075	47.089	57.921	61.821	67.371	75.008	78.111	80.888	498.11	556.044
IRR (1)	10.42										
IRR (2)	13.19										

Figure 13.1 LOTUS Spreadsheet 'MINT'

produced by the Battelle Institute and the PREDICT package produced by Risk Decisions Ltd in the UK.

The BASICS package allows the user to input 'descriptors' – factors relating to some future state or event. A range of values for each of the descriptors is also input to the program, together with an assessment of the statistical probability of each of those values occurring. The user then estimates the statistical probability of any one value for each variable affecting each of the others. This process of 'cross-impact analysis' continues until the cross-impact matrix is complete. The computer then calculates the most probable combinations of factors and outcomes. This technique is used to build 'scenarios', or pictures of alternative futures, for long-range planning and decision making. 'What if' questions can be asked by inputting new values to the model and then recalculating the 'occurrence matrix'.

PREDICT is a spreadsheet-type model. Unlike LOTUS its cells can contain more than one value. Each cell of the model can contain a list of values, or a statistical distribution. The normal mathematical, financial and statistical functions are available to create relationships between rows, columns and cells. A random number generator is used to select values from each cell to perform calculations, so that if the user decides to perform 100 iterations of the model a whole range of output values will be obtained. In fact the output from such a model is itself in the form of a statistical distribution. By this means a great number of possible options and outcomes can be tested and the decision maker is presented with a mathematical picture of the likelihood of success or failure of a project.

Figure 13.2 shows a PREDICT worksheet with the contents of one cell displayed. Figure 13.3 shows the results of calculating that simple model 200 times in the form of probability distributions.

At the most senior level of the organization, the strategic management level, considerable degrees of uncertainty will surround long-range forecasts. Management information will be treated much more subjectively than is the case with short-term matters. Indeed, a recent *Financial Times* article revealed that research among senior managers had shown that important decisions were often made wholly subjectively, the decision maker then seeking data to justify the decision. Strategic decisions are complex, often covering a wide range of disciplines and needing considerable amounts of information from outside the organization. As well as using numerical, quantitative, information managers may wish to explore qualitative issues to do with the policies, objectives and values of the organization as well as taking account of their own experience.

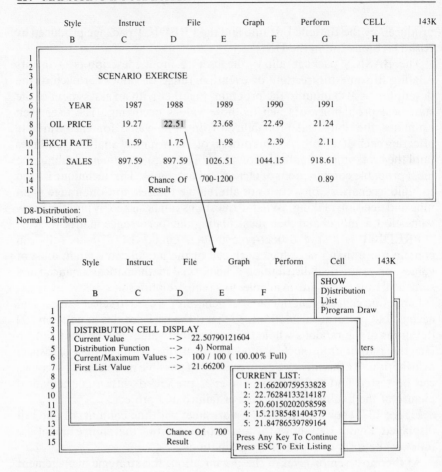

Figure 13.2   PREDICT worksheet (one cell displayed)

Qualitative methods

Techniques of qualitative analysis and decision making are less well-known than the familiar spreadsheets and business planners but they are a powerful means of bringing qualitative information to bear on management decisions. An example of the qualitative approach is seen in 'COPE' (COgnitive Policy Evaluation), originally developed at the University of Bath by Dr Colin Eden, now at the University of Strathclyde[2,3] In this technique situations or problems are described in short statements, or concepts. A discussion about a problem can be represented as a series of concepts, each leading from another as explanations or consequences. Eventually a map of the problem is built up of concepts and the causal links between them. Figure 13.4 shows

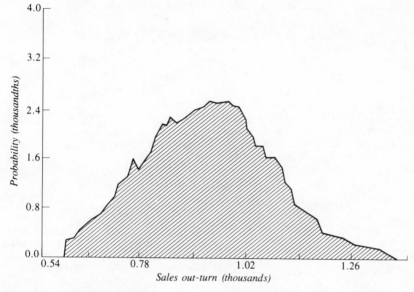

Figure 13.3   PREDICT graph

a typical COPE map. Each concept is in two parts, a positive pole and a negative pole. The two parts represent either alternative views of a concept or opposite views. This representation allows the analyst to explore alternative solutions. The concepts and the links between them are entered into a computer which stores the map as a kind of ideas database. The program is then able to group concepts into topic areas, to explore alternative routes between key concepts, to suggest alternative strategies and to draw the user's attention to key issues. If required, the user can engage in a dialogue with the computer, developing a model by means of a question and answer session.

The COPE technique is wholly qualitative, it contains no numbers or weightings which might otherwise inhibit the exploration of ideas and alternatives. LOTUS 1–2–3 and COPE are evidently at two ends of a spectrum of decision-support techniques. At one end of the spectrum are wholly numerical models, at the other end are wholly qualitative models. Probabilistic and scenario programs such as PREDICT and BASICS, are near the middle of the spectrum. Expert systems, with their combination of qualitative opinion, judgement and quantitative rule bases, also belong in the middle part of the spectrum. The bringing together of such techniques, through sharing of common databases and by transferring data from one type of analysis to another, promises to provide immensely powerful tools for management decision makers in future.

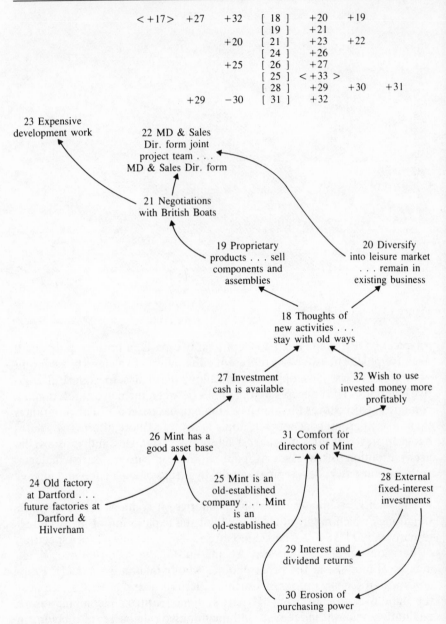

```
        < +17 >   +27   +32   [ 18 ]   +20   +19
                              [ 19 ]   +21
                        +20   [ 21 ]   +23   +22
                              [ 24 ]   +26
                        +25   [ 26 ]   +27
                              [ 25 ]  < +33 >
                              [ 28 ]   +29   +30   +31
                  +29   -30   [ 31 ]   +32
```

23 Expensive
development work

22 MD & Sales
Dir. form joint
project team . . .
MD & Sales Dir. form

21 Negotiations
with British Boats

19 Proprietary
products . . . sell
components and
assemblies

20 Diversify
into leisure market
. . . remain in
existing business

18 Thoughts of
new activities . . .
stay with old ways

27 Investment
cash is available

32 Wish to use
invested money more
profitably

26 Mint has a
good asset base

31 Comfort for
directors of Mint

24 Old factory
at Dartford . . .
future factories at
Dartford &
Hilverham

25 Mint is an
old-established
company . . . Mint
is an
old-established

28 External
fixed-interest
investments

29 Interest and
dividend returns

30 Erosion of
purchasing power

Figure 13.4   COPE map 'MINT'

13.4 Looking at the information

Displaying the information

Modern computers and information systems are capable of turning raw data into attractive graphs and charts, which themselves can be incorporated into written reports or can be turned into slides for projection. Recent developments in hardware and software put 'desk-top publishing' within the reach of most businesses. Managers can therefore prepare high-quality presentations of business material for their colleagues to inform, challenge or to exhort them. The transfer of data into graphs and charts is eased by the adoption of one of the 'standards' for database format, such as those used by LOTUS 1–2–3 or DBASE 111. Graphs derived from spreadsheet programmes can be imported into specialized graphics programmes: the user can then add special symbols, colours, etc. to improve the appearance and impact of the presentation. Figure 13.5 is a version of the COPE map from Fig. 13.4 imported into FREELANCE, then enhanced and printed on a laser printer.

The computer screen itself is a powerful medium for the communication of management information. Information derived from a company database may be extracted, formatted and presented on the screens of desk-top computers in the managers' offices. Alternatively, screens of information may be downloaded from the computer and projected onto large display screens, either from a TV-projector device or from a specially-equipped overhead projector.

The TV projector devices are large, heavy and very expensive, costing in the region of £10 000, but they can display full colour pictures. The overhead projector device is a liquid crystal screen, connected to the video output from a computer, which is mounted on top of the screen of an ordinary OHP. Computer displays are shown in various shades of blue and care must be taken to avoid certain colours in the computer output that will not be projected. This device is simple, but is portable and cheap, costing less than £1000.

Information centres

The advantage of using the computer as a processing and communications aid for management information is that the process may be made interactive. Managers can experiment with computer models, ask 'what if' questions and explore alternative strategies before making decisions. No commercial risks are involved and even the most unlikely scenarios can be explored without risk.

Following the military example, of equipping command and control centres and operations rooms, some organizations have developed the

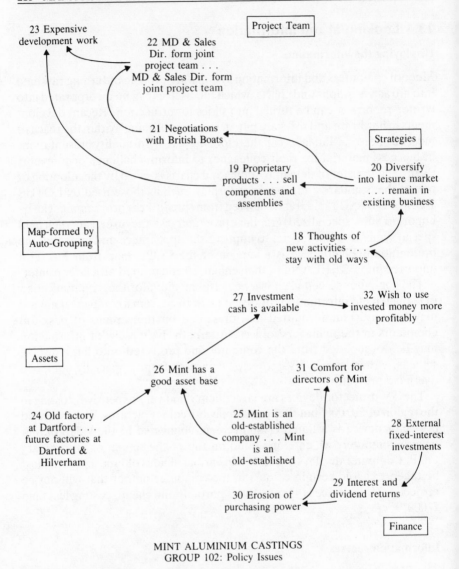

MINT ALUMINIUM CASTINGS
GROUP 102: Policy Issues

Figure 13.5 COPE map redrawn in 'FREELANCE'
Source: Smith and Ray, 'Mint aluminium castings, a case study', Henley – The Management College, 1987.

process of communication even further. Special 'decision centres' have been constructed in which computer-generated information can be projected onto the walls of a conference room. Computer consoles inside the room are used to control and to explore the company database and external information sources. Such facilities can be used for decision-making, strategic planning, or other information-rich processes.

The computer company ICL have developed a facility called 'The POD'. This is a small octagonal room, occupying a site only 6 metres square. The room is equipped with an octagonal central table surrounded by swivel chairs. Each wall of the room is equipped with some form of display surface, a whiteboard, a projection screen or a computer screen. Visual aids, such as 35mm projector, overhead projector, etc. are installed in a ceiling unit. All the equipment in the room can be controlled from a hand-held infra-red controller. Adjacent to the room is a small bay containing audio and computer equipment which may be operated either by a secretary or by an 'information engineer'. In this self-contained environment managers can be immersed in the information required for decision making and can interact with computer models and simulations.

One way of using a facility like the POD, apart from real-time decision making, would be to set up an information centre in an organization where information relating to some proposed strategic decision could be displayed. Managers could then explore the information in advance of the decision-making meeting and become familiar with the options available and their consequences using some of the techniques described above. In this way the decision-making process would be greatly enhanced.

13.5 Applying the information

Management information systems exist to further the aims of the business. If applied at the operational level they can improve productivity and efficiency. At the management level they may open up new ways of doing business, tackling problems and making decisions. At the strategic level they permit simulation and experimentation.

Ideally, the processes that give rise to different types of management information should be iterative and adaptive, meaning that they should 'learn' and develop as they are used. Users of database programs can save a great deal of time if they record commonly-used search strategies. Similarly, programmes designed to extract and present management information and models to simulate business activities should become more refined and powerful as the strategies to extract and to process information from them are refined. The manager will then be able to predict the future activities of the organization more and more accurately. Just as organizational development is an essential process for the future success of any business, so the development and refinement of information systems has a vital role. As information handling and communications processes improve within the organization so more and more information becomes available to be effectively processed. The organization learns and improves its performance through the growing effectiveness of its management and use of information.

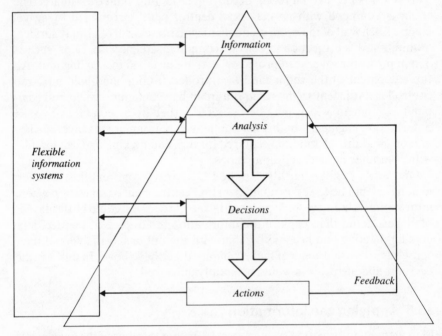

Figure 13.6 The learning organization

13.6 Conclusion

The efficient extraction and effective presentation of information is vital to the success of the organization, raw data is of little use unless meaningful information is extracted from it. A great advantage of information technology and systems is that they allow managers to experiment and to simulate business situations. While many operational decisions may be made with quantitative information, senior managers making strategic decisions will need means of dealing with qualitative information also. Business information can be effectively communicated in graphical form. Organizational learning and performance improvement comes through the effective use of information for planning and decision making.

References

1. J. E. Smith and G. H. Ray (ed. P. J. A. Herbert), *'Mint Aluminium Castings, A Case Study'* Henley, The Management College, 1987
2. Colin Eden, Sue Jones, David Sims, *Messing About in Problems*, Pergamon, 1983
3. Colin Eden, Sue Jones, David Sims, *Thinking in Organisations*, Macmillan, 1979

14.
The Future of
Information Systems

14.1 Introduction

Modern information systems, although firmly founded on well-established basic technologies, have only a short history. It is unwise to base predictions about the future on trends established over a short time, but given the kinds of technological developments described in Chapter 7 it is possible to outline the future course of development of information systems.

Not only the systems will change. We have already seen how the nature of an information system is closely related to the organization that it serves. Organizations will change in the future, but now the impetus for change may be reversed. Whereas early information systems followed organizational change it is now more likely that developments in information systems will, in future, facilitate organizational change. Today, an organization wishing to improve its competitive position will devise an information system that enables it to act faster and more effectively than a competitor. The capability of future systems will be such that business activities may be seen as adding value to business. This concept will be discussed in more detail later.

14.2 The information organization

Conventional organizational structures, like those discussed in Chapter 8, are based on hierarchies of management. Those hierarchies are themselves based on seniority, experience and knowledge. Those at the top of the organization are assumed to have broad experience and extensive knowledge about the business and its environment. The bringing together of that knowledge and experience constitutes wisdom which is used to direct the affairs of the organization.

Wisdom is applied knowledge which itself is applied information. If some way could be found of making information and its processing available to everyone in an organization what kind of structure would develop? Imagine the situation in which an organization has an extensive database of information about all its activities. Details of customers, clients, stocks, orders, costs, prices, performance, forecasts and other items of management information are readily available through an information system. Many of the day-to-day decisions about company operations have been programmed into PDSs, all transactions are handled by TPSs, decision support systems help with short- and long-term decision-making and planning. What need is there now for a management hierarchy? What need is there for the organization to be in one place? Figure 14.1 illustrates the 'data-based organization'. Just as the developments in telecommunications and computing technologies are making the virtual network possible, as described in Sec. 11.6, so they make possible the 'virtual firm', an idea introduced in Sec. 8.11. This would be an organization that exists in name only. Its employees would offer their professional services on a daily, or even an hourly, basis and would work remotely over an information system. An entrepreneur wishing to set up some business operation requiring specific business skills could advertise for experts to provide those skills on an occasional basis. Once hired, those persons would be given access to the company database

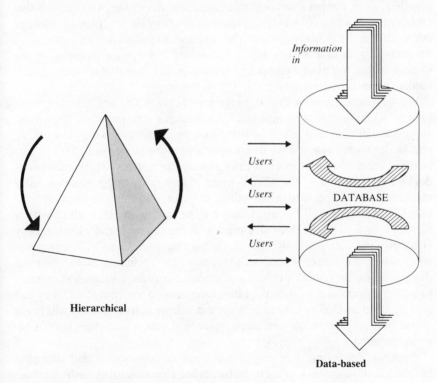

Figure 14.1 Data-based organization

and would then start to interact with other remote colleagues and with the information system. Provided matters of security and contract could be effectively dealt with this would be a good way of involving the housebound or disabled in business activities.

14.3 Transparent networks

The successful development of remote working, or 'networking', depends largely on the successful implementation of open systems architectures for information systems. Ideally the computing and communications networks of the world should be transparent to the user. In other words, it should be possible to connect a business or domestic computer terminal to any network or information source, anywhere in the world, without needing to know how that connection is made. That is what happens today with international telephone calls and it is only a matter of time before the spread of digital systems allows data 'calls' to be handled in the same way.

Universal networks could simply provide the means of connecting users together, or of connecting users to commercial databases. They could also add significant value to data traffic themselves. If intelligent processors were embedded in the public networks then even small businesses and individual users could gain access to powerful processing and storage facilities, in the same way that telephone customers can use public operator services, voice-banks and information services.

We have already seen the convergence of computing and telecommunications technologies that makes computer networks possible. That convergence will continue as public networks are converted to digital working and as the technology becomes cheaper and more powerful. There is currently a great revival of interest in facsimile, the electronic transmission of documents, because of the achievement of standards that make dissimilar machines compatible with each other. It is possible that the conventional facsimile machine will be overtaken by the microcomputer fitted with a facsimile unit. This enables documents to be scanned and electronically encoded. The electronic signals are then transmitted to another computer where they are reconstituted as plain text, in the image of the original document, on the computer screen. Electronic document scanners are likely to become popular as a means of inputting data to the computer, they can also be used as part of a facsimile system. Other convergencies will bring about the integration of text, data, voice and image into one multi-functional terminal.

Another interesting convergence is seen in automotive and domestic building technologies. Car manufacturers are experimenting with electronically-controlled electrical accessories, such as lights, locks, radio and engine controls. One electrical distribution 'ring' will carry current to all parts of the vehicle and will be switched to the appropriate devices by electronic signals carried on a data-link. Exactly the same technique is being proposed for houses and office premises. The electrical mains will be wired to all the electrical fittings which will then be controlled by data signals. To control such networks a computer of some kind is required. In the case of a domestic installation one can envisage the home computer controlling lighting levels, heating, security devices and the cooker while at the same time setting up long-distance data links to some remote database or dealing with the household's electronic mail.

14.4 Decision support systems

In Chapter 13 was saw how information and information technology could be used for supporting managers in the decision-making process. The nature of the technology at present is that data for decision-making must be collected from a number of sources, stored, processed and communicated almost every time a model is needed or a decision made. Once powerful simulation models of an organization's activities are constructed there is no reason why they should not run automatically. The system would contain details of information required from different worldwide sources. It would know what calculations to perform and what forecasts to make. Each manager could define a portfolio of information that was required for any special function or decision-making activity. The information system, using alternative futures or scenarios, could present alternative pictures of the future of the organization, perhaps offering them on a continuous basis in a decision support room like the POD.

14.5 The universal database

The success of all these future developments will, of course, depend on their usefulness to the business and domestic user. Essentially it is information that users want, presented in a wide variety of different forms. At present that information comes from a number of different places. Imagine carrying out a literature search on some business topic. It is necessary to go to a number of libraries and when there to examine a large number of different books, journals and papers in order to find the required information. Now that data storage is so cheap and convenient, using technologies such as the CD-ROM and digital paper, it can only be a matter of time before libraries, particularly those like the British Library that provide a comprehensive reference facility, begin to store their information in electronically-readable form. Public databases could be provided, based on optical or high-density magnetic storage technologies, giving access to enormous quantities of reference material. The researcher would then need a system that could be connected to any of these databases to perform searches for particular items of information. Searching techniques, using free text retrieval, are now very fast and with the advent of parallel processing will become faster still. It is possible to imagine a literature search, say for a PhD thesis, being done automatically overnight while the researcher sleeps peacefully in his or her electronically-controlled house.

14.6 What next?

Information systems have developed at a remarkable pace, but as this book has attempted to demonstrate, there is a human element in their use that is just as important as the technology. One could almost say that there were no more technical problems. Almost any desired network configuration or information requirement can be satisfied by existing technologies. Later generations of systems will be much faster, more powerful, and will be ubiquitous. It is the human element that is perhaps the chief determinant of change. The design, implementation and application of information systems is only limited by the imagination and ingenuity of the human beings that control them.

15
Conclusion

The three main parts of this book have identified the problem of information management, outlined the tools now available, and pointed the way for managers to find solutions relevant to their business. In this short concluding chapter we recap some of the main points, to consolidate the material and equip the manager to approach the information problems of his own organization with greater confidence.

Information is one of the main resources available to managers. It helps them achieve business results. Information is becoming more important because it is now a commodity in its own right – in fact the largest commodity in the economies of developed countries. For managers, information makes possible better decisions, which in turn lead to better actions and thus better results. Business information, and business information systems, must therefore be judged by the extent to which they lead to better decision, better action, and better business performance.

Information management is becoming more important on managers' agendas. The value of information itself, and the power of modern information technology for handling it, make this a more important subject for senior management than it was even five years ago. Information systems can affect the organization externally: the strategic relationship with the environment and the customer. They can affect the organization internally: the balance between task, team, and individual in getting the job done. They can affect people individually: the way they do their work, interact with colleagues, and develop the workstyle and lifestyle which suits them and the organization best. The senior manager must be concerned to draw all these facets together when making a strategic review of a business. We have reviewed some methods by which managers can make such a strategic review. The human aspect of this is vital. Senior managers, middle managers and IT professionals all have a different perspective. The insights from each corner of this ITernal Triangle need coordinating, rather than being allowed to come into conflict.

In Chapter 2 we examined three sectors of industry, and five functional areas which are found in most organizations. Together, they illustrate the changing nature of the business environment, the way organizations must continually change to meet fresh challenges, and the often vital role which information systems can play. Whether the enterprise is profit-making or service-providing the principles still apply. Chapter 3 brought the problem into sharper focus with some definitions. Information management is the informed response of the general manager to the opportunities of Information Technology (IT). It requires knowledge of the potential and limitations of IT; knowledge of the information systems currently available and the legal framework within which they operate; and the skill to relate this to the needs of business and then deal with specialists who will design and implement systems. These information systems comprise people, procedures and technology. They usually involve more than one mode of information handling from the basic list of four: text, data, voice, and image. It is important not to confuse data (often masses of numbers relating to detailed facts) with information (which has some useful relevance to a management problem).

Part 2 of the book looked more closely at IT. The emeregence of the electronic microchip has had a dramatic effect on IT. Handling information in the digital rather than analogue form, chips have become the underlying technology for both computing and telecommunications. Computers have developed more recently although the idea of a general purpose machine programmed to perform the task in hand is much older. We have examined both the hardware and software aspects of computing technology, illustrating the rapid advances in terms of the Personal Computer (PC) often used by managers. The emergence of application packages which meet the common needs of the office has been very important: word-processing, database, spreadsheet and graphics. The development of computers has meant that in most organizations they have penetrated bottom-up through the structure, starting with transaction processing systems and developing through information provision systems and now decision-support systems. There is likely to be a second wave of systems, making programmed decisions, and based on human knowledge rather than just on storage, calculation, and reporting. As management information systems like these become more numerous in the organization, it becomes more important to have a corporate database to hold the store of underlying facts about the business.

Telecommunications is a much older technology but there have been dramatic advances in recent years. It helps to keep in mind the way that human beings communicate with each other. Signs, language and pictures are all used in ways which suit the way our brains work. Modern IT should take account of this, rather than impose what happens to be technically convenient. The impact of digital technology on telecommunications has been gradual, because the largest system of all (the telephone network) still has a heavy investment in analogue technology at its edges. Transmission media have developed in capacity, notably with satellite communication and fibre-optic cable systems. Communication switching is now based on digital technology, under software control. Nevertheless, we still live in a mixed analogue and digital world. For digital data transmission, modems or separate data networks have to be used. The hope for the longer term is the Integrated Services Digital Network (ISDN) and the emerging Open Systems Interconnection (OSI) standards.

The legal framework for information systems is important. In several countries the deregulation of telecommunications has brought competition to the provision of basic telecommunication services. In a larger number of countries there is competition for the provision of Value-Added Networks and Value-Added Services which build upon basic telecommunications. The other legal development is data protection, which for an increasing community of nations imposes legal obligations for the protection of data about living identifiable individuals. Not only must the data be accurate and relevant for the legitimate registered purpose, but its transfer to other people or countries is strictly controlled.

Chapter 6 brought together the two technologies, to consider the current range of information systems available to business. There are several recent and important developments such as cellular radio and Local Area Networks which extend and integrate older systems. As the capacity of communications and of processing increase, the trend towards voice- and image-based services will continue. In countries like the UK the play of market forces means that economic arguments for particular types of system must be kept under regular review. The option of running private networks is still open, but not as attractive as it once was. There is a new category of managed networks which are attractive to some businesses who do not wish to rely totally on the public networks.

The future of IT is difficult to predict. The technology itself is still advancing at a dramatic rate, but its application in the form of working systems is controlled by economic factors which are often more difficult to judge. The perspective of the past teaches us to be cautious about saying that a new information age is imminent. Nevertheless some of the technical developments under the Fifth Generation Computing System project have already made an impact on business. More powerful chips, practical forms of parallel processing, and optical technology are examples of this. More powerful machines will support new kinds of software which will more closely emulate the way human beings solve problems and build up their knowledge and experience. Knowledge-based systems in the form of expert systems are already practical tools of management, enabling scarce human expertise to be encapsulated, formalized, and applied by people with lower levels, or different types, of skill.

Other developments are in the field of information security. Information can be abused by subverted people, and its protection is as necessary as the safeguarding of documents and cash in the normal office environment. To counter the threats of eavesdropping, illicit access, logic bombs and spoofing a range of measures, both technical and administrative, is necessary. Technology gives important new tools for this, but the personnel and procedural aspects remain of the greatest importance. Taken overall, developments in IT will continue to affect the way we conduct our business and domestic lives.

Part 3 of the book related the technology to the problems of business. In Chapter 8 we examined the relationship between organizational structure and information systems. Information flows in and around organizations performing an essential function, that of providing energy to business operations. It was emphasized that formal organization structures do not necessarily represent what really goes on and that information structures were a more realistic way of understanding the activities of an organization.

The organization was likened to a system that behaves in certain ways when information is input to it. It is important to know just what happens to the information inside a business, there may be losses or distortions. The nature of information itself was examined and it was emphasized that managers often have to deal with information that is incomplete or imprecise. Managers should always question the source and accuracy of information that they deal with. The computer will process whatever is given to it, often without comment. The information must be as accurate as possible, timely and appropriate for its purpose.

Chapter 9 introduced the idea of the 'project life cycle', a disciplined way of designing an information system project. Essential features of such projects were identified, such as gaining senior management support, consulting the users, defining the design requirements, etc. The importance of consulting everyone with an interest in the project was emphasized. Ways of looking at the organization were suggested. Input–output analysis, relevance analysis, and the information systems matrix were all offered as structured ways of defining the nature of the information system. These solutions are not meant to be prescriptive, they represent an ordered and thorough approach to system design.

The stages of the project outlined in Chapter 9 were all concerned with preparation: they were the 'thinking' stages. Time spent in thinking about projects is time well spent. It is easy to make expensive mistakes with information technology and systems and then to be stuck with them for long periods. Careful analysis and assessment of needs and opportunities for information systems in an organization will pay off handsomely in future.

The practical aspects of implementing information systems projects were dealt with in Chapter 10. Again, the importance of involving the potential users of the system in all stages of the project was emphasized. Project control was discussed, and two techniques, the Gantt chart and the critical path diagram were described. Again, these descriptions were not meant to be prescriptive, although they are extremely useful. They illustrated the need for order and discipline in establishing and controlling projects. The different types of project control charts are, in fact, simply a means of communication. They serve to keep all those involved in a project up-to-date with what is going on and to focus attention on problem areas. The charts should not be allowed to rule the project; on the other hand, they must not simply be updated every time there is a slippage. They are an information system in their own right and must be allowed to communicate their message effectively.

Chapter 11 attempts to bring together the technologies of communications and computing into information systems and networks. In doing so it repeats material from earlier chapters, but tries to add practical interpretations in a business context. The need for compatibility between systems and equipment was stressed. The only effective way of constructing large-scale systems and of sharing information within them is to ensure that the systems are 'open'. Being tied into one proprietary system or another closes off development options for the future. The possibility of a worldwide 'virtual network' is a real one. Digital systems will enable computers and telecommunications facilities to be directly connected together. Today's hardware, software and systems will look very quaint and limited in only a few year's time.

Chapter 12 attempts to deal with what are perhaps the most important issues relating to any information system, the problems of the people who have to use them. The information revolution has caused many casualties as it has displaced many office and less-skilled workers from their jobs. That was the result of 'office automation' and 'mechanization'. There is much more to come. The latest technologies and systems operate at the middle and senior levels of organizations and are likely to have a great effect on employment there.

The chapter suggests that peoples' fears about information technology may not easily be dispelled. Rather they must be dealt with head-on. Through programmes of information and consultation much of the resistance to new technology can be overcome and dispersed.

Perhaps easier to deal with, but just as vital, are issues of security. Information is the lifeblood of modern business and it must not be shed. Taking care of information, however it is stored, should be second nature to all information workers. It was emphasized that security is now the concern of everyone. Distributed information systems have shifted the burden of responsibility from the data processing experts to ordinary office workers. All information workers need to be aware of the risks arising from unattended terminals, unprotected disks, unsaved files, power failures and all the other dangers that are so easy to overlook.

Information systems are useless if they do not assist the organization in the achievement of its objectives. Chapter 13 looked briefly at ways in which information could be made to work in decision making. The techniques described, ranging from the wholly numerical and quantitative to the wholly non-numerical and qualitative are only examples of a wide range available to managers. The intention of the chapter was to encourage managers to think about ways in which information could be better employed and more powerfully communicated in their organizations. Computers are good at number-crunching. With expert systems and qualitative modelling techniques they will soon be as good at manipulating ideas. Bringing all these techniques together will provide managers with enormously increased capability for planning and decision making. Information systems are not just for the middle managers, the accountants and the shop-floor. They are becoming an essential feature of senior management activities. Present restrictions on computer hardware make some of the processes clumsy to use and senior people are naturally reluctant to waste their time in working a machine. The latest developments in communications, parallel processing and computer graphics, promise to open up a new world of information for all levels of business.

Chapter 14 is a brief excursion into that future for information systems. It envisages a universality of systems and information. What is not clear is whether or not the human element in systems is going to be able to develop at the same speed as the technology. When information becomes a commodity, who will control it? How will information providers make money when information is essentially free? What patterns of organization will evolve to make use of the capabilities of the new technologies?

These are rather philosophical questions, but so were questions about computing for managers only 10 years ago. The pace of change is so rapid that this book can only hope to offer a snapshot of the world as it is and a glimpse of the world as it might be in, perhaps, no more than a few years, or even a few months time. We hope that readers will have been encouraged to take a practical interest in information systems and that some of the mystique that has surrounded them in the past has been dispelled. The underlying theme of the book has been to examine information systems from the point of view of the *practical* manager. Now it is up to you to put the lessons into practice.

Glossary

Note: Words set in italic are cross-references.

A

Acoustic coupler   A device that allows a telephone to be used for transmitting data. The telephone handset fits into the coupler, which connects it to the transmitting network and at the same time blocks out external noise.

Activator   In systems theory, activator, *comparator* and *sensor* are the names given to the parts of a feedback mechanism. The 'activator' is the part that adjusts the system to give the required output.

Address   A number or label used to identify a location containing data or a program instruction, in a computer's memory.

AI   See *Artificial Intelligence*

ALU   Arithmetic and logic unit; the part of the computer's control processor that carries out arithmetical and logical operations on data sent to it.

Analogue   A form of *signal* in which a smoothly-varying physical quantity is represented by a smoothly-varying electrical voltage. An example is the signal from a microphone, which varies in accordance with the air-pressure variations (sound) reaching the microphone.

Apple   The American company that produced one of the earliest microcomputers, the Apple II, and currently produces a range including the Apple IIe, Macintosh and Macintosh XL.

Application   The practical use for which a computer program is designed. Word-processing, stock control and wage payment are all examples of applications.

Application program   A computer program that supplies a particular service to the end-user. Examples are stock control and payroll programs.

Array   An orderly set of *data*, where each item is identified by a subscript. The dimension of the array is the number of subscripts needed to identify an item. For example, the array could consist of days of the year. If it is one-dimensional, Friday, February 3rd will be identified by the number 34. If it is two-dimensional, the same date would be identified by day and month (32).

Artificial Intelligence (AI)   In a sense, there is no such thing as artificial intelligence. However, computers with very large memories can be programmed with sufficient data to make a series of decisions from one initial input, and to act in a manner which we can call intelligent. An *expert system* can demonstrate artificial intelligence. For example, an expert medical system can diagnose a patient's illness, on the basis of information fed into it by the patient.

ASCII   American Standard Code for Information Interchange. This is a system for representing alphanumeric characters and other symbols with binary numbers. For example, the letter J is represented in this system as 1001010.

ATM   Automated Teller Machines, often called cash dispensers.

B

Babbage Charles Babbage was the British engineer and mathematician who effectively invented the digital computer. Around 1833, Babbage put forward his design for an Analytical Engine, which incorporated all the basic concepts of computing. Not all Babbage's ideas could be put into practice in his time, since many of them required the power of electronics. Babbage was assisted in his work by Ada, Lady Lovelace, niece of Lord Byron, the poet.

Backing store The part of the computer's memory that contains programs and data not immediately needed for processing. The backing store has larger capacity, but slower access-time, than the computer's *main memory*. When needed, programs and data are transferred to it from the main memory. The backing store is also known as 'backing memory', 'secondary store' and 'auxiliary store'.

Backup storage A section of computer memory not generally available to users. It is used to provide security copies of certain classes of file.

Bar code A set of thick and thin printed black bars, representing a string of numbers, used for product identification in many stores. Each product has a unique bar code which is printed on the product itself, or on its wrapping. At the *point of sale*, the bar code is 'read' by a light-sensitive device called a *bar code reader*, linked to a computer. The computer cross-references the code with a price table in its memory, and prints out the details on the receipt. The computer also records details from the code, for updating the company's stock list. The result is that stock can be finely controlled, and popular items quickly spotted.

Bar code reader A light-sensitive device linked to a computer, for reading *bar codes* on items at *point of sale*.

BASIC A high-level programming language widely used on microcomputers. The initials stand for Beginners' All-purpose Symbolic Instruction Code. BASIC is designed to be easy to learn and use, for people with no previous programming experience.

Batch processing A method of data processing in which a large number of tasks are collected together, then processed in a batch. Tasks may be batched on a daily or weekly or monthly basis. Batch processing is therefore not suitable for applications that require processing in 'real time', for example airline bookings.

Baud A unit used to measure the speed of transmission along a communication line. The baud rate is the number of pulses that can be transmitted per second. Often 'baud' is the same as 'bits per second', so that a line with a baud rate of 2400 carries that many bits per second. However this is not always true, since bits can travel down a line two or more at a time.

Benchmark A test to gauge the performance of a computer system. Usually the benchmark is a program or group of programs with well-known results. When run on several different systems, it allows them to be compared. Benchmarking is sometimes used by purchasers to help them decide what system to buy.

Binary system A system of counting in which only the digits 0 and 1 are used. In the binary system:

> decimal '1' is represented by binary '1'
> decimal '2' is represented by binary '10'
> decimal '3' is represented by binary '11'
> decimal '4' is represented by binary, '100', and so on.

The binary system is a convenient basis for computing, where 1 can be represented by an electric pulse or magnetic charge, and 0 by the absence of a pulse or charge.

Bit Abbreviation for 'binary digit', that is 0 or 1. The bit is the basic unit of information storage in a computer. 1 is represented by an electric pulse or magnetic charge, and 0 by the absence of a pulse or charge.

Black Box   A term that can be used for any piece of apparatus that carries out a particular function within a system. The term is generally used to simplify discussion when the emphasis is on the input and output of the apparatus, and its function rather than its internal design.

Block   In computing, a block is a group of words, characters or digits that is treated as a unit of *data*. Data is transferred in the discrete blocks between the parts of the computer system.

Branch   A computer program may be able to take two or more possible directions, depending on some condition, or the result of a computation. The resulting program sequences are called branches.

Bubble memory   A compact way of storing large volumes of computer data. The bubbles are magnetized spots or domains in a thin film of magnetic material. A bubble in any location represents 1 and its absence 0. Bubbles can be moved around magnetically.

Buffer   In computing, a buffer or buffer store is a temporary storage location for data that is being transmitted between different units of the system. The buffer compensates for the different speeds at which the units can handle data. For example, a printer may accept data from a computer's central processing unit at a rate of 240 characters per second, but print it at only 30 characters per second. The data is stored in the printer's buffer while waiting to be printed.

Bug   An error in a computer program, or a fault in a computer system. Getting rid of bugs is called 'debugging'.

Bus   In a computer system, a bus is a conducting route along which signals can travel from one of several sources to one of several destinations. A bus is also known as a 'trunk' or 'highway'.

Byte   A binary number which represents a symbol or character (A–Z, a–z, 0–9, –, $, % and so on). A byte usually consists of 8 binary digits or bits. There are two common systems for translating characters into bytes: *ASCII* and EBCDIC. ASCII (American Standard Code for Information Interchange) is the international standard; EBCDIC (Extended Binary Coded Decimal Interchange Code) is an alternative which is less common now.

C

CAD   Computer Aided Design; use of computer systems to help the designer. CAD systems often provide data for subsequent automated manufacture.

CADCAM   Computer Aided Design and Manufacturing; see *CAD*.

CAE   Computer Aided Engineering; see *CAD*.

Cartridge   Container for magnetic disks or tapes, or for programmed chips, which are easily inserted into a computer and easily removed again.

Cathode ray tube   A device used to display information. The information is input at one end of tube in electrical form, and converted to light on a luminescent screen at the other end. Television sets and VDUs are built around cathode ray tubes.

Central Processing Unit (CPU)   This is the 'brain' of the computer. It has three parts:
- the primary memory unit,
- the arithmetic and logic unit (*ALU*),
- the control unit.

The memory sorts program instructions, data to be processed, and the results of the processing. The arithmetic and logic unit carries out the arithmetical and logical operations on data taken from the memory. The control unit fetches instructions in sequence from the memory, decodes them and activates the circuits needed to carry them out.

Chip A thin piece of semiconductor material (usually silicon), a few millimetres in each direction, on which are etched tens of thousands of electronic circuits. Chips are the basic components of modern computers. A single chip containing the central processor unit of a computer is called a *microprocessor*. *Microcomputers* are small computers built around microprocessors.

CIM Computer Integrated Manufacturing; see *CAD*.

Clock The rate at which a computer performs operations is controlled internally by a clock. The clock is an electronic device that generates signals at regular intervals. Each signal initiates an action within the central processing unit.

COBOL Common Business Oriented Language, a high level programming language designed for business applications.

Coding The writing of instructions for a computer. It is part of programming.

COM Computer Output to Microform; automatic recording of computer output on a photographic image. The images may be held on a strip (microfilm) or on a sheet (microfiche).

Communication The transfer of *information* between people, or of data between machines.

Communication network A system which provides, on demand, telecommunication between users. Users may be people or machines. The main elements of a communication network are signals (to represent the information), transmission (to convey the signals between predetermined points), and switching (to connect particular users for the duration of a call). An example is a telephone network: the audio/electrical interface is in the telephone handset; transmission is over cable or radio paths, and switching is done in the telephone exchanges.

Communications protocol A set of rules defining the way information will flow in a system. In all forms of communication, a protocol must be observed to ensure that the sender and receiver interact properly. The protocol may include rules on the structure of commands and responses, and the order in which they can occur.

Comparator In systems theory, comparator, *activator* and *sensor* are the names given to the parts of the feedback mechanism. The comparator is the part that compares the output of the system with the required output.

Compiler A compiler is a program for translating programs written in high level languages (such as *COBOL* and *BASIC*) into machine code. The compiler translates a complete program before running it. It therefore works faster than an *interpreter*, which translates programs one instruction at a time.

Computer A collection of components which enables you to put data in store, modify it, and get information out. Computers are usually divided into three classes:
- mainframes
- minicomputers
- microcomputers.

These divisions reflect the power, size and cost of the machines. Mainframes are large-scale computers. They can carry out up to 100 million instructions per second. They are generally used by large organizations which have centralized processing and storage requirements. Minicomputers are medium-scale. They are used within smaller organizations that still need powerful data processing facilities. They are capable of carrying out several million instructions per second. Microcomputers are at the lower end of the scale. They are used individually or in the networks and small operations.

Convergence   Three major industries, the computer, telecommunications, and office supply industries, are working towards the same point in their efforts to serve a common market: information management. This phenomenon is called convergence, and is made possible by a convergence of the underlying technologies of computing and communications, based on modern digital electronic circuits (chips).

Core memory   Computer memory was once composed of magnetic cores. This was the standard form of internal computer memory until the 1970s. The cores were tiny doughnut-shaped circles of magnetizable material threaded on wires. The term 'core memory' is still used to describe the fast working memory of a computer, even though is now comprises electronic chips.

CP/M   Control Program for Microcomputers; an operating system for microcomputers before *DOS* became the industry standard.

CPU   See *Central Processing Unit*

Cursor   The flashing symbol which draws attention to an active place on a computer display (VDU). It often indicates where the next character you type will appear on the screen.

D

Daisy wheel printer   A high-quality printer, so called because the print wheel is shaped somewhat like a daisy, with the characters round the outside of a disk.

Data   Numbers representing an observable object or event.

Database   A collection of related data held in a computer system, and organized so that many users can draw on it. A database usually needs large backing memories and a filing system developed with all potential users and applications in mind. The emphasis is on the sharing of data.

Database Management System (DBMS)   A software system for designing, setting up, and subsequently managing a *database*.

Data capture   The collection of data at the instant a transaction occurs. For example, a *bar code reader* at a checkout can capture all the data needed to identify a product, record its price on the customer's receipt, alter the stock figure for it, and even order a replacement from the warehouse.

Data dictionary   Part of a *database management system*. It is a record of each item of data held in the database and its characteristics (i.e. type and length).

Data protection   The safeguarding of data held on computer systems and which relates to living, identifiable, individuals. In the UK the 1984 Data Protection Act controls the automatic processing of personal data. This Act requires all users of automated personal data to register their systems with the Data Protection Registrar and to comply with specified principles of data use.

Data transmission   The transfer of data between computers or between a central computer and its terminals via a telecommunications network, such as the telephone system.

DBMS   See *Database Management System*

Decision Support System (DSS)   Software designed to help a manager carry out strategic planning. It does this by interacting with a *database* of past and current data. It allows the manager to identify trends, project into the future and examine the likely outcome of various courses of action. Some DSS even suggest courses of action for consideration by the manager.

Decision table   An 'if . . . then' table showing the action to be taken when certain conditions are met. Decision tables are used to help in problem solving and in documenting computer programs.

Digital   A form of *signal* in which a physical quantity is represented by a set of numbers. The numbers are usually in the *binary system*, i.e. patterns of 0s and 1s only.

Digital switching   See *communication network, digital*, and *switching*. The process of connecting digital transmission paths together, on demand, in order to establish telecommunication between persons or machine which require it. The telecommunication is wholly digital, so that patterns of 0s and 1s (binary signals) can be transmitted without corruption.

Digitizing plotter   Equipment for inputting drawings to a computer. It consists of a board and electronic 'pen'. By pressing a button on the pen, its position is recorded in the computer in digital form.

Direct access storage   Storage from which data can be extracted in a very short constant time, regardless of location. Compare with serial access, as on magnetic tape.

Disk/Disc   A flat circular device for storing *data*. The disk is coated with magnetizable material. Data is stored on it by selective magnetization of the surface. Disks can be 'hard' (made of coated metal) or 'soft' (made of vinyl). The latter are termed 'floppy disks', or 'diskettes'.

Disk drive   A mechanical device used to record data on, and retrieve data from, a magnetic disk. A disk drive includes a unit for rotating the disk and a read/write head.

Distributed data processing   Organization of data processing resources so that they are brought closer to the place where processing is required. The term is used to describe many different systems, such as: many terminals connected to a mainframe; a network of minis each with several terminals; a network of micros, sharing resources such as disk drives and printers.

DOS   Disk Operating System; an operating system for microcomputers held on a *disk*. Usually the one produced by Microsoft and which has become the industry standard; it is used on the first generation of IBM personal computers.

Dot matrix printer   A dot matrix printer forms each character from tiny dots. These are printed on the paper by print needles. The more dense the dots, the better the quality of the printed character.

Downloading   The process of moving data or programs from one system to another in electronic form.

DSS   See *Decision Support System*

E

EFT   Electronic Funds Transfer; a payment system which uses electronic information systems instead of paper-based information systems. For example, payments between banks can be made electronically instead of by a written instrument such as a cheque.

EFTPOS *Electronic Funds Transfer* at Point of Sale; a system in which a customer authorizes an EFT payment for goods at the place where they are sold to him.

Electronic office General term for the office fitted with electronic equipment: private branch telephone exchange, telex, electronic typewriters, copiers, computers, printers and so on. Most electronic offices of today are organized in a compartmentalized fashion, with the computer separated from other machines such as telex and facsimile. The result is that the office activities remain fragmented. An improvement is the integrated electronic office, where all the equipment is interlinked, so that data can be transmitted directly from one device to another. The office desk will become a multi-function work station, from which the user has access, at the touch of a button, to all the office facilities.

E-mail Electronic mail; a system which enables users at simple terminals in offices to send messages to each other electronically. Only if users wish to, need they make a 'hard copy' of such messages, on paper.

ENIAC The first electronic computer completed at the University of Pennsylvania in 1946. The initials stand for Electronic Numerical Integrator And Calculator. ENIAC was programmed by direct wiring, and had over 18 000 valves.

Entropy In information theory, entropy means the degree of 'mixed-upness' of information. The more mixed up it is, the less useful it becomes (like a jumble of letters, compared with clear written English). Any information system should be structured to ensure that entropy is at a minimum.

EPOS Electronic Point of Sale system; one which records electronically the details of sales made at a check-out point. Often the data is read from a *bar code* on the item sold, using a light-wand or laser-scanner. The data thus collected may be used for stock control, market research, and other purposes. An extension of EPOS is where the customer authorizes electronic payment; see *EFTPOS*.

EPROM Erasable Programmable Read Only Memory. A memory device can be read during use, but not written to. The contents of EPROM can, however, be erased and replaced using a special machine. Erasure is by means of ultraviolet light.

ESPRIT The European Strategic Programme for Research and Development in Information Technologies. This ten-year European (EEC) project started in 1984. It recognizes information technology as an area of major importance in the coming decades. The project's main areas of activity are: advanced microelectronics; software technology; advanced information processing; office systems (advanced integrated work stations, etc.); and the use of computers in manufacturing.

Ethernet A *local area network* (LAN), developed by Xerox, commercially available since 1980. Ethernet is basically a system for linking computers, word processors, printers, copiers, and all the other electronic devices within an organization, so that data can be transmitted between them. Ethernet has become the basis for a standard used by several manufacturers of LAN equipment.

Expert system A software package that provides 'expert' advice, and help with problem solving, in a specialized field such as mathematics, engineering or medicine. Knowledge is put into the system by a human expert, or a team of human experts, and this is added to in the light of experience so that the performance gradually improves.

F

Facsimile (FAX)   A method of transmitting copies of original documents electronically, using either the telephone network or modern digital data networks. Text, graphics, diagrams and handwritten copy are all transmitted equally easily, since they are all treated as pictures and automatically scanned.

Failsafe system   A computer system which is able to close itself down, without loss or disruption of data, in the event of a power failure or other breakdown. When started up again, it will resume processing at the point at which it ceased.

Feasibility study   Research into possible ways of solving a practical problem. In information management, it could be an assessment of the feasibility of using modern information systems to support the organization's activities, and a survey of available *hardware* and *software*, to see whether it matches the identified needs.

FGCS   Fifth Generation Computing Systems; see *Generation*. A type of computer system now being developed which has more powerful hardware, new types of software systems which emulate human problem-solving and intelligence, and interface with human users in convenient ways such as natural language, speech, and pictures.

Fibre-Optic Cable (FOC)   See *Optical Fibres*.

Field   An item of computer data. For example, a payroll record might have these four fields: employee number, gross pay, deductions, and net pay.

File   The familiar paper file is simply a collection of related data, kept together under a file name. It could be a file on customer orders, or personal details of employees. A computer file is much the same. It contains related data, held in electronic form, and is given a file name.

Firmware   Computer software sorted on a chip, so that it can be read, but not written to, during use. It could be a word-processing chip fitted into the computer, for example. Firmware is held permanently in ROM (*Read Only Memory*) or semi-permanently in *EPROM* (Erasable Programmable Read Only Memory).

Flexible Manufacturing Systems   Automated production systems which can easily be re-programmed to make a different product; computer-controlled production.

Floppy Disk   See *Disk*.

Flowchart   A computer program flowchart is a diagrammatic representation of the sequence of operations in the program. A system flowchart shows the flow of data through the system.

FOC   Fibre-Optic Cable; see *Optical Fibres*.

Font reader   A light-sensitive device that can scan printed pages and feed the information from them directly into a computer; an *Optical Character Reader* (OCR).

FORTRAN   A high-level computer language used mainly for scientific and engineering applications. Its name comes from FORmula TRANslator.

G

Generation   Term describing the stages in the development of computer systems. First generation machines used thermionic valves, second generation machines used transistors, and third generation machines used *integrated circuits*. Present state-of-the-art computers are fourth-generation. The Japanese and western nations are currently involved in a ten-year project to develop the fifth generation; see *FGCS*.

Geostationary satellite Satellite in orbit around the earth, moving so that it always appears to be above the same point on the earth's surface. This makes it particularly useful for telecommunication purposes.

GIGO 'Garbage in, garbage out'. The principle stating that results produced from unreliable data are equally unreliable.

Graphics Graphs, pie-charts and other diagrammatic ways of presenting *data* so that it becomes useful *information*. Computer graphics are classed as high-resolution, medium-resolution, or low-resolution. High-resolution graphics can show fine lines and smooth curves. In low-resolution graphics lines are thicker, and curves can only be approximated by a string of small blocks.

H

Hard copy Printed copy of messages, data, etc. output from a system. Compare with more transient forms of display, such as a VDU screen.

Hard disk A magnetic storage device; see *Disk*.

Hardware The electrical circuitry and physical devices that make up a computer system.

High Level Languages (HLLs) Computer languages that are close to ordinary English, and match the application for which they are used. *FORTRAN, COBOL* and *BASIC* are all high-level languages designed for particular applications. COBOL, for example, was designed for business use. A COBOL payroll program might contain these instructions:
  Multiply hours by rate giving gross pay
  Subtract tax from gross pay giving net pay
Such instructions can easily be understood by the business user.

I

IBM International Business Machines, an American electronics company that has achieved the largest share of the world computer market (over 60 per cent). In the field of personal computers (PCs), the IBM standard soon became a standard for most of the industry; hence the term 'IBM-compatible'.

ICL International Computers Ltd, a British computer company that makes mainframes, minis, and micros.

Index An index in computing is in many ways like the index of a book. It is an ordered reference list for the contents of a computer file, and enables the user to have rapid access to the required data.

Information Human significance associated with an observable object or event. Often comprises *data* selected to be relevant to a particular purpose.

Information system A collection of procedures, activities, people and technology set up for the collection of relevant *data*, its processing to help provide answers to a specific set of questions, and the *communication* of the resulting *information* to the people who need to act upon it.

Information Technology (IT) All the *hardware* and *software* that has been developed for the collection, storage, processing, and communication of information. It includes computers, word processors, private automatic branch exchanges, photocopiers, fax machines, bar code readers and so on. A formal definition of IT is 'The convergence of computing and telecommunications made possible by modern microelectronics'. The UNESCO definition is 'Scientific technology, engineering disciplines, and the management techniques used in information handling and processing; their application; computers and their inter-action with men and machines; and associated social, economic and cultural matters'.

Information theory   Theory concerned with the rate of transmission of information over a *communication network*. It treats information as a collection of symbols or signals.

Input device   Device for the input of *data* to a computer system. Keyboards, mice, light pens, joysticks, and touch-sensitive screens are all input devices.

Input–output (I/O) device   A device that can be used for both input and output in a computer system. The visual display unit (*VDU*) is an example. The keyboard is the input portion while the monitor is the output device.

Integrated Circuit (IC)   A small *chip*, usually made of silicon, which contains a number of interconnected electronic components. In the chip industry, the current trend is towards *Very Large-Scale Integration* (VLSI), which means packing tens of thousands of components into the same small chip.

Interface   The point of contact, connection, or interaction between different de-vices. There is much effort to formulate standards for interfaces, rather than standardizing the devices themselves. See *OSI*.

Interpreter   *Software* for translating a computer program from a *high-level language* to *machine code*. Each instruction is translated and then executed very quickly, thus speeding up the development process. Compare with a *compiler*, which translates a complete program before executing any of it.

ISDN   Integrated Services Digital Network; a *communication network* which oper-ates wholly in the digital mode, from user to user. It offers high speed (64 000 bits per second) switched connections, which can carry digital signals representing information in any of the four modes: text, data, voice, and image.

J

Joystick   See *input device*

K

Keypad   Device for inputting data to a computer or microprocessor. It is similar to a keyboard, but with many fewer keys. An example is the remote control keypad used for television control.

Keyword   A word or phrase in a document that is chosen as the key for retrieving that document from a computer's memory.

Knowledge   Theoretical or practical understanding of a subject. Encapsulates indi-vidual or collective human experience.

L

LAN   See *Local Area Network*.

Laser printing   A very fast method of printing, using a laser. The laser, under computer control, 'paints' the required image on the printing drum, to a very high degree of accuracy. Laser printers use plain paper, or acetate sheets, but can only print one copy at a time.

Light Emitting Diode (LED)   A device made with semiconductor material that glows when an electrical voltage is applied. LEDs are used in the display panels of equipment such as TVs and video recorders for displaying time, channel number, etc.

Light pen   A pen-shaped device attached to a computer. The pen has a light-sensitive tip. When it encounters a flash of light, it sends a signal to the computer. *Bar code readers* at supermarket check-outs are a special type of light pen which also incorporate the light source.

Line printer   A printer that prints a complete line at a time rather than character by character. Used for bulk printing from larger computers.

Liquid Crystal Display (LCD)   A method of data display. 'Liquid crystals' are substances that become transparent to light when an electric current is applied to them. They are used in pocket calculators, digital watches and similar devices. More recently LCD screens have become large enough for use in VDUs.

Local Area Network (LAN)   A *data transmission* system designed to link computers, word processors, printers, and other electronic devices within a restricted geographical area such as an office complex. See also *MAN* and *WAN*.

Logic gates   Switches in electronic circuits that control the passage of current. The logic gates enable the computer to carry out arithmetical and logical operations.

Loop   A loop is a sequence of instructions in a computer program that may be executed more than once before the program continues.

M

Machine code   The detailed set of instructions that a computer *CPU* can carry out directly. The computer must translate any computer program into machine code before executing it. Translation into machine code is carried out by another computer program – either a *compiler* or an *interpreter*.

Mainframe computer   A large powerful computer built on a large frame or chassis. Mainframes are used by large organizations that need centralized data processing and storage. Mainframes can carry out many millions of instructions per second. They require specialist operating and maintenance staff.

Main memory   The memory in the *central processing unit* of a computer. It stores only the instructions and data currently in use. When required, new instructions and data are transferred from the *backing store* into the main memory. Main memory is also known as 'primary memory' or 'working memory'.

MAN   Metropolitan Area Network; a *communication network* which links devices within a single town or sector of a city. It is larger than a Local Area Network (*LAN*) and smaller than a Wide Area Network (*WAN*).

Management Information System (MIS)   An integrated network of people, activities, procedures and technologies, designed to provide management with all the information it needs. The term is often used to denote electronic information systems which present information relevant to the tasks of management.

Mean   A mathematical term denoting the average of a group of numbers. To find the mean of ten numbers, you simply add up the numbers and divide by 10.

Megabyte   Mega- usually means 1 million. However, in computing it means 1 048 576. So a megabyte of information is over a million *bytes* or characters.

Memory   The part of the computer that stores instructions and data. The memory has two sections, the main or working memory and the backing store. The *main memory* stores the data and instructions in immediate use. Other data and instructions are held in the *backing store* until needed.

Menu system   A menu system allows a user to interact with a program by presenting a menu of options from which the user can choose.

Microcomputer   Microcomputers are at the lower end of the computer range. They are small, relatively cheap, and suited to individual needs.

Microprocessor A single *chip* containing all the circuitry of a *central processing unit*. Microprocessors are used in microcomputers and in such devices as automatic washing machines, digital watches, pocket calculators and so on.

Microwave transmission Microwaves are radio waves of very high frequency and short wavelength. Their transmission requires line-of-sight contact between transmitter and receiver; hence the use of tall towers (such as the Telecom Tower) and satellites. Satellites can handle thousands of communications at a time, and transmit signals very rapidly between microwave stations on land. Microwaves are used for transmitting all forms of data, including text, graphics, and voice in digital form.

Minicomputer A medium-scale computer that provides a powerful data processing facility for a large number of users. Minis are capable of executing a few million instructions per second.

MIPS Millions of Instructions Per Second. A measure of a computer's processing power. A modern large computer would be rated at over 10 MIPS, with some up to 100 MIPS.

MIS See *Management Information System*.

Modem A modem (derived from 'MODulator-DEModulator') is a device that enables *digital* data to be transmitted over *analogue* communication links. For example, a modem is used to convert a digital signal from a computer into an analogue signal for transmission across the public service telephone network.

Mouse An *input device* for a computer. A mouse is about the size of one's palm. It has a ball on the underside, and a set of buttons. The unit is rolled over a flat surface. The position of the ball is fed into the computer by pressing a button. The mouse can be used for manipulating text on a screen display, choosing an option from a menu, or entering graphics into the computer.

N

Network See *communication network*.

Noise In a general sense, noise is the term for unwanted signals in any form of communication. In information management, it refers to anything that interferes with the communication of information. For example, unnecessary data, unfamiliar jargon, and even crackling on the phone line can all be considered as noise.

Non-volatile Describes computer memory where the data is not lost when the power is switched off. A computer's working memory is volatile, while *ROM* chips and *bubble memory* are non-volatile.

Normal distribution The distribution obtained by random sampling which represents many natural phenomena and commercial situations. Its graph is a bell-shaped curve.

O

OA Office Automation; see *electronic office*.

OCR See *Optical Character Recognition*.

OEM Original equipment manufacturer, or a company which buys equipment and relabels or repackages it before resale.

Off-line Any part of a computer system is off-line if it is not under the control of the central processor.

Off-line storage   Storage not under the control of the central processor. For example, floppy *disks* in a box on a shelf are off-line, as is a switched-off printer, or one under local control to replace the paper.

On-line   Any part of a computer is on-line if it is under the control of the central processor.

On-line storage   Storage under the direct control of the central processor. A floppy disk is on-line when it is in use.

Operating System (OS)   An operating system is a set of programs that manage the basic operation of computer hardware, so that the machine can run other programs (usually *Application Programs*).

Optical Character Reader (OCR)   Devices capable of 'reading' characters on paper and converting the optical images into binary coded data. The most advanced OCR systems are approaching the ability to decipher normal handwriting.

Optical Fibres   Fine flexible glass fibres used for transmitting pulses of light that represent binary data. A hair-thin optical fibre can carry as many signals as a copper cable made of several thousand wires.

OSI   Open Systems Interconnection; an initiative from the International Organisation for Standardisation (ISO) to agree *interface* standards for the interworking of computer systems across communication networks.

Output device   A device for converting binary data into a form readily understood by humans – such as print, visual display or sound – or into a form for controlling a mechanical device. Printers, pen plotters, voice synthesizers and *VDU* screens are all output devices.

P

PABX   Private Automatic Branch Exchange; an electronic telephone exchange serving users at a single location, and offering more features than are usually available on the public network (e.g. call transfer, ring-back-when-free).

Packet switching   A method of *data transmission* in which data is divided into small packets of standard size and format, transmitted through a network at high speed, and reassembled at the point of receipt. Each packet contains control information, including the destination address. Several countries have national Packet Switched Systems (PSS), and they are linked by an international service (IPSS). Such networks are very effective at handling different kinds of digital data traffic.

Packet switching protocol   A set of rules for sending messages over *packet switching* systems. A standard protocol, called X25, has been internationally agreed.

Parallel processing   Using several microprocessors, working together, to increase the capacity of a *CPU*.

Pascal   A *high level language* specially designed to produce a well-structured program.

PBX   Private Branch Exchange; a telephone exchange serving users at one site. Usually now a *PABX*.

PC   Personal Computer; a *microcomputer* designed for individual use.

Peripherals   All the *hardware* connected to a computer system (apart from its *central processing unit*). Examples are *VDUs*, and *disk drives*.

Physical circuit protocol   A set of rules for connecting the devices in a communications system.

Pixel   For the display of characters and graphics, a screen has to be divided up into dots, or into tiny squares called pixels. Each dot or pixel is under computer control, and can be given a different colour or shade. A typical arrangement for a video screen is 25 lines of 80 characters, displayed on 400 lines of 640 pixels.

Point of Sale (POS)   The area in a store where goods are paid for. Ordinary cash registers at point of sale are being replaced by devices that do the same job, but also collect information about what has been sold, and for how much. The information may be stored on a cassette and removed at the end of the day, or fed directly into a computer. Either way, it allows management to keep a close watch on sales, daily takings, and stock position. See *EPOS*.

Prestel   The public *videotex* service operated by British Telecom. The user can call up information from the videotex computer onto a television screen, and can feed information to the computer (orders for goods, holiday bookings, and so on) by means of a *keypad*.

Program   A set of instructions telling a computer what to do. The instructions are in the form of *software* and are normally listed in a numerical order corresponding to the order in which the computer will execute them when the program is 'run'. Often a program requires the computer to do some operations many times in succession; this is known as a 'loop' in the program.

Programmed Decision System (PDS)   *Software* with pre-programmed criteria built in to enable it to initiate a particular course of action without human intervention. One example is the software for monitoring a manufacturing process. If a fault is detected, the PDS can make projections as to the likely effects of the fault and then 'decide' whether or not to shut the process down.

PROM   Programmable Read-Only Memory. A read-only memory that can be programmed just once by the user; it is then permanent. See also *EPROM*.

Protocol   A set of agreed rules by which communications may be established between devices. See also *OSI*.

PSS   See *Packet Switched Service*. Also stands for Packet Switch Stream, British Telecom's commercial packet switched data network.

PSTN   Public Switched Telephone Network; the public telephone network.

Q

QWERTY Keyboard   The layout of keys in the conventional UK typewriter. The term is derived from the letters displayed in the top row of the keyboard, reading across from the left-hand side. The same layout is often used on computer keyboards, even though it is a poor one from the point of view of ease of learning and speed of operation.

R

RAM   See *random access memory*.

Random access   A feature of a memory device where there is a direct access to any given memory location, regardless of its physical location. It is not necessary to skim past other locations: the read/write head goes directly to the required one.

Random Access Memory (RAM)   Memory with a *random access* capability which is used by a computer for internal, fast storage purposes. The RAM usually stores the current program and immediately associated data. The amount of RAM limits the complexity of programs, speed of operation, and volume of data which can be handled by the computer.

Read Only Memory (ROM)   A computer needs to store a great deal of unchanging information, such as instructions for decoding a programming language. This information is stored in permanent form in the computer's ROM, where the information can be read but the writing of the data is not allowed. The data in ROM is held even while the machine is turned off; it is therefore permanent.

Real time operation In many cases, a computer has all the necessary *data* in store before it begins to execute a program. In real time operation, however, data has to be fed in at various stages if the program is to continue. The booking of airline flights via computer is a real time task. So is the monitoring and control of equipment and procedures by a computer, as on a modern assembly line.

Record A company's paper file on personnel will probably contain a record of each employee. Each record will consist of data such as name, date of birth, date of employment, salary, and so on. In the same way a computer file is made up of records, and each record is made up of related items of data, called *files*, often as part of a *database*.

Redundancy The provision of additional equipment or information over and above that needed to carry out a piece of work. A certain amount of redundancy is useful in most systems to provide backup should anything go wrong. However, beyond a certain level of redundancy a system becomes inefficient.

Ring A configuration, or topology, of *communication network* where each device is connected to a single transmission line in a ring arrangement. Each device is able to gain control of the ring and send a message to any other device in the ring. Messages are broken into packets of data and sent at high speed. This technology, called token ring, for a *Local Area Network* (LAN) is an alternative to *Ethernet*.

ROM See *Read only memory*.

S

Semiconductor A conductor is a material that conducts electricity easily. An insulator does not conduct. A semiconductor can act as either conductor or insulator, depending on the controlled addition of impurities. Silicon is a semiconductor; 'doped' silicon is an even better semiconductor made by adding substances such as boron or arsenic to pure silicon. Silicon chips are made of doped silicon and form 'active devices' which are the basis of electronic technology.

Sensor In systems theory, sensor, *comparator*, and *activator* are the names given to the parts of the feedback mechanism. The sensor is the part that monitors the output of the system.

Sequential access Refers to *memory* where the data can be accessed only in the order in which it is stored. To access data at the end of the sequence all that comes before it must be accessed first. Magnetic tape provides sequential access. Contrast with *Random access*.

Serial processing Processing records in a data file in the order in which they occur in the storage device.

Service bureau An organization which provides computer processing services, usually '*on-line*' over a communications link.

Signal A representation, usually electrical, of *data* or *information*. See *transmission*.

Software One of the two main components of a computer system, the other being the *hardware*, or physical machine. Software comprises instructions (a *Program*) or *data* for the computer. The value of software lies in its intellectual content rather than in the physical form of storage. Software has to be stored in some way, usually on magnetic media, but the cost of storage and of replication is very small compared with the cost of generating the software in the first instance. Today, the software costs of computing systems often exceed the hardware costs.

Software package   Commercially-available *software* which is ready to run, and which performs some commonly-required task such as *word processing, spreadsheet, database,* or *graphics.*

Solid state technology   Technology based on devices with no moving parts and without electronic valves, e.g. using silicon chips. See *semiconductor.*

Spreadsheet   A general-purpose program that provides a large table for the entry of data in rows and columns, for example for accounting purposes. These programs are generally used on *microcomputers.*

Star   A configuration of *communication network* where all communication between users takes place via a central computer. Each user has a direct link to that computer. It is one configuration for a *local area network.*

Statement of User Requirements (SUR)   When designing an information system it is essential to analyse and define the user's needs. This allows the most appropriate hardware and software to be chosen.

String   A sequence of characters that is handled as a unit by the computer.

Subroutine   A sequence of instructions within a program that can be called up and repeated as and when necessary.

Switching   That part of a telecommunication system which enables *signals* to be directed to the intended recipient, using available *transmission* facilities.

Syntax   The rules governing the structure of a natural or programming language.

System   A set or assemblage of things connected, or associated, or interdependent, so as to form a complex unity; a whole composed of parts in orderly arrangement according to some scheme or plan.

Systems analysis   The process of analysing a problem into its basic operations and specifying them in programmable form.

Systems software   A collection of programs designed to control a computer system. It would include a *compiler* or *interpreter* for translating a *high level language* into machine code, and a supervisor for managing and scheduling tasks.

T

Telematics   General name for the broad range of applications of modern *information technology*; from the French 'Telematique'.

Telesoftware   A technique for the transmission of computer programs from a central computer 'library' to individual computers via *videotex* or *teletext.*

Teletex   A business communication service offered by carriers such as British Telecom. The terminals involved are usually word processors, and transmission is at high speed (2400 bits per second) from the memory of one machine to the memory of the other. Producing *hard copy* is done after electronic reception of the message. Teletex has a greater character-set than earlier systems. It should not be confused with *teletext* or *telex.*

Teletext   A system for displaying broadcast information on modified television receivers. Ceefax from the BBC and Oracle from ITV are two examples. The information is transmitted in parts of the TV signal not needed for the picture and sound. The user retrieves the 'frame' of interest to him by selection using a keypad.

Telex   Short for 'Teleprinter Exchange'. A text service similar to the public telephone service except that it carries teleprinter signals rather than speech signals.

The speed of transmission is low, and the character set limited. A more modern version is *teletex*, based on the use of word processors rather than teleprinters.

Template   A list of commands used in a spreadsheet or other program to do a particular sequence of operations. Often called up by depressing a single function key.

Terminal   An input/output device connected to a computer system via a communications link.

Time-sharing   In a time-sharing system, several users are connected on-line to a central computer, which shares its time between them. The computer services each user in turn, but so fast that each of the users appears to have an exclusive service and is unaware of the presence of the others. Eventually, too many users trying to do too much will degrade the service.

Touch-sensitive screen   A display screen which enables you to interact with a computer program simply by touching the screen at the appropriate point. A less precise pointing system than using a *mouse*.

Transmission   That part of a telecommunication system which enables *signals* to be sent from one predetermined point to another. Examples of transmission media are cable, radio, satellite, optical fibre.

Turing, Alan, M.   English mathematician (1912–54). He put forward the idea of a general-purpose computer that could be programmed to solve mathematical and logical problems. One of his legacies was the Turing Test for assessing computer 'intelligence'.

U

UNIX   An *operating system* developed by the Bell Telephone Laboratories in the US. It enables multiple tasks to be performed for many users of a single computer installation.

User-friendly   Describes any computer system that is designed to be used without much training and by the non-specialist.

V

Variable   In computing a variable is simply a location in read/write memory. It is given a name to identify it. For example it could be called *score* and be used for storing a student's marks as he or she works through a test.

Very Large Scale Integration (VLSI)   The manufacture of between 10 000 and 1 million electronic components on a single microchip. The *chip* industry reached the VLSI stage in the late 1970s.

VDU   Visual Display Unit or Video Display Unit. An input/output device in which the input is by means of a keyboard and the output is displayed on a screen.

Videotex (Viewdata)   Interactive two-way system for transmitting data between computer databases and television sets or monitors via the telephone network. The British Prestel system was the world's first public videotex system (1979). Prestel provides financial information, timetables and schedules, news, sport and weather reports, government statistics, holiday information, mail order, and games.

Virtual memory   A memory management system which cuts down on the need for increasingly large *main memory*. A program and its associated data are broken into small segments and stored in the *backing store*. Only the segment currently in use is kept in the main memory. In some systems a large part of the *operating* *system* is also segmented in this way, with only the core being permanently held in main memory.

VLSI See *Very Large Scale Integration*.

Voice input/output Interfacing a computer system using the human voice. Voice input to computers is limited at present; voice output (synthesis by a computer) is easier.

Volatile Describes computer memory where the data is lost when the power is switched off. A computer's working memory is volatile, while *ROM* is not.

von Neumann, John Mathematician (1903–57) who put forward the concept of the stored-program computer, which has been the basis for almost all subsequent computer designs.

W

WAN See *Wide Area Network*.

Wang American company, named after its founder Dr An Wang, which manufactures word processors, minis, micros, and office automation systems.

Wangnet A *local area network* system produced by the Wang Company. It is capable of carrying data, voice, and video signals on the same co-axial cable.

Wide Area Network (WAN) A *communication network* which extends nationally, and through gateways internationally. Larger than *Metropolitan Area Networks* (MANs) or *Local Area Networks* (LANs).

WIMPS *Window*, Icon, *Mouse*, Pull-down *menu*, Screen-based computer systems. Features of modern *software* intended to make computers more *user-friendly*.

Winchester Disk A class of hard *disk drive* in which the platters and read/write heads are enclosed in a sealed unit at the time of manufacture. Winchesters are typically used with small business computers needing greater storage capacity than that provided by floppy disks.

Windows A feature of a computer system in which the screen of the *VDU* is split up into several areas, or windows, within each of which a different job or aspect of a single job can be displayed simultaneously. The feature makes it easier to handle complex tasks, or transfer data between tasks.

Wisdom Experience and knowledge judiciously applied. The highest level of a hierarchy which attaches human significance to objective fact; see also *data, information*, and *knowledge*.

Word A group of *bits* which the computer treats as a unit for storage and processing purposes.

Word length The number of *bits* in a *word*. If a computer can handle words of 8 bits, then the word length is 8 bits (1 byte). Word length is a measure of the power of the computer. 8-bit machines are obsolescent; most are 16-bit; and newer machines handle words of 32 bits.

Word processor A special-purpose computer designed for the manipulation of text. The input device is a keyboard and the text is displayed on a monitor. Text can be stored and manipulated in various ways to give the desired product. The output device is a printer. An appropriate *software package* can enable a personal computer (PC) to be used as a word processor.

Work station Apparatus from which a user can communicate with the various devices linked in a *local area network*.

WYSIWYG What you see is what you get. A type of *word processor* or other system in which what you see on the screen is similar to what will be printed on the page as hard copy.

Bibliography

'Delivering the goods in style', reported in *IMPAQ*, 2Q87, p. 16.

Adair, John, *Training for Leadership*, Macdonald, 1968.

Burch, J. G. and G. Grudnitski, *Information Systems: Theory and Practice*, Wiley, 1986.

Child, John, *Organization*, Paul Chapman Publishing Ltd, 1986.

Davis, G. B. and M. H. Olson, *Management Information Systems*, McGraw-Hill, 1985.

Eden, Colin, Sue Jones and David Sims, *Thinking in Organisations*, Macmillan, 1979.

Eden, Colin, Sue Jones and David Sims, *Messing About in Problems*, Pergamon, 1983.

Handy, Charles B., *Understanding Organizations*, Penguin, 1985.

HMSO, *Britain – an Official Handbook*, HMSO, 1965, and 1985–89.

King, D. W. and J. -M. Griffiths, 'Measuring the value of information and information systems, services, and products', AGARD Conference Proceedings, No. 385, January 1986.

Oborne, David J., *Computers at Work*, John Wiley & Sons, 1985.

Parkinson, L. K. and S. T. Parkinson, *Using the Microcomputer in Marketing*, McGraw-Hill, 1987.

Peters, Glen, 'Evaluating your computer investment strategy', *Journal of Information Technology*, Vol. 3, No. 3, September 1988, pp. 178–88; *Accountancy Age*, October 1987, p. 58.

Porter, M. E. and V. E. Millar, 'How information gives you competitive advantage', *Harvard Business Review*, July–August 1985, pp. 149–60.

Rogers, E. M., *Communication Technology*, The Free Press/Collier Macmillan, 1986.

Smith, J. E. and G. H. Ray (ed. P. J. A. Herbert), '*Mint aluminium castings, a case study*', Henley – The Management College, 1987.

Further reading

The following books complement the material in this book, and are suitable for managers wishing to widen their knowledge of particular aspects of the subject.

Davis, G. B. and M. H. Olson, *Management Information Systems – Conceptual Foundations, Structure and Development*, McGraw-Hill, 1984, 693pp.

Doswell, R. and G. L. Simons, *Fraud and Abuse of IT Systems*, NCC Publications, 1986, 143pp.

Eaton, John, Jeremy Smithers and Susan Curran, *This is IT*, Philip Allan, 1988, 335pp.

Forester, Tom, *The Information Technology Revolution*, Blackwell, 1985, 674pp.
Harmon, P. and D. King, *Expert Systems – Artificial Intelligence in Business*, Wiley, 1985, 283pp.
Michie, D. and R. Johnston, *The Creative Computer*, Viking, 1984, 263pp.
Zorkoczy, P., *Information Technology – an Introduction*, 2nd ed., Pitman, 1985, 164pp.

Index